My Life

My Life

by George Sand

Translated from the French
and adapted by
Dan Hofstadter

Harper & Row, Publishers
New York, Hagerstown, San Francisco, London

FIRST EDITION

Designed by Gloria Adelson

Library of Congress Cataloging in Publication Data

Sand, George, pseud. of Mme. Dudevant, 1804–1876.
  My Life.
  Translation of Histoire de ma vie.
  Includes index.
  1. Sand, George, pseud. of Mme Dudevant, 1804–1876—
Biography. 2. Novelists, French—19th century—
Biography. I. Hofstadter, Dan. II. Title.
PQ2412.A2E5 1979   843'.7 [B]   77-3770
ISBN 0-06-013767-3

79 80 81 82 83 10 9 8 7 6 5 4 3 2 1

Contents

Translator's Note

George Sand's *Story of My Life (Histoire de ma vie)* first ran from 1854 to 1855 in 138 installments in the Parisian newspaper *La Presse*, amounting altogether to about half a million words. With almost no delay it was published in twenty octavo volumes by Victor Lecou et Alexandre Cadot. A contemporary critic wryly observed that George's memoirs might more aptly have been titled *Story of My Life Before My Birth*, for almost a third of the mammoth affair contained nothing of George's life at all, but a doctored version of her father's correspondence with her grandmother. The title was a misnomer in other ways, too: at publication a major portion of George's career still lay before her, and in any case the sections on her life were greatly outweighed by lengthy homilies and digressions. Written to raise money for her daughter's dowry and to settle pressing debts, *Story of My Life* was mercilessly padded. Yet if the book was not a "life" in the accepted sense, it was indeed "her story," the controversial woman's experience transformed by self-advocacy into melodrama.

This volume is, so far as I know, the first translation into English of any substantial part of George Sand's memoirs. Probably no such translation would have been feasible before Gallimard's publication in 1970 of Georges Lubin's lovingly definitive edition of the *Oeuvres autobiographiques*. That model of French textual scholarship not only makes the labyrinthine historical details of the work comprehensible to the translator, it also eliminates any urgent need for a complete edition in English. In effect, the full *Story of My Life* would probably be so confusing to most nonspecialists that they would require a second life to figure it out; and since specialists now have a definitive French edition readily available, the editors and I have decided to present a version made up of what we believe are the most interesting sections of George's actual narrative. The core of a major document of literary history and women's emancipation is thus offered to the general reader. While the paragraph headings herein are George's own, the numbered chapters are my device, and merely suggest convenient stops.

George Sand the stylist was a distinguished innovator—as in *Francois le champi,* which she composed at least five years before her memoirs—but *Story of My Life* was a different kind of writing: tossed off nightly for the press, rolling rhythmically but inexactly forward, essentially unrevised. Where the adjectives pile up, I have tried to use one or two English ones to match them; where the same information is conveyed several times—the result of hasty writing, perhaps, or of a desire to remind readers of things they had read about months before—I have rendered it only once; where the episodes grow too long to sound natural in English, I have broken them up. At the same time I have tried to be accurate, by accuracy meaning not microscopic closeness but fidelity to big things, to George's Romantic themes, to her feeling for rhythm and tonality. The text is quaint, garish, at times even droll, full of self-regarding modesty and feigned folksiness. I read it as a period piece, and to render its time-bound color I've resorted to a hybrid style reminiscent of some mid-nineteenth-century American magazine and diary writing.

My thanks for advice on the way go to Richard Balkin, Jacques Barzun, Professor Carl Hovde—who brought Sand's influence upon Margaret Fuller's English style to my attention—and Cynthia Merman, Patricia Oxelgren, and Roger Shattuck, none of whom bears any responsibility for any errors in the translation.

My Life

Prologue

I WAS BORN in the year of Napoleon's coronation, Year XII of the
French Republic (1804). My name is not Marie-Aurore de Saxe, Marquise of Dudevant, as several of my biographers have asserted, but
Amantine-Lucile-Aurore Dupin, and my husband, M. François Dudevant, claims no title: the highest rank he ever reached was that
of infantry second lieutenant. He was no more than twenty-seven
when I married him; in representing him as an old colonel from
Napoleon's army they have confused him with M. Delmare, a character in one of my novels. How easy it is to write a novelist's biography:
you present her fiction as the truth about her life, with little expendi-
ture of imagination.

My descent, for which I have been so often and so singularly reproached by persons on both sides of my family, has caused me to devote much thought to the question of class origin. I suspect my foreign biographers of being excessively aristocratic, because all of them have favored me with an illustrious bloodline, not caring to notice—well-informed though they surely must be—a glaring stain upon my coat of arms. For one is not only Papa's child, one is Mama's too—I daresay even more so: we are directly beholden to the woman whose womb has borne us. Now, though my father was indeed a great-grandson of Frederick Augustus II, King of Poland, and thus I have some illegitimate cousinage with Louis XVIII, it is just as true that the People's blood runs in my veins; and besides, there is no bastardy on that side.

My mother was a penniless child of the old cobbled streets of Paris; her father, Antoine Delaborde, was a "master fowler," which means merely that he sold canaries and finches on the Quai des Oiseaux; earlier he had kept a billiard saloon in some corner of Paris, where, I may add, he failed to make his fortune. My mother's stepfather, however, had a big name in the bird trade: the name Barra is still to be seen in the Boulevard du Temple above a huge stack of cages wherein crowds of songbirds twitter away as gaily as ever.

On my paternal side, Frederick Augustus, Elector of Saxony and King of Poland, was the most amazing profligate of his time. It is no honor to have his blood in one's veins, for they say he had several hundreds of bastards. Aurore de Koenigsmark, that beautiful and accomplished courtesan, bore him a son whose intrinsic nobility by far surpassed his own, though this son was no prince but merely a French field marshal. He was Maurice de Saxe, the victor of the Battle of Fontenoy, who was as dashing as his sire and no less debauched, though he was a better general and also luckier and more competently staffed. Yet his glory was stained by his love affairs, such as his adventure with Mme. Favart, which was recounted with such noble feeling in Favart's letters.

One of his last affections was Mlle. Verrières, euphemistically known as a "dame of the Opéra." Their daughter, Aurore, my grandmother, was not acknowledged as the marshal's child until fifteen years later, when she was allowed by a high court to bear his name. One proof of a blood tie was her marked resemblance to Maurice de Saxe; another was her virtual adoption by the Dauphine, King

Augustus's daughter and the mother of Louis XVIII. This princess placed her in the convent of Saint-Cyr, forbade her to see her mother, and took charge of her education and marriage.

At fifteen Aurore de Saxe left Saint-Cyr to marry the Count of Horn, a bastard son of Louis XV who was Louis XVI's newly appointed deputy in Alsace. She first beheld him on the eve of her wedding and took mortal fright, believing she saw the late king's portrait come to life, so striking was the resemblance. The Count of Horn was actually taller and more handsome, but he was also harsh and insolent. On the wedding night a valet approached my great-uncle de Beaumont (Mlle. Verrières's son by the Duke of Bouillon), who was then scarcely more than a child, and told him to do anything to stop the young countess from spending the night with her husband. The count's doctor was called in, and the count acquiesced.

Consequently Aurore was her husband's wife in name only; they saw each other only once more, during the princely reception they were given in Alsace, replete with garrison troops in full review order, speeches by the city bigwigs, night illuminations, fancy-dress balls at the town hall—all the vain bustle with which folk seemed to want to console the poor little girl for belonging to a man she did not even know, and whom she had had to flee as if he were Death himself.

My grandmother told me how amazed she was—she who was just out of her convent—at the pomp of this reception. She was in a gilded four-in-hand drawn by white horses; His Lordship her husband was on horseback, his uniform plastered with military decorations; the noise of the cannon frightened her almost as much as her husband's voice. One thing exalted her: that she was given to sign, by the king's order, a general amnesty. At once a score of prisoners came out of the prison to thank her. She began to weep; and perhaps her innocent joy was credited her by Providence, and repaid during the Terror, when she herself was delivered from a brief imprisonment.

A few weeks after her arrival in Alsace, His Lordship the governor vanished in the midst of a ball. Madame his wife was still dancing, at three in the morning, when someone whispered to her that her husband begged to see her in his bedchamber. She went up. At the door to his room she remembered that her little brother had

3

made her swear never to go in there alone; but she grew bold as the door opened and she saw light and people. The valet who had warned her on her wedding night was supporting the Count of Horn in his arms. A doctor was by the count's side.

"Show her out!" cried the valet. "The count has nothing to say to the countess now!"

She saw nothing but her husband's great white hand dangling over the bedside; it was quickly restored to the attitude proper to a corpse. The Count of Horn had just been killed in a duel by a fierce sword thrust.

That was all my grandmother was to know of the matter. Perhaps the only wifely duty she ever performed was to mourn her husband; dead or alive, it was always fear alone that he inspired.

If I mistake not, the Dauphine was still living, and returned Aurore to a convent. Soon the young widow obtained leave to see her mother, whom she had always loved.

Mlle. Verrières lived in affluence, indeed on a rather grand scale. She was still beautiful, yet old enough to be surrounded by disinterested men. She lived pleasantly, in the insouciance which the lax morals of the era permitted, and "cultivated the Muses." Aurore was lovely as an angel, she had a superior intelligence and an education on a level with the most enlightened minds of her day, and these were developed still further by her mother's conversation and entourage. She had, moreover, a splendid voice; at her mother's they performed comic operas, and she played Colette in *Le Devin du village*, Azémia in *Les Sauvages*, and all the leading roles in Grétry's operas and Sedaine's plays. In her old age I often heard her sing airs by the old Italian masters, which she'd made her daily fare: airs by Leo, Porpora, Hasse, Pergolesi. By then her hands were palsied, and she accompanied herself with a few fingers on a tinkling spinet. Her voice trembled, but it was always accurate and of wide range: age cannot affect phrasing and accent. She sight-read the scores, and I've never heard a better singer or accompanist. She had that classic breadth, that simplicity, that pure taste and clear enunciation which no one would even recognize today. When I was a child she had me join her in an Italian duet:

> *Non mi dir, bel idol mio,*
> *Non mi dir ch'io son ingrato.*

She sang the tenor part, and one day, though she was about sixty-five, her voice rose to such powerful expression that I dissolved in tears. I'll have occasion to return to my first impressions of music, the dearest of my life; but now I want to continue the story of my dear grandmama's youth.

She never had any passion but maternal love, and never knew what an "adventure" was. Yet hers was a tender and generous nature, and an exquisite sensibility. She was no bigot, her only religion being that of the eighteenth century, the deism of Rousseau and Voltaire. Poised, clear-sighted and very taken with a certain ideal of self-respect, she knew nothing of coquetry, being too well endowed to need it, and this system of provocation offended her dignified thought and habits. She made her way through a licentious world without losing a feather from her wing; and condemned by fate never to know love in marriage, she solved the problem of how to escape ill will and calumny.

She was about twenty-five when her mother died. Mlle. Verrières was getting ready for bed, without the slightest indisposition save to complain that her feet were cold. She sat down by the fire, and while her maid was heating her slippers she gave up the ghost without a sigh. When the slippers were warm the maid asked her how she felt, but getting no reply, she looked at her face and saw that the final sleep had closed her eyes. I believe that in those days, for certain natures perfectly keyed to their philosophic salons, everything was easy, even death.

Aurore retired to a convent: that was what you did if you were a young girl or widow without relations to steer you through the world. You settled in with a certain elegance; you received, you went abroad in the morning, even in the evening, with a suitable chaperone. It was an affair of etiquette and taste.

Toward the age of thirty Aurore decided to marry M. Dupin de Francueil, my grandfather, who was then sixty-two. M. Dupin, the same mentioned by Rousseau in his memoirs and Mme. d'Épinay in her *Correspondence*, was the embodiment of what the last century called a "charming man." He was not of high birth, being the son of a farmer-general who had traded the sword for public finance; he himself was a receiver-general when he married my grandmother. But his was an ancient and well-connected family, with four folios of lineage scrawled in heraldic gibberish with lovely tinted vignettes. For all this, my grandmother demurred. Not that M. Dupin's age was a capital objection; but her entourage held him too lowly a personage to set beside a Mlle. de Saxe, Countess of Horn. This prejudice was scuttled for money reasons: M. Dupin was then very rich. Yet with my grandmother, the assiduous favors, and the grace, wit and charm of her elderly suitor, carried more weight than the baited hook of wealth; and after two or three years of wavering, during which he came every day to the convent parlor to lunch with her, she accepted his love and became Mme. Dupin.

She often spoke to me about this long-pondered union, about this grandfather whom I never knew. She said that during their ten years together he was—along with their son—the darling of her life; and though she did not use the word "love," which I never heard escape her lips concerning him or anyone, she smiled when I said that I could not see how she could have loved an old man.

"An old man loves more than a young one," she replied, "and it's impossible not to return the love of one who loves you perfectly. I called him my old husband and my papa. He wanted it so, and always addressed me as his daughter, even in society. Your grandfather, my sweet, was handsome, elegant, well-tailored, gracious, perfumed, amusing, fond, even-tempered, and lovable until the hour of his death. Had he been young, he'd have been *too* lovable to have so calm a life, and perhaps I shouldn't have been so happy with him—I'd have had too many rivals! I'm convinced I had the best years of his life, and no young man ever made a woman as happy as he made me; we were always together, and I was never bored. His mind was an encyclopedia, and he had the gift of knowing how to devote himself to others' needs as well as to his own. During the day he made music with me—he was an excellent violinist; indeed, he made his own violins—and he was besides a fine clockmaker, architect, painter, locksmith, decorator, cook, poet, composer and cabinet maker; and he was first-rate at embroidery! The pity of it was that he threw away his fortune on his various gifts and experiments; but it only dazzled me, and we ruined ourselves in the most delightful fashion. In the evening, if we weren't out, he'd sit beside me and draw while I unraveled damask; or we'd take turns reading to each other; or perhaps some friends would be seated about us, keeping his rich and subtle mind in good fettle with their charming conversation. I had young friends, splendidly married, who never stopped telling me how much they envied me my husband.

"In those days we knew how to live, and how to die," she said. "We had no importunate illnesses. If you had gout you walked anyway, without grimacing; your breeding made you hide your pain. And we had no money worries to spoil the inner life; we knew how to ruin ourselves without showing it, like cardsharps who lose without betraying their anxiety. We thought it better to die at a ball than in bed amid candles and nasty men in black. We were philosophical; we did not play at austerity, but we were austere, sometimes, without flaunting it. If we were chaste, it was by inclination, not out of prudery. We enjoyed life, and when the hour to depart it came, we didn't try to make others lose their taste for it. When my husband said farewell, he prayed me to survive him for years, and to be happy. That's how to make people regret you, my dear: have a generous heart, like his."

It is certainly seductive, this philosophy of wealth, independence, tolerance and graciousness; but you needed an income of six thousand pounds to support it, and I don't quite see what it did for the wretched and the downtrodden.

It went by the board, this philosophy, in the expiations of the Revolution, and those who had been so happy in the past kept nothing of that past but the art of gracefully mounting the scaffold; which is much, I cannot deny, but they were able to display this final valor because of their disgust at a life in which they no longer found the means to amuse themselves, and because of their consternation at the thought of a society in which they would have to admit the right of every man to comfort and leisure.

Nine months to the day after her wedding, my grandmother gave birth to a boy, her only child, who received the name Maurice in memory of Maurice de Saxe. She wanted to nurse him herself; this was still an eccentric wish at that time, but she had read *Émile* religiously, and wanted to set a good example. Besides, she had a highly developed maternal sense, which became a passion that stood her in stead of all others.

But nature scorned her zeal. She had no milk, and for several days, despite the pain she inflicted on herself by suckling her child, she fed him only with her blood. She had to give up, a wrenching agony; and this seemed a bad omen.

7

My grandfather died after ten years of marriage, leaving his accounts with the government and his personal affairs in great disorder. My level-headed grandmother gathered persons of good counsel about her and took charge of everything herself. She settled the debts promptly, and when all were paid, to the government as well as to private parties, she found herself "ruined," commanding an income of seventy thousand pounds a year!

The Revolution soon abridged her resources, and she did not regain her balance so easily after this second stroke of ill luck; but she met the first with her chin up, and though I cannot understand how one can be anything but immensely rich on seventy thousand pounds, all is relative, and she accepted this "poverty" with philosophy and dignity.

After leaving M. Dupin's seat at Châteauroux, she lived in the Rue de Sicile in a "little apartment" which, to judge by the quantity and size of the furniture in my house today, contained rather enough to fall back on. She engaged for the education of her son a young man whom I knew when he was old, and who was my tutor also. This personage, at once serious and comical, looms too large in my memories for me to pass him over.

His name was François Deschartres, and as he had worn the collar at the Collège du Cardinal Lemoine, he entered my grandmother's household with the habit and the title of "abbé." When the Revolution came caviling at titles of all kinds, the Abbé Deschartres prudently became Citizen Deschartres. Under the Republic he was M. Deschartres, mayor of the village of Nohant; under the Empire he wanted "abbé" back, for he had not swerved in his love for the forms of the past. But he had never taken holy orders, and besides, he could not shake a nickname I had tagged him with for being such a self-important know-it-all; so that ever after he was called the Great Man.

He had been a pretty lad, and was so when my grandmother took him on: tidy, clean-shaven, bright-eyed, and strong at the calf. In all, a fine figure of a tutor. But I'm sure that no one ever saw him in his heyday without laughing, so clearly was the word "cad" spelled out in all the lines of his face and in all the gestures of his person. To perfect the role he should have been illiterate, greedy and craven. But in fact he was learned, sober and madly brave. He had all the great qualities of soul conjoined to an unbearable character and a conceit bordering on lunacy. He had the most absolute ideas, the most uncouth manners, the most overweening language. But what devotion, what zeal, what a generous and sensitive soul!

My grandmother, in entrusting to him her son's education, hardly divined that she had just bought the tyrant, the savior and the great friend of his life.

In his free hours Deschartres continued to take courses in physics, chemistry, internal medicine and surgery. Later, when he was my grandmother's farmer and the mayor of the village, this knowledge made him useful to the district, especially as he practiced without taking fees. He was so big-hearted that there was no stormy night, no heat or cold or ungodly hour, that could keep him from dashing, for miles sometimes, along forgotten lanes to bring succor to some thatched cottage. But as he must be ridiculous as well as sublime in all matters, he took professional ethics so seriously as to thrash his patients when they returned cured and offering money! Nor could he be got around with presents, for I don't know how often I saw him fly downstairs at the poor devils and belabor them with the very geese, turkey hens and hares they had brought in homage to their savior. Insulted and injured, the good people would go off heavy-hearted, saying, "How ill-tempered he is, the dear fellow!" though a few would angrily add, "There's one I'd lay out, if he hadn't saved me life!" Then Deschartres would bellow from the head of the stairs, "How's that, you swine, you cur? I helped you, and you'd pay me for it! You'd rather be quits with me, eh? Be off with you, or I'll beat you black and blue—and guess who you'll have to send for!"

During the Terror, Deschartres guarded my father's and my grandmother's interests like a watchdog; but it seems that his passion for anatomy drove him now and again into the hospital wards and amphitheaters for dissection. Despite the dreadful bloodletting, his love for science kept him from philosophic reflection upon the heads which the guillotine provided the 'prentice sawbones of the time. One day, however, he had a little shock that greatly discomfited his observations. To a student's enthusiastic cry: "Freshly cut!" a few human heads had just been placed on a laboratory table. A cauldron of water was being brought to a boil to skin the heads for dissection. Deschartres was submerging them one by one.

"Why, here's a priest's head," said the student, handing him the last one. "Look—it's tonsured." Deschartres turned and recognized the head of a friend whom he had not seen for a fortnight.

"I was speechless," he told me. "I stared at the poor head with its white hair; it was still beautiful, and it seemed to be smiling at me. I waited till the student's back was turned, and kissed its forehead. Then I put it in the cauldron with the others and dissected it, keeping the skull for myself. I had it awhile, but soon it became too dangerous to have sitting about. I buried it in a corner of my garden. The incident upset me so much that I was long unable to continue my research."

My father hated Deschartres's lessons. Deschartres dared not handle him roughly, for though he was one of the "old school," my grandmother's love for her son forbade him the use of "proper discipline." He tried to make up with zeal for what he believed to be the strongest lever of the intelligence—the cane. He took lessons with my father in German, music, whatever he couldn't teach him, and coached him in his masters' absence. Out of devotion he even took up fencing, and had Maurice practice parry and thrust between lessons. My father, who was lazy and in a decline, perked up at fencing school; but when Deschartres butted in, with his gift of making the most fascinating subjects dull as dishwater, the child fell asleep on his feet.

One day he asked Deschartres, "Sir, when I fight in real earnest will it be any better fun?"

"I think not, little friend," replied Deschartres. But he was wrong. It was not long before my father came to love war. He never felt so calm, so gently roused, as during a cavalry charge.

But the future warrior was still a weak and spoiled child—when he came down with a child's complaint he would ring for a servant to pick up his pen—yet he soon recovered, and was among the first to be infected with patriotic enthusiasm when the French nation manned its frontiers.

When the Revolution began to rumble, my grandmother, like all the enlightened aristocrats of her day, watched it approach without fear. She had fed too long on Voltaire and Rousseau not to hate the abuses of the court. She detested the queen's coterie, and at her house I found boxes full of couplets, madrigals and satires directed at Marie Antoinette and her favorites. It was "the quality" who copied and passed round these libels. The most telling among them were in my grandmother's hand, and perhaps she had composed them; it was in the best taste to write an epigram upon some gallivanting in the court, and it was the philosophic opposition of the day which took up this characteristically French literary form. Some of these epigrams were most unusual and daring. They rhymed in the language of the streets, and the jargon of the markets was borrowed for ditties upon the paternity of the Dauphin or the dissipations of "the German woman"; both mother and child were threatened with the cat-o'-nine-tails. Oh, don't imagine these songs issued from the People! They came from the salons, and went down into the streets.

My grandmother was forced to accept the considerable reduction which the Revolution effected in her resources. From the remains of what she considered the remains of her initial fortune, she bought the estate of Nohant, not far from Châteauroux; her relations and her way of life attached her to the province of Berry.

I shall now say a few words about this estate, where I was reared and spent most of my life, and where I should like to die.

The income is modest, the house simple and comfortable. The countryside is plain though situated in the Noire valley, a vast and admirable site. It is just this central location in the most level part of the country, in a large belt of grain land, that deprives us of the various prospects one may enjoy from heights or slopes. Yet we have a wide blue horizon, and some shift of terrain about us, and compared with Beauce and Brie, the view is magnificent. It pleases us, and we love it.

My grandmother loved it too, and my father repaired here amid the troubles of his life to seek hours of sweet repose. The rich brown furrows, the great walnut trees with their full crowns, the shaded lanes, the tousled bushes, the overgrown churchyard, the little tiled belfry, the ancient portico, the tall, half-ruined elms, the peasant cottages behind their retaining walls, arbors and green hemp patches—all grows fair to the eye and dear to the heart when one has lived so long amid these humble, calm and quiet surroundings.

The chateau—if one may call it so, for really it is only a mediocre manor from the time of Louis XIV—abuts on the hamlet, forming, with no more pomp than any house in the village, one side of the rustic square. The hearths of the commune, no more than two or three hundred, are sparsely sown throughout the countryside; but there are some twenty clustering about the manor, like neighbors, so to speak, and we must be on good terms with the peasants. We've always been very comfortable here, and though the well-to-do proprietors deplore the proximity of the day laborers, there is less reason to complain of the children, fowl and goats of these neighbors than there is to praise their kindness and good nature.

The people of Nohant, all peasants, all smallholders, have a certain wry jocosity beneath their dour exterior. They have sound traditions, some vestige of piety without bigotry, great modesty of dress and bearing, slow but steady work habits, orderliness, great cleanliness, and much mother wit and candor. With one or two exceptions, I have always had pleasant dealings with these good folk. Yet I have never wooed them, nor demeaned them with what some call benefices. I have rendered them certain services, and they have readily repaid me, according to their means, and in the measure of their good will and intelligence. They owe me nothing. They neither flatter nor cringe, and I've seen them gain more well-grounded pride and initiative each day without ever abusing the trust we've shown them. Nor are they uncouth. They have more tact, reserve and politeness than I have seen among those who consider themselves well-bred.

Such, too, was my grandmother's opinion. She lived twenty-eight years among them and had nothing for them but praise. Deschartres, with his bad temper and ticklish self-importance, had harder times with them, and always inveighed against the guile, knavery and stupidity of the peasant. My grandmother repaired his blunders, and he, too, was forgiven his outbursts because of his essential humanity.

My father studied much with Deschartres, but did not become learned in the classics. His was an artist's nature, and here he profited only by his mother's lessons. Music, modern languages, drawing, literature—it was these that thrilled him. Music always triumphed over the rest; his violin was his boon companion. Besides, he had a magnificent voice, and sang admirably. He was all heart; more republican by instinct, if not by principle, than his mother, he personified the chivalrous phase of the first wars of the Empire. But in 1796 he was still an artist by temperament.

In the fall of that year my grandmother sent him to Paris, perhaps to enjoy himself during a long period of rest, perhaps for more serious reasons, which their correspondence suggests but which I cannot divine.

LETTER
from my father to his mother

Paris, 6 Vendémiaire, Year VII
[September 7, 1798]

I am writing you, my dear Mother, from the home of our "Navarrais."* The Law of Universal Conscription promulgated this morning, which requires reply within twenty-six days, has prevented me from awaiting your answer, and has determined me to take the steps I have mentioned. This morning we shall go together to the captain of the chasseurs and conclude the matter. Do not worry, my dear Mother: there's no question of my joining the Brussels garrison, nor of my facing enemy fire. I'll probably have a leave, or an order *forcing* me to come and embrace you! All the young men here are in a daze. All the pretty women and the loving mamas are in tears. Without cause, I assure you. I shall don the green dolman, take up the saber and let my mustaches grow. Lo, you are the mother of a defender of the fatherland, with the right to his share of the national restitution fund—a net profit! Come now, dearest Mother, do not worry. You shall see me soon.

LETTER
from my father to his mother

7 Vendémiaire, Year VII
[September 8, 1798]

I am an enlisted man. I have a long saber, a red cap, a green dolman. As for my mustaches, they are not so long as I might wish: but that will come. Already folk "tremble at my aspect"—at least, I hope they do. Come now, dearest Mother, do not worry.

I am a private soldier; but did not Marshal Saxe serve gladly in this rank for two years? You agreed that I was old enough to seek a profession. I beat about the bush awhile because you were afraid of war, but at heart I hoped that circumstances would force me to follow my true calling. And now it has come to pass. I'd be happy but for the sorrow of leaving you disquieted, which rends my heart; but I assure you that whither I'm going they don't fight, and that I'll often

---

* His uncle, the abbé de Beaumont.

13

have long leaves to see you. Come now—your own chasseur embraces you with all his heart! There's a place for a bugler in the regiment; suggest it to Deschartres! I kiss you, dearest. Farewell, I love you!

I have before my eyes a portrait of my father, and I want to describe this young man whose letters reveal such a good heart, and a mind so frank and gay. Five feet three inches tall, wasp-waisted, well-built, pale-complexioned, the nose aquiline and delicately chiseled, the mouth intelligent and candid, the eyebrows and mustaches as black as lines drawn with ink, the eyes big and black and gentle and brilliant—really the most beautiful eyes you could imagine—and the hair thick and powdered, and falling loosely upon the brow, which the locks wholly cover without being plastered down (this mass of powered hair, almost touching the jet-black eyebrows, is very becoming and enhances the brilliance of the eyes)— in brief, my father's soul and face at that time were most delicate, and the reader may well conceive that despite his masculine figure General Harville once took him for a woman in disguise. He had tiny feet besides, and hands of perfect beauty.

Later my father grew a trifle stout, though without losing his elegant figure. His face filled out, his features grew more defined. He became one of the most dashing officers in the army. But for me his ideal beauty and most affecting charm reside in the portrait I have just described.

LETTER
from my father to his mother

Cologne, 19 Floréal

Whatever you think, my dear Mother, I don't smell so awfully of the stable! Grooming my horse is the least of things. You need only an improvised apron, and if a bit of the perfume lingers about your person, faith! our lovelies haven't the air of being too bothered by it. Besides, they'd best get used to it: in the field we'd stink even more. Permit me to say, my dear Mother, that your idea of raising my allowance so that I may engage a servant doesn't suit me at all. You're not so rich you can afford the sacrifice; also, a cavalryman who had his boots shined and hair queued by a lackey would be the laughingstock of the army. I laughed at the notion of having a flunky, in the position I'm in; but I was even more touched by your solicitude. If the idea of seeing me with currycomb and pitchfork in hand drives you to despair, it would be very easy for me to get my horse tended by one of the general's stableboys for six francs a month.

Women are born to console us for all the evils of this world. Only in women do we find those charming favors to which sensibility attaches so high a price. I first recognized them, my dear Mother, in you; and now you repair my follies. Oh, if only all mothers were like you, happiness would never forsake a family! Each letter from you increases my gratitude and love. No, we must not abandon this frail creature! I know you will not abandon her! To profess and to practice virture, that is your lot and wont. Farewell, my dearest Mother, my excellent and beloved Mother! I have only time to kiss you—with all my soul!

Here is the explanation of the preceding paragraph. A housemaid at Nohant had just given birth to a baby boy, who later became my playmate and friend. This lovely person had not been seduced; she had yielded, like my father, to youthful abandon. My grandmother had gently dismissed her, provided for her, and reared the child.

Under her supervision he was given to a clean peasant wet nurse who lived nearby. My father received news of this child from his mother; they referred to him discreetly as "the rustic cottage." Not that anyone actually had the sort of rustic cottage that the squires of the Old Regime used to visit on the sly; there was indeed one in the case, but it was only the meeting place of a tender grandmother, a village wet nurse and a bouncing boy. This child was not given to the orphanage, but brought up with as much care as any legitimate son. A day's abandon was repaired with the solicitude of an entire life. My grandmother had read and cherished Rousseau, and she had profited not only by his truths but also by his errors; for to make use of a bad example to set a good one is to turn evil to the advantage of good.

In another letter, which my father wrote from Ivrea to the elder of his nephews, he recounts the crossing of the Saint Bernard Pass and the assault on the Fort de Bard. The fragments I've transcribed reveal how gaily men acted, and without the faintest thought of boasting, in this fine moment of our history.

. . . I arrived at the foot of a rock, beside a precipice where the general staff had pitched camp. I called on the general; he received me. I settled in; I presented my respects to Bonaparte. The same night, he ordered the storming of the Fort de Bard. I found myself in the van with the general. Bullets, bombs, grenades and shells were thundering all about us. We were thrashed (but I am unhurt). . . .

We evaded the fire from the fort by climbing over boulders and vaulting crevices. Bonaparte was climbing with us. Some men fell over the precipices. At last we descended into the plain, where they were fighting. A hussar had just seized a fine horse; I stopped him, and gained the saddle—a rather necessary location in war! This morning I took an order to the forward outposts and found the way strewn with corpses. Tomorrow, or tonight, we shall have a pitched battle. Bonaparte is impatient, he will absolutely advance. And so will we all. . . .

We are laying waste a beautiful country. Slaughter and desolation follow at our heels; we leave ruins and corpses in our tracks. We've tried in vain to spare the population, but the Austrian's tenacity compels us to bombard everything. I'm the first to deplore this state of affairs, yet also the first to be seized by this damnable passion for conquest and glory, which makes us so impatient to fight and to advance. . . .

LETTER
from my father to his mother

At the General Staff Headquarters, Torre di Garofolo
27 Prairial, Year VIII

Historians, trim your quills; poets, mount Pegasus; painters, poise your pencils; journalists, lie as you please—never was finer subject proposed! I shall relate the feat as I saw it, and as it happened.

After the glorious engagement at Montebello we arrive at Voghera on the 23rd. We're off at six in the morning, led by our hero, and at four in the afternoon we reach the plains of San Giuliano. We find the enemy, trounce him, bring him to bay at La Bormida; then night sunders the two armies. The First Consul and the Commander in Chief are quartered in a farm at Torre di Garofolo. We lie on the ground without supper, and sleep. In the morning, the enemy attacks; we deploy our troops along a two-league front. What bombs and bullets! The oldest veterans have never seen an enemy so strong in artillery. By nine o'clock the slaughter is so great that two columns of wounded and their bearers have formed rearward upon the road leading from Marengo to Torre di Garofolo. Already our battalions have been repulsed from Marengo. The right flank are turned by the enemy, and his artillery open a crossfire together with his center. Bullets rain every which way. The general staff meet. A bullet whizzes under the horse of General Dupont's aide de camp, another grazes the crupper of my own. A shell falls in our midst, explodes; no one

16

is hurt. We deliberate. The Commander in Chief sends one of his aides de camp to the left flank, but he does not make a hundred paces before his horse is shot out from under him; so Lieutenant General Stabenrath replaces him. On the way we find a platoon of the First Dragoons. The officer approaches us, downcast, and points to the ten men he has with him; they are the survivors of the fifty who composed his platoon at dawn. While he's talking, a bullet whizzes under my horse's nose, making him rear and throw me. He falls upon me, I adroitly free myself. Miraculously, he's on his feet unhurt. I remount, and we find the left flank in retreat. We rally a battalion, but hardly have we done so when we see a column in rout, running as fast as their legs can carry them. The general sends me to halt them: impossible! I find infantry tangled with cavalry, field gear and pack horses, and the wounded forsaken and mangled on the road, run over by caissons and artillery. Horrid screams, the dust so thick you can't see two feet ahead! In this extremity I dash off the road and ride forward, crying, "Halt up in front!" At last I find a fellow officer. We strike some men with the flat of the saber, others we praise and cheer; for among these desperate runaways is many a brave fellow. I dismount, unlimber a cannon, regroup a platoon. I'm beginning to regroup a second, but the first have already decamped. We give up and join the Commander in Chief. Bonaparte gives the order to beat a retreat.

It's two o'clock; we've already lost twelve cannon. The consternation is general, the horses and men exhausted, the wounded congesting the road. Already I see us refording the Po and the Tesina, crossing a country whose every native is our enemy, when a soothing thunder gives heart: the Desaix-Kellermann Division are here with thirteen cannon! We halt the rout. The division arrive, an attack is sounded, we turn in our tracks, we drive on the enemy, he flees in turn, we laugh as we charge. We take eight standards, six thousand men, two generals, twenty cannon, and only night can despoil our furor of what remains.

The next morning, General Melas raises the white flag and sends a general to parley with us. We receive him in the courtyard of our farm, to the music of the Consular Guard. He brings propositions. They will cede us Genoa, Milan, Tortone, Alessandria, Acqui, Pizzighettone and a part of the Milanese. Today we shall dine with them at Alessandria; the armistice has been concluded; General Melas's palace is ours. The Austrian officers ask me to represent them to General Dupont. Faith! it is my pleasure! They're in a huff to be given the law, but let them snort, they're done for. *Vae victis!*

One

First passion.—Incidents from a novel.—Deschartres's unhappy expedient.—The Black Head Inn.—My father's wedding.—My birth.—My appearance.—Heartbreaks.—Maternal diplomacy.—My mother's character.—My aunt Lucie and my cousin Clotilde.—My first stay at Chaillot.—Beginning of my own story.—First memories.—Novels from the foot warmer.—Soldier games.—Chaillot.—Clotilde.—The Emperor.—The flute.

LETTER
from my father to his mother

Asola, 29 Frimaire, Year IX
[December 1800]

How long it has been, my dear Mother, since we last exchanged our thoughts! But whose fault, you will ask, is that? Truth is, not altogether mine. Since we have come to Asola we do nothing but scout the enemy's positions, and once returned, we keep a joyous and noisy company whose revels and laughter last far into the night. We go to bed exhausted, and next morning ride off again. You scold me, and tell me I'd do better to go to bed early. But were you of warrior stamp, you'd know that fatigue brings excitation, and that our profession calls for coolness only where there is danger. Where there is none we are mad, and must be so. Besides, I have good news for you, which I have only just heard myself. The general has just presented me with an aide de camp's commission, a yellow plume, and a fine red sash with a gold fringe.

Now I am one of Lieutenant General Dupont's aides de camp, and so you must address me on your letters, so they may reach me the sooner. At last I am in a position of some charm; respected, esteemed and loved—yes, loved! by a dear and charming woman—and my complete happiness wants only your presence, though that is wanting so much!

You must know that since Dupont's general staff and the Watrin Division joined forces here, we gather every evening, and Mme. Watrin, radiating youth and beauty, shines like a star. Oh, she is not the one! A softer star burns for me.

In Milan I fell in love. You knew it—my silence gave it away. At times I thought I was loved in return, and then I saw, or thought I saw, that I was not. Seeking to deaden my pain, I departed, and tried to put the matter out of mind. The charming woman came here too, but we hardly talked; indeed, we hardly looked at each other. I was spiteful, perhaps, though that is scarcely in my nature. She, too, behaved proudly toward me, though her heart is tender and passionate. Then, at lunch today, we heard artillery reports from afar. The general told me to find out what was happening. I flew downstairs and dashed to the stable. As I was about to mount I turned, only to see this dear woman standing close behind me, flushed and confused, and gazing upon me with anxiety, concern, love. The only answer was to take her in my arms, but that was impossible in the courtyard. I contented myself with tenderly holding her hand after I had leaped upon my noble steed, who reared magnificently three times as he gained the road. In a trice I reached the place whence the noise proceeded. Finding the Austrians already being driven back in a skirmish which they had provoked, I returned to inform the general. *She* was still there. Oh, what a welcome! What delicate favors she lavished upon me!

This evening, by an undreamed-of chance, I found myself alone with her. The others, weary from the day's taxing rides, had retired. I told her at once that I loved her, and she fell into my arms. Then she escaped and shut herself in her room. I tried to follow; she begged, implored, ordered me to leave. And I, already the submissive lover, obeyed. As we must saddle at daybreak to reconnoiter, I stayed to share the day's emotions with my dear mother. How delightful was your eight-page letter! What joy it gave me! How sweet it is to be loved, to have a dear mother, good friends, a beautiful mistress, a taste of glory, fine horses, and enemies to fight! Of all these I have somewhat; but what is best is my dearest mother!

For the first time Maurice had felt the pangs of a lasting passion. This woman of whom he writes with mixed levity and excitement, this gracious dalliance that he thought he might forget was to draw him into a struggle against himself, a struggle which harrowed and ennobled his last eight years. From that instant his honest heart, which a sole attachment, filial love, had preserved in its precious unity, was rent asunder by two irreconcilable affections. The proud mother was tormented by a jealousy which preyed on her the more for that maternal love had been her one passion, and to this anguish was added the spleen of ruffled prejudices.

The charming woman whom the young man had dreamed of in Milan and conquered at Asola was none other than my mother, Sophie-Victoire-Antoinette Delaborde. I mention all three of her given names because during her troubled life she bore them successively, and these three names symbolize three eras. In her childhood Antoinette was preferred; it was the name of the Queen of France. During the period of imperial conquests, Victoire naturally prevailed. After their wedding, my father always called her Sophie. All is emblematic in the most seemingly fortuitous details of human life.

My grandmother would have preferred that my father find a companion of his own rank, but she did not worry much over what was known in her circle as "marriage beneath one's station." She did not make more of birth than it warranted; and as for a fortune, she herself had done without one, and, had always managed to settle her son's debts. But it pained her to accept a daughter-in-law whose youth had been given over to frightening hazards. When she heard that her son had married my mother she was in despair, and wished to dissolve with her tears the contract cementing their union. It was not that her reason coldly condemned it, simply that her heart misgave her concerning the consequences; for his sake she feared the storm and struggle of so bold an alliance, and the censure he was sure to receive in some circles.

From late in the year 1800 to shortly after my birth in 1804, my father's spirit was torn between a beloved mother and an adored wife. Not until 1804 did he find strength in the satisfaction of having done his duty by marrying the woman he had so often tried to sacrifice for his mother's sake.

Maurice arrived in Nohant in early May 1801. After the first joyful embrace, his mother looked him over with some surprise. The Italian campaign had altered him: he was taller, thinner, stronger, paler; he had grown an inch since his enlistment, a rare occurrence at the age of twenty-one, probably caused by the taxing marches he had been forced to make when captured by the Austrians. Despite the gaiety which filled the first days of his return to his mother, she soon saw that he was beset by some secret sorrow. One day he went visiting in La Châtre and stayed longer than necessary. He went the next day under some pretext, and the day after, he confessed to his downcast mother that Victoire had come to join him. She had sacrificed everything to an unselfish love, of which she had given him undeniable proof. He was dazed with gratitude and tenderness; but he found his mother so set against their reunion that he hid the strength of his affection. Seeing that she was alarmed by the scandal that this adventure was causing in the little town, he promised to induce Victoire to return straightaway to Paris. But he could not persuade her to do so save by promising to join her. He had to choose between mother and mistress: between breaking the heart of the one or of the other. Victoire had sacrificed everything; she had burned her boats; her only joy, her only fortune, was to live with her lover without regrets. But how could this fine son, lately returned from a campaign during which his mother had suffered so, leave her after a few days? And how, just when Victoire was showing him such devotion, could he send her packing like a hussy who has pulled an impertinent stunt? There was more at stake than the contest of two loves: there was the contest of two duties.

The dilemma was insoluble. It was his friend Deschartres who settled the matter by an enormous mistake which released the young man from his scruples.

In his devotion to Mme. Dupin, in his contempt for love, which he had never known, and in his respect for the proprieties, the poor tutor hit upon a disastrous scheme for setting things right at one blow. One morning he left Nohant before his former pupil had wakened and betook himself to the Black Head Inn at La Châtre, where Victoire was still enjoying the delights of sleep. He introduced himself as a friend of Maurice Dupin, and the young wayfarer bade him wait while she hastily dressed to receive him. Unaffected by her beauty, he greeted her with his characteristic surliness, and began to cross-examine her. Amused by his demeanor, the young woman replied gently at first, then coyly, and finally, taking him for a lunatic, burst out laughing. Deschartres, who until then had kept a pompous tone, lost his temper and started to scold her. His reproaches turned to threats; his heart was not tender enough to advise his conscience of the cowardly act he was committing by insulting a woman whose protector was absent. Flying into a rage, he ordered her to take the Paris road that day.

Undaunted, Victoire lost patience in turn; now it was she who sauced and taunted the tutor. Her retorts were rather fast than wise, and her Parisian wit could not be matched by the stammer that always came over Deschartres when his dander was up. She stoutly showed him the door and slammed it in his face, vowing through the keyhole that she would indeed leave that day—with Maurice. Deschartres, disarmed by her nerve, thought for a moment, then took a fatal step: he fetched the mayor and another town official who was a friend of the Dupins. The Black Head Inn was instantly invaded by these two worthies, and the town buzzed with rumors of a new revolution.

Alarmed by Deschartres's report, the two gentlemen marched bravely to the fore, prepared to face an army of furies. Deschartres, by now bloated with rage, whipped them up, demanding a company of gendarmes. However, the military was deemed dispensable; the officials entered the inn, and over the protests of the innkeeper, himself smitten with his lovely guest, climbed the stairs, with equal courage and coolness.

No barricade waited them; they found not the harpy described by Deschartres, but a tiny lady, pretty as an angel with her bare arms and tousled hair, weeping at the edge of her bed.

This sight eased their minds; they grew gentle, even tender. One of them fell in love with the wicked creature, and the other had no trouble seeing how Maurice might adore her with all his heart. They began delicately to question her. She proudly refused to answer; but when she saw that they took her side against the ranting pedagogue, silencing him and even rather fancying her in a fatherly sort of way, she calmed down and answered them sweetly. She hid nothing; she related how she had met Maurice in Italy, how she had loved him and left a generous protector for his sake; and she added that she knew of no statute that forbade her to sacrifice a general for a lieutenant, or the one's fortune for the other's love.

The officials cheered her, and warning Deschartres that he had no right to bully the young woman, they got him to leave, promising to use friendly persuasion to obtain her departure.

Deschartres left, hearing, perhaps, on his way out of town, the approaching gallop of Maurice on his way to his sweetheart. At length all was amicably settled with Maurice's help, though at first he was so indignant at his churlish tutor that the two men could barely restrain him. Luckily Deschartres was already far away. Tactless as always, he was now compounding the mother's sorrows by painting a horrible portrait of the "adventuress," and predicting a dire fate for the son yoked and blinkered by this dangerous woman.

Meanwhile Maurice and Victoire were being calmed by the two officials. The young couple excited their sympathy, but they could not forget the modest and decent mother; they wanted to respect her repose and to spare her nerves. Maurice did not need their affectionate coaxing to see where his duty lay. He explained it to his companion, and she promised to leave that evening. Nonetheless, when the two officials had gone, the lovers arranged to meet at Paris in a few days. This was Maurice's right; and, already, his duty.

Maurice went on writing to his mother. Sophie, as he now called her, had joined him in the army camp at Boulogne. As she was already pregnant, I, too, was there. My mother returned to Paris to lie in, and my father followed on 12 Prairial. On 16 Prairial, they went secretly to the municipal hall of the second ward.

On that day my father was reborn; yet, at the same time, sick unto death. He had done his duty by the woman who loved him so deeply, and who was about to make him a father. But if he was happy to bow to a love which had become his conscience, he was also sad to have secretly disobeyed his mother, like a browbeaten child. This deception was his big mistake: his mother would not have browbeaten him, but pardoned him out of her infinite tenderness, if he had done the simple thing, and told her the truth.

He had not the courage. Not that he lacked frankness; but he would have had to sustain an irresistible assault, to see tears the very thought of which troubled his mind. For this he was wanting in strength; and who can blame him? How he must have suffered when, concealing everything from kith and kin, he gave his mother's name to a bride worthy in her love to share it! But give it he did;

though sad and frightened, he did not falter. At the last moment Sophie Delaborde, in a dimity frock and with merely a gold thread on her finger, trembling with joy, and heedless of the future despite her condition, offered to forgo a consecration which, as she said, could not add to their love. He insisted; but when they came home he wept for an hour at having disobeyed his beloved mother. He tried to write her, but managed only a few lines, which betrayed his fear and remorse. He posted the letter, begged his wife's forgiveness for abandoning her at this hour, hugged my sister Caroline—Sophie's child by an earlier union—and vowed to love her as much as the child about to be born. Then he prepared to leave for Nohant, where he was to spend a month in hopes of confessing what he had done and winning acceptance of it.

These hopes were vain. He did manage to blurt out to his mother that Sophie was pregnant, and fondling my brother Hippolyte, the child of "the rustic cottage," he pointedly reminded her how saddened he had been by the birth of this little boy. He also spoke of the duty imposed by a woman's devotion. But at his first word my grandmother burst into tears, and refusing to hear him out, trotted out her well-worn speech.

"You love another more than me," she said, "and so you really don't love me at all! Where are the days when you loved me alone? Oh, how I wish I'd died in ninety-three, like so many others! You'd have borne me in your heart as I was, and I'd never have had a rival!"

How to reply to such passionate love? Maurice wept, said nothing, and entombed his secret. He returned to Paris and lived calm and secluded in his modest home.

My aunt Lucie was about to marry one of my father's fellow officers, and they gathered with a few friends for a little family celebration. On another such occasion soon after, they were dancing a quadrille, my mother in a pink dress and my father improvising a dance air on his Cremona fiddle, when my mother suddenly felt a stab of pain and left the dance for her room. Since she had not paled, and had left calmly, the dancing went on. As the final "Allemande right!" was sounded, my aunt Lucie went into my mother's bedroom and cried, "Maurice, Maurice, come quick! You have a daughter!"

My father took me in his arms. "We'll call her Aurore," he said, "after my poor mother, who is not here to bless her—but who shall bless her one day."

It was July 5, 1804, the last year of the Republic and the first of the Empire.

"She was born to music, and 'in the pink,'" said my aunt. "She will be happy."

I had a sound constitution, and as a child seemed likely to become beautiful, a promise I did not keep. This was perhaps my fault, since at the age when beauty blossoms I was already spending my nights reading and writing. As the daughter of two perfectly beautiful people, I should not have occasioned such degeneration, and my poor mother, who admired beauty more than anything, often naïvely reproached me for doing so. But I've never been able to preen my person: much as I like cleanliness, I find studied elegance unbearable.

Not to work so that my eyes would sparkle; not to run and play in the sun when God's good sun attracts me so; not to walk in sturdy wooden shoes for fear of deforming my ankles; to wear gloves, that is, to renounce the quickness and strength of my hands; to doom myself to be clumsy and feeble; never to tire myself, when everything urges me to use up my energy; to live, in short, under a bell jar; to be neither burned, nor chapped, nor faded before my time—such things were always impossible for me. I was fresh only for a moment, never beautiful. My features were regular enough, but I never thought to give them any vivacity; and the habit of daydreaming, formed from the cradle, gave me my well-known "silly look" already at an early age.

On the whole, with decent hair, eyes, teeth, and no deformities, I was neither ugly nor beautiful in my youth—a serious advantage, I think, since ugliness prejudices people one way and beauty another. They expect too much of a radiant face, and distrust a repellent one. It is best to have a face which neither dazzles nor frightens, and with mine I get on well with friends of both sexes.

My grandmother came to Paris in the month of Ventôse with the intention of annulling her son's marriage. She thought he would give in, because she had never seen him resist her tears. She arrived in secret, without notifying him as was her custom, and went straight to her lawyer, whom she consulted as to the validity of the marriage.

He called in two other distinguished lawyers, and they concluded that there was indeed a case (there is always "a case" in this world), but that the marriage would almost certainly be upheld by the courts, that my birth certificate proved my legitimacy, and that even supposing an annulment could be obtained, my father would both desire and feel in duty bound to contract marriage anew with the mother of his child.

My grandmother probably never intended to enter a formal plea against her son. Still, she wanted to spend several days without seeing him, to exhaust her resistance and also to find out more about her daughter-in-law. But my father, hearing she was in Paris and realizing she knew everything, engaged me to plead his case. He took me in his arms, hailed a cab and rode to the house where my grandmother was staying. Winning over the concierge with a few words, he handed me to her, and she proceeded to carry out the scheme he had devised.

She went up to my grandmother's rooms, and using the first available pretext, asked to speak to her.

"Just look at my pretty little granddaughter," she said. "Her nurse left her off with me today, and I can't get enough of her."

"My, my, she *is* fresh as a daisy," said my grandmother, reaching for her bonbonnière.

At that moment the good concierge—who was playing her part to perfection—sat me upon my grandmother's lap. My grandmother gave me a sweet and began to scrutinize me with a certain astonishment. All at once she held me at arms' length.

"Liar!" she said to the concierge. "This child doesn't look a bit like you!"

Startled, I began to weep bitterly, and she was touched.

"Come, little pet," said the concierge, taking me back. "She'll have none of you, so let's get along."

But my grandmother was won over at last. "Stay; give her to me," she said. "Poor mite, it's hardly her fault! But tell me, who brought her here?"

"Your son, ma'am. He's waiting downstairs, and wants his daughter back. I meant no offense, ma'am. I expected you'd be pleased."

"I understand, dear. Go fetch my son, but leave the child with me."

My father leaped up the stairs. He found me on my grandmother's lap, pressed tightly against her bosom. Though she was trying to make me laugh, she herself was crying. My mother, who told me about this adventure, said that when my father brought me back I had in my hands a pretty ring with a big ruby, which my grandmother had slipped off her finger, telling me to put it on my mother's.

Some time passed before my grandmother agreed to see her daughter-in-law, but already word had spread that her son had made a "lopsided" marriage, and her refusal to meet my mother caused people to draw embarrassing conclusions about my mother and hence about my father. My grandmother grew worried that her antagonism to the marriage might end by harming her son. She therefore received a jittery Sophie, who disarmed her with her candid deference and her tender embraces. A church wedding was held under my grandmother's supervision, and a family repast signaled my mother's official adoption, and my own.

Later I shall relate how these two women, so different in habits and in tastes, affected each other. It is enough now to say that each behaved civilly, and that the sweet names "mother" and "daughter" were exchanged. Although my father's marriage had caused a minor scandal in my grandmother's little entourage, it made not a ripple in the circles he frequented, where my mother was welcomed without having to display either a bloodline or a fortune. But she never liked society, and later, when my father joined Murat's staff, he had virtually to drag her to that prince's receptions.

My mother was not one of those bold schemers whose secret passion is to wrestle with the prejudices of their time, and who believe they will find a place in the sun by clinging, at the risk of countless affronts, to the specious grandeur of society. She was far too proud even to risk being snubbed. She was so reserved as to seem shy, but if anyone tried to patronize her she just froze him out. Yet she was cordial toward those she respected, and proved attentive and charming in their company. She was lively, teasing, hostile to social constraints. Big dinners, long at-homes, tedious visits, even balls—all these she hated. She was the woman by the hearth, the woman abroad on a bracing walk. But in her own household she needed intimacy, trust, sincerity, freedom to do what she wanted when she wanted. Thus she always lived a little apart, more careful to refrain from tiresome acquaintances than eager to form new ones. In this she was very like my father, and never was a couple better matched in this regard. They were happy only in their family circle; everywhere else they stifled melancholy yawns.

My father returned to camp with General Dupont. My mother followed him in the spring of 1805, staying there two or three months, during which interval my aunt Lucie took care of my sister and me. (My sister Caroline, whom I've already mentioned, was five or six years older than I.)

The first memory of my life dates from my second year, when a maid dropped me against the chimney piece. I was cut on the forehead and frightened. This shock jolted me into awareness of life, and I clearly saw, I still see, the rosy marble of the chimney piece, and my blood running down it, and the distraught look of the maid. I also remember the doctor's visit, the leeches he applied behind my ear, my mother's anxiety, and the maid's dismissal for drunkenness. We left that house, wherever it was; I've never been back, but I feel that I'd immediately find my way about it.

Thus it's not surprising that I remember perfectly the apartment we occupied one year later in the Rue Grande-Batelière. It is from there that my first precise and continuous memories date. Yet from the chimney-piece accident until the age of three, I can retrace only a blurred train of hours spent sleepless on my little bed and filled with gazing on some curtain fold or flower in the wallpaper.

At the same time that my mother married my father, my aunt Lucie married M. Maréchal, a pensioned officer. Five or six months after I was born, Aunt Lucie had a daughter. This was my dear cousin Clotilde, perhaps the best friend I've ever had. My aunt lived in a little house my uncle had bought out in the country, in Chaillot.

Very early my mother took charge of my upbringing, and while I put up no resistance, nothing much was achieved. Had I been left alone I'd have been very slow to develop. I walked at ten months. I began to talk fairly late, but once I could say a few words I learned the rest very quickly, and at four I could read quite well, as could Clotilde. Our mothers took turns teaching the two of us.

Thus we went often to Chaillot, and even after I'd learned to walk I still wanted to be carried by our friend Pierret, who found me too heavy to tote all the way back to town in the evenings. To get me to walk, my mother began to tell me that if I dawdled she'd leave me behind, halfway home. This scene usually occurred where the Rue de Chaillot crosses the Champs Élysées, and one evening it took place just as a little old lady was lighting the street-lamp. No fool, I refused to budge, and my mother went on a few steps with Pierret to see how I liked being left behind. As the street was almost empty, the lamplighter could overhear our dispute.

"Watch out!" she croaked at me. "I'm the one who snatches all the naughty little girls, and I lock them up in my lamp for the rest of the night!"

The devil must have whispered her those words, for none could have frightened me more. At once the streetlamp with its shimmering reflector took on a nightmarish quality, and already I saw myself shut up in its crystal prison, licked by the flame which flared at the will of that petticoated Punch. I ran shrieking after my mother. Behind me the hag cackled, and I shuddered at the squeak of the lamp as she turned it up.

Perhaps it was my upbringing; perhaps the inspiration of what I'd seen and heard; perhaps some innate trait of my own—whatever the case, I was passionately taken with the novel before I'd fully learned to read.

I had long had a craze for playing with the saucepan on the fire, and my mother, who was always sewing or fussing with her soup pot, could get rid of me only by keeping me in a sort of jail consisting of four chairs, with an unkindled foot warmer in their midst for me to sit on when I got tired. They were cane chairs, which had been sacrificed to keep me busy, for I always tried to unravel the caning with my nails. I was still so little that to enjoy this amusement I had first to stand on the foot warmer, and then to rest my elbows on the seats; yet while yielding to my need to occupy my hands, a need I've always had, I was weaving endless tales, which my mother called my "novels." I can't remember anything about these amusing compositions, but my mother told me a lot about them. She declared that they were terribly dull because of their length and the scope I gave to digressions. This is a fault I've retained, I'm told; for my part, I confess that I'm almost unaware of what I do, and that I have today the same irrepressible abandon in such storytelling that I had when I was four.

It seems that my tales were a kind of mishmash of everything that haunted my little brain. They were patterned after fairy tales, and the chief characters were always a fairy, a good prince and a beautiful princess. There were few wicked beings and no great mishaps. Everything always came right, guided by notions as happy as childhood itself. What was curious was the length of the tales, and what you might call their serialization; for I could pick up a story wherever I had been cut off the night before. Perhaps my mother, who listened mechanically to these long ramblings, helped me find the thread without my knowing it.

I recall more clearly the enthusiasm with which I took to games that imitated adult behavior. I was often grumpy, and when my sister or the glazier's eldest daughter came to coax me into such classic games as blindman's buff or hot potato, I found none of them to my liking or quickly tired of them. But with my cousin Clotilde or other children my age I at once found games which flattered my fancy. We simulated the battles and flights through the woods that played so large a part in my imaginings. One of us would go astray, and the others would search for her and call her. She would perhaps be asleep under a tree (that is, under a sofa). We would come to her rescue; one of us would be the mother of the others, or a general, maybe, for impressions of the military world about us had inevitably penetrated our nest, and more than once I was the Emperor, and commanded our troops on the battlefield. Puppets, dolls, dollhouses—we tore them all to shreds, and they suffered the carnage so patiently that we never knew our ferocity. But galloping on our imaginary chargers, and striking toys and furniture with our invisible sabers, we were seized by a feverish enthusiasm. We were scolded for playing boys' games, and it is true that my cousin and I were eager for boyish excitements. One autumn day comes to mind: dinner was being served, and night had invaded our room. We weren't in our home; no, we were out at my aunt's house in Chaillot, for there was a bed curtain, which my mama didn't have. Clotilde and I were chasing each other through the trees—that is, among the curtain folds—and the room had disappeared, and we had come to some dark countryside, just as night was falling . . . and then someone called us to table. We did not hear; my mother had to carry me there, and I shall always remember how shocked I was to see the lights, the table, the real objects about me.

Now that the things in my memory appear in their true dimensions, I see that the house in Chaillot was a very modest dwelling. But to a child it was paradise. Today I could still draw a ground plan of the premises; they are that clear in my memory. The garden was best of all, because it was the only garden I'd ever been in—my mother never took me to the Tuileries to flaunt borrowed turn-outs or to teach me a mincing gait while I bowled a hoop to impress the strollers. We left our sad retreat only to go to the theater, which my mother greatly fancied, as already I did too; or, more often, to Chaillot, where we were always received with shouts of joy. Clotilde bade me into her Eden with the warmth and gaiety that she has never lost. I adored her, despite an occasional set-to always provoked by me, which she would finish by jeering me silly. When she was angry at me she called me "horror" instead of Aurore, a taunt which infuriated me. But how could I sulk with a green arbor before me, and a terrace lined all round with pots of flowers? It was here that I saw my first gossamers, white and ashimmer in the autumn sun; my sister must have been with us on that day, because it was she who explained that the Blessed Virgin herself had spun these threads on her ivory distaff. I dared not break them, and made myself tiny to pass under them.

The garden was a long rectangle, quite small but immense to me, though I made its rounds two hundred times a day. It was laid out in the old way; there were flowers and vegetables; no view at all, since it was enclosed by walls; but at the end was a sandy terrace, reached by stone steps, with, on each side, the classically silly earthen vase, and it was on this terrace that all our alarums and excursions took place.

It was here, too, that I saw my first butterflies, and sunflowers which seemed a hundred feet tall. One day we were interrupted at play by a clamor outside. We heard cries of "Long live the Emperor!" and hurried footfalls, which grew fainter; but the cries continued. The Emperor was indeed passing by at some distance, and we heard the clopping of the horses and the shuffle of the crowd. We could not see over the wall, but it made quite a sight in my imagination, and we, too, vibrating with a sympathetic fervor, cried with all our might, "Long live the Emperor!"

Did we know who the Emperor was? I don't remember, but we must have heard talk of him all the time. Shortly thereafter I formed a clear notion of the Emperor—I can't say just when, but it must have been toward the end of 1807.

He was reviewing the troops on some avenue near the Madeleine. My mother and Pierret had succeeded in penetrating the crowd as far as the soldiers, and Pierret lifted me above their hats that I might see him. This little body rising over the rows of shakos caught the Emperor's eye. "He's looking at you!" cried my mother. "Remember this—it'll bring you good luck!" I think the Emperor heard those naïve words, for just then he did look me right in the eye— I can still see that hint of a smile drift over his wan countenance, whose cool severity frightened me. I shall never forget his face, especially the expression of his eyes, which no portrait has caught. He was rather stout, and wore a greatcoat over his uniform. He had his hat in his hand when I saw him, and I was fairly hypnotized for an instant by his piercing gaze, so harsh at first, then suddenly kind and caring.

A memory which dates from my first four years is that of my first feeling for music. My mother had gone to visit someone in a village near Paris. The apartment was high up, and since I was too little to look down into the street I could see nothing from the window but the rooftops of the surrounding houses and a large piece of sky. We spent much of the day there, but I noticed nothing; I was too charmed by the many wonderful airs someone was playing on a wooden flute. The sound came from a high garret and a remote one too, for my mother could hardly hear it. My own hearing must have been more acute, because I didn't miss a quaver from this little instrument, and I was spellbound. I seemed to be hearing it in a dream: the delicate melodies hovered along the rooftops and vanished into the bright blue sky. Perhaps an inspired artist was playing, who had no other audience than myself; or perhaps it was a cook's boy practicing the theme from *Monaco* or *Les Folies d'Espagne*. Whoever it was, I felt an inexpressible musical pleasure. There, for the first time, I vaguely sensed the harmony of external things, my soul being equally ravished by the music and the beauty of the sky.

Two

Pierret.—We depart for Spain.—Asturias.—Morning glories and bears.—The bloodstain.—The talking magpie.—The Queen of Etruria.—Madrid.—Godoy's palace.—The white rabbit.—I become Murat's aide de camp.—His sickness.—Weber.—First solitude.—Mamelukes.—Afterimages.—The echo.—My brother's birth.—He is discovered to be blind.—We leave Madrid.—Letter from my father to his mother.—Leopardo.—Memories of a bombardment and a battlefield.—Embarkment and shipwreck.

I HAVE VERY FEW memories of my father before the Spanish campaign. He was away so often that I must have lost sight of him for long intervals. Yet he did spend the winter of 1807–1808 with us, for I dimly remember quiet, candlelit dinners, and a modest tidbit of vermicelli cooked in sugared milk which he made as if to eat by himself, just to tease me in my childish greed. I also remember that he folded his napkin into the figure of a monk, rabbit, or Punch, which made me laugh and laugh. He must have spoiled me horribly, for my mother had to step between us to keep him from encouraging my freaks instead of curbing them. I've been told that during the short periods he spent with us he couldn't bear to let his wife or daughter out of sight, that he played with me all day long, and that even in full uniform he didn't hesitate to carry me out into the street and down the boulevards.

Doubtless I was very happy, for I was much loved; we were poor, and I utterly unaware of it. My father drew a soldier's pay, on which we could have lived comfortably had not his expenses, as one of Murat's aides de camp, exceeded his means. My grandmother stinted herself to help him, yet still he left debts for uniforms, horses and horse furniture. Often my mother was accused of adding a certain slovenliness to the family difficulties; but I can still picture our dwelling clearly enough to warrant that the charge was undeserved. A woman of great industry and courage, she made the beds, swept the rooms, mended our clothes and did the cooking. All her life she rose with the sun and retired at one in the morning, and I don't recall seeing her idle at home for an instant. We received no one but our kin and our friend Pierret, who always showed me a father's tenderness and a mother's loving care.

It is time I told the story and sketched the character of this priceless man whom I shall remember fondly my whole life. Pierret was the son of a small vintner in Champagne. From the age of eighteen he had been employed in the Treasury, where he had a modest position. He was the ugliest man you could lay eyes on, but his ugliness expressed such kindness that it called forth trust and warmth. He had a huge, flattish, flabbergasted sort of nose, blubber lips and tiny eyes; his blond hair was always in frizzy revolt, and his skin was so white and rosy that he looked young all his life. At forty he flew into a rage because an official at the municipal hall, where he was acting as a witness at my sister's wedding, asked him if he was not a minor. Yet he was tall and fat, and his face was always in wrinkles on account of a nervous tic which wrung it into frightful grimaces; perhaps it was this tic which prevented you from knowing just what sort of face he really had. But I think it was mostly the frank and naïve look on his countenance, in its rare moments of repose, that lent the illusion of youth. He hadn't an ounce of what they call wit; but as he judged all things with his heart and conscience, you could ask his counsel on the touchiest tangles in life.

His tastes were prosaic. He liked wine, beer, his pipe, billiards and dominoes. All the time he was not with us he spent in a public house in the Rue du Faubourg Poissonière under the sign of The

White Horse. This tavern was his family circle, and for thirty years he was there most every day. His life went by obscurely, and with little variation; but he was happy, and how could he not have been? All who knew him loved him, and no thought of evil ever passed through his honest, simple soul.

He was very nervous and hotheaded, but his kindness showed through anyway, for he never succeeded in offending anybody. What tirades I had to take from him! He stamped his foot, he rolled his little eyes, he grimaced and went red in the face. My mother ignored all this. "It's one of Pierret's conniption fits," she would say. "We're in for some funny faces!" and at once Pierret would drop his dramatic tone and laugh. She teased him endlessly, so it was little wonder that he often lost his temper. During his last years he became even more irascible, and every day he would grab his hat and storm out, swearing he'd never darken her threshold again; but by evening he was back, forgetful of the morning's bitter farewell.

He claimed fatherly rights over me that would have verged on tyranny had he been able to exercise them. For it was he who had weaned me, which astonishing fact may furnish an idea of his character. My mother, exhausted yet unable to ignore my crying, and fearing, too, that her maid did not tend me at night, had grown unable to sleep just when she needed to most. Observing this one night, Pierret took me home. He kept me there two weeks, so busy with me that he hardly slept, and fed me sugared milk as carefully as any wet nurse might have nursed me. He brought me back to my mother each morning, and then went to his office; in the evening he'd come from The White Horse to fetch me. He was then a strapping fellow of twenty-two, but he carried me about without caring what anybody thought. When my mother made a show of resisting, he went red in the face and accused her of "imbecile weakness"; and when he brought me back, my mother had to admire my freshness and good humor. It is so unlike a man—especially a tavern-haunter like Pierret—to wean a child of ten months that it is a marvel not only that he did it but that the idea came to him at all.

Is it surprising, then, that he always saw me as an infant? When I was forty he still addressed me as if I were a child: he wanted not gratitude but love. And when I asked him why he wanted to be loved, he had but one answer: "Because *I* love *you*," said in a furious tone and with a nervous grinding of teeth. If in a note to my mother I forgot to include a salutation to Pierret, and presently encountered him, he turned me a cold shoulder. Explanations were of no avail; he called me a "bad heart" and vowed eternal hatred. He said it all so comically that you'd have thought he was a fair-ground mummer if you hadn't seen the tears in his eyes. My mother, who knew his nervous states, would say, "Hush up, Pierret, you're raving"; and she would pinch him hard to bring him round. Only then would he deign to listen to my excuse, and one heartfelt word was enough to reassure him.

He had met my parents in a way that had at once drawn them together. One of his relations lived in the Rue Meslay, on the same floor as my mother. This woman had a child my age which she neglected, and which cried all day for its milk. My mother would go into the room where the poor thing was dying of hunger and nurse it in secret. One day Pierret caught her in the act. Deeply touched, he became devoted to her and her family.

He conceived a great affection for my father at first sight. He took charge of his papers, rid him of malicious creditors, and with his clerical skills, helped him appease the others little by little; and so he freed him of all the material cares he was capable of managing, for he was at home with the details of other people's welfare. It was he who chose my father's servants and picked up his pay, making sure it would reach him wherever he was. My father never left on a campaign without saying, "Pierret, I commend to you my wife and children, and if I do not return, remember it's for your whole life." Pierret took this responsibility seriously: after my father's death he devoted his whole life to us. Of course, tongues wagged about these domestic relations—what soul is judged pure by those that are not?—but to me such suppositions will always seem an outrage. He was not seductive enough to make my mother unfaithful even in thought.

It was Pierret who prepared our departure when we resolved on a journey to Spain. This was hardly a prudent enterprise for my mother, already seven or eight months pregnant; she even wanted to bring me, though I was still a rather troublesome little person. But my father had written that he would remain awhile in Madrid, and I believe she entertained some jealous suspicion on this score. Whatever her motive, she was bent on rejoining him, and yielded to what was probably the first temptation to do so. The wife of an army purveyor whom she knew was traveling post to Madrid, and offered her a place in her carriage. For her sole protector this lady had brought along a twelve-year-old stableboy. So there we were on the road together: two women, one of them pregnant, and two children, of whom I was not the silliest or unruliest.

Except for the thought of a certain doll, which pursued me for some time, I remember nothing of our journey before we reached the mountains of Asturias. But I can still feel my astonishment and terror at those towering heights. The road wound through an amphitheater of peaks which obscured the horizon, and with each moment some sharp turn surprised and dismayed me. Often it seemed we were imprisoned amid these crags, that there was no road forward or back.

It was here, beside the way, that I first saw wild morning glories in bloom, and I wondered greatly at their pink bells with dainty streaks of white. From my tenderest infancy my mother had instinctively guided me into the world of beauty by sharing her impressions with me. Whenever a pretty cloud appeared, or a striking effect of light, or clear and running water, she would say, "Look—there's something fine!" and at once these objects revealed their beauty to me.

But since her memory was infirm and she could never follow any train of recollections, she tried to fight this tendency in me, though in many ways it has proved hereditary. She was forever saying, "You must remember what you see here," and each time she urged me to, I did. When she saw the morning glories she said, "Smell them, they have a honey scent; and don't forget them!" This was the first revelation of smell I can recall; and by one of those chains of memory and sensation which everyone knows but no one can explain, I never smell wild morning glories without seeing that spot in the Spanish mountains, and that roadside where I first plucked them.

Another incident I shall never forget is one that surely would have astonished any child. We were in a level place, not far from some dwellings. The night was clear, but dense trees bounded the road, and now and then they obscured it. I was on the box with the stableboy; suddenly the postilion slowed his horses, turned to him and shouted, "Tell the ladies not to fear—my horses are first-rate!" There was no need to pass the word, for my mother had heard. Thrusting her head out the carriage window, she saw, as I did, three figures: two on one side of the road and the other directly across from them, about ten paces from us. They seemed small and did not move.

"Bandits!" cried my mother. "Driver, turn back—I see their muskets!"

The postilion, who was French, began to laugh, for this vision of muskets showed him that my mother had no notion what sort of enemies we were up against. He judged it best not to enlighten her, whipped up his horses and passed the three figures at a smart trot. They did not budge. My mother, seeing them through her fright, thought she made out pointed hats, and took them for armed men. But when the horses, skittish and frightened for their own sakes, had coursed awhile, the postilion reined them to a walk and hopped down.

"Well, now, my ladies," he said, still chuckling, "did you see their muskets? They clearly had some mischief in mind, because they stood there as long as they could see us. But I knew my horses wouldn't blunder. If they'd upset us there, they'd have finished us off."

"But who were they?" asked my mother.

"Three big mountain bears—with all due respect, my little lady."

My mother was even more frightened than before. She implored the postilion to climb back up and drive us at top speed to the first inn. But the man seemed used to such encounters. He told us that the brutes could do no harm unless one fell, and drove us on to the next post-house without mishap.

My mother had another fright, much less founded, in a perfectly respectable-looking inn. I was very weary, for we had traveled in stifling heat, and no sooner had we been shown to our room than I was asleep.

My mother went out into the passage; but a moment later she screamed and rushed back into the room. On the floor outside she'd seen a large bloodstain, and it was enough to convince her that she had fallen into a den of cutthroats. Mme. Fontanier, our traveling companion, only laughed at her; but my mother could not go to bed until she had searched the house. For my mother, though a coward, was a coward of a very peculiar sort: she continually imagined terrible dangers, but at the same time her presence of mind gave her the courage to confront whatever frightened her. She was one of those women who always fear something because they fear death, yet who never lose their head because they have the genius of self-preservation.

There she was, then, already armed with a torch and beckoning Mme. Fontanier on toward the discovery. But the latter, neither so timid nor so daring as my mother, remained unruffled. Suddenly some great courage came over me, and seeing my mother about to march off alone on an expedition from which her companion shrank, I caught firm hold of her petticoat. The stableboy, a cunning, fearless rascal, followed with another torch.

Thus we set off to reconnoiter, on tiptoe so as not to arouse the suspicions of our hosts, whom we could hear chatting in the kitchen. My mother showed us a bloodstain before a door, to which she pressed her ear, her imagination being so overwrought that she fancied she heard groans. "I'm sure it's some poor devil of a French soldier whose throat has been slit by these wicked Spaniards," she said to the stableboy. With a trembling but determined hand she opened the door upon what turned out to be three huge corpses—of swine freshly murdered for the larder and the travelers' table!

My mother burst out laughing and returned to mock at her own fear with Mme. Fontanier. As for me, I was more frightened by the sight of those eviscerated, bloodstained hogs, squalidly hanging from the wall with their scorched snouts touching the floor, than by anything I could have imagined.

Toward Burgos or Victoria we encountered a noblewoman who must have been the Queen of Etruria. It is said that the flight of this princess was the immediate cause of the revolt of May 2: thus we probably saw her as she was heading for Bayonne, whither King Charles IV had summoned her that he might gather his family under the talons of the imperial eagle.

We had stopped for dinner in a hamlet. At the inn there was a post chaise, and at the back of the courtyard I saw a large garden with sunflowers which reminded me of those at Chaillot. In the corner of the courtyard was a magpie in a cage, and to my astonishment this magpie talked. He was saying something in Spanish which probably meant "Death to the French" or perhaps "Death to Godoy." The only word I caught was the first, which he repeated in an affected and diabolical tone: *"Muera, muera . . ."* Mme. Fontanier's stableboy said that he was angry with me and wished me dead. I was so amazed to hear a bird talk that my "novels" began to seem more realistic than I had hitherto believed. Since he talked, he must think, and I was aghast at this evil genius who knocked his beak against his cage, repeating, *"Muera, muera!"*

But a fresh commotion distracted me. A large carriage followed by two or three others had just entered the courtyard, and the horses were being rapidly changed. The people of the hamlet were trying to break into the courtyard, crying, *"La reina! La reina!"* but the innkeeper and some other men held them back, denying it was the Queen. They changed the horses so quickly that my mother, who was upstairs, did not have time to come down. Besides, no other carriages were permitted to approach, and the hostlers seemed in on some secret, for they kept insisting to the people outside that it was not the Queen. But one of their wives carried me up to the main carriage, whispering, "Look—that's she!"

There had always been kings and queens in my "novels," and I'd pictured them as beings of extraordinary radiance and luxury. But this queen wore only a thin white dress, fashionably tight at the waist but yellow with dust. Her daughter, who was perhaps eight years old, was similarly attired, and both seemed dark and ugly. They were a sad and anxious pair, and I do not recall that they had either escort or retinue. They fled rather than departed, and when they were gone my mother casually remarked, "Another queen takes to her heels." Indeed, these poor queens were hieing to Bayonne to beg of Napoleon a protection which was to seal their political doom. Of course, when I witnessed the scene I was not old enough to sense that this fugitive queen was frightened, and trying to preserve her incognito; but I have never forgotten her grim expression, which betrayed at once a fear of remaining and a fear of leaving.

We arrived in Madrid sometime in May. Reaching our goal safe and sound was almost a miracle in itself, for uprisings had already broken out in several parts of Spain, and the lowering storm was heard everywhere. To be sure, we followed a supply line protected by the French army; but nowhere were the French safe from vengeance-seekers, and my mother, with one child in her arms and another in her womb, had good reason to be afraid.

My weariness vanished the moment I saw the magnificent apartment we were to occupy. I was entering the palace of the "Prince of the Peace," just as if my "novels" had come true. Murat himself had the lower floor of this palace, which was the richest and most comfortable in Madrid, for he had protected the queen's passion for her lover. This abode boasted greater luxury than the house of His Majesty. Our own apartment was situated on the fourth floor. It was immense, and entirely hung with crimson silk. The cornices, beds, armchairs and divans, all gilded, seemed to me of solid gold, just as in my "novels" once again. There were also great pictures which terrified me. Massive heads that seemed to pop out of their frames and follow me with their eyes oppressed me greatly, but I soon grew used to them. Another marvel was a cheval glass in which I saw, toddling about the carpet, a child whom at first I could not recognize; I'd never seen myself top to toe, and had no notion of my stature, which was slight even for a child my age. Yet I looked so tall that I was frightened.

For all my wonder, it may be that this splendid palace was really in the most vulgar taste. Certainly it was very untidy, and full of pets, rabbits among others, who scurried about without attracting notice. I wonder if these tranquil hosts, the only ones who had been robbed of nothing, were wont to be admitted to the apartments, or if they had merely slipped from kitchen to salon during the general bustle. There was one, ruby-eyed and white as snow, who forthwith became my friend. He took over the corner of the bedroom behind the cheval glass, and there our intimacy grew, unchallenged by anyone. Still, he was very grumpy, and several times he scratched the face of one come to dislodge him; but in his moods he never turned on me, and slept hours on my lap while I told him my finest tales.

Soon I had the prettiest toys in the world: jumping jacks, doll furniture and horses, all in gold leaf, fringes, spangles and brocade. These were the playthings left behind by the infantes of Spain, who'd half-broken them. I deftly finished the job, for I found them grotesque. Yet they must have been valuable, for my father rescued two manikins of painted wood and brought them back to my grandmother as objects of art. She kept them awhile, and everyone admired them, but somehow after my father's death they again fell into my hands. I recall one little fellow in rags who doubtless had remarkable truth of expression, for he frightened me. Was it only by chance that this clever simulacrum of a haggard old beggar stretching out his hand had entered the glittering trove of the Spanish infantes? What a strange toy, this personification of poverty, for a king's son—and what food for his thoughts!

Though I'd already seen Murat in Paris and played with his children, I did not remember him. Probably I'd seen him in mufti; in Madrid, in gold and plumes, he struck me as very grand.

Perhaps he'd expressed some displeasure that an aide de camp had brought his wife and children to the ordeal in which he now found himself, and perhaps my parents had deemed that the whole family should assume a military aspect in his eyes; in any case, I was obliged to put on a uniform every time I appeared before him. This uniform was a treasure that we kept long after I outgrew it, and I can remember it in detail. It consisted of a dolman of white cashmere wool with braids and buttons of real gold, a matching pelisse trimmed with black fur, and a pantaloon of purple cashmere with gold embroidery after the Hungarian fashion. I also had boots of red morocco with gilded spurs, a saber, a braided baldric of crimson silk with enameled gold lanyards and canions, and a saber knot with an eagle embroidered in real pearls. Seeing me so attired, the very image of my father, Murat was gratified by this little flattery of my mother's; and either taking me for a boy or pretending to, he presented me laughingly to his callers as "my aide de camp."

Then he fell ill; from debauchery, they said, but this is false. Like many in our Army of Spain, he had an inflammation of the vitals, and he suffered terribly without ever taking to his bed. He thought he'd been poisoned, and did not endure his sickness patiently, for his cries echoed through that grim palace where none slept anyway but with one eye open. I remember being wakened by my parents' worried voices the first time he howled in the night. Thinking he was being murdered, my father leaped out of bed, seized his saber and ran half-naked to his apartment. Then I, too, heard the cries of this poor hero, so terrible in war, so cowardly off the battlefield: I was frightened half to death and began to shriek myself.

Our sojourn in Madrid lasted no more than two months, yet it seemed long to me. I had no playmates my own age, and I was often alone for a large part of the day. My mother was obliged to go out with my father every morning, and she left me with a Madrilenian maidservant who had been recommended to her as highly reliable but who bolted the moment they were gone. My father had a valet called Weber who was worth his weight in gold and who often came to look after me at the Plaza de Teresa; but this good German, who knew hardly a word of French, spoke to me in double Dutch and smelled so foul that, without my knowing the cause of my sickish feeling, I would faint away when he carried me. He dared not betray my maid's negligence, and as for me, it never crossed my mind to complain of her. I thought Weber was appointed to watch over me, and I only wished he would stay in the antechamber and leave me alone. Thus my first words to him were, "Weber, I like you, but do go along." And Weber, the proverbial docile German, departed. When he saw how well behaved I was when left alone, he took to locking me in and going off to tend to his horses, who probably received him more gently than I. So it was that I first knew the pleasure of finding myself alone, and far from being frightened, I was, rather, unhappy when I heard my mother's carriage return.

No sooner did I see that I had the run of this vast apartment than I began to mime theatrical poses before the cheval glass. Then I tried to force my white rabbit to do likewise, or feigned to offer him as a sacrifice to the gods on a stool which did me for an altar. I wrapped myself in my mantilla to play priestess, so savoring my ability at mime that, seeing myself and the rabbit in the glass, I believed I was playing in a scene with four actors. Then the rabbit and I would hail the mirror folk, or threaten or implore them. Or we would dance a bolero, for the Spanish dancers had enchanted me, and I aped their graces with a child's facility of imitation. And so I quite forgot that the figure dancing in the glass was my own, and was surprised that it stopped when I did.

When I'd had enough of dancing these ballets, I went out to daydream on the terrace, which ran along the whole façade of the palace and was unusually spacious and elegant. The balustrade was of white marble, and grew so hot under the sun that I could not touch it. I was too small to see over it, but in the spaces between the balusters I could make out whatever was happening in the plaza. In my memories that plaza is magnificent. There were other palaces and fine mansions all around it, but I never saw the city's people; in fact, I do not believe I saw a single Madrilenian there all the while I was in Madrid. Probably after the insurrection of May 2 the populace were no longer allowed near the palace of the French commander in chief. All I saw, then, was French uniforms, and more splendid still, the Mamelukes of the Guard, one of whose contingents occupied the building facing us. In their turbans and rich Oriental costumes, these copper-skinned men came to water their horses at a great basin in the middle of the plaza, forming groups on which I never tired of gazing.

To my right an entire side of the plaza was bounded by a massive church, topped by a cross planted in a gilded globe. This globe and cross, set agleam by the sunset and relieved against a heaven bluer than any I'd ever seen, made a sight I shall never forget. I stared at them until there appeared before my eyes those red and blue balls which, by an excellent word derived from Latin, we call *orblutes* in our Berrichon dialect. These afterimages vastly amused me, for I could not understand their entirely natural origin. I enjoyed seeing the colors float before my eyes and even persist when I closed them. But soon I discovered a more exciting phenomenon on the terrace. The plaza was often deserted, and even in broad day a gloomy silence reigned in the palace and its vicinity. One day this silence scared me, and I called out to Weber, whom I saw passing below. He did not hear me, but a voice just like my own repeated his name on the other end of the balcony.

This voice reassured me: I was not alone; but curious to know who was mimicking me, I went into the apartment, expecting to find someone there. There was no one, so I returned to the terrace and called for my mother; the voice repeated her name, soft and clear, quite bewildering me. Louder, I called my own name, and presently got it back, but blurred. I repeated it lower, and the voice returned, also low, but sharper, as if talking in my ear. Baffled, I thought someone had joined me on the terrace; but seeing no one, and squinting vainly along the rows of closed windows, I puzzled over this prodigy with great delight. The oddest thing was to hear my name repeated by my own voice. Then I hit on a droll explanation: I was double, and somewhere nearby was another me whom I could not see, but who could see me always, since she always answered. At once I conceived this as a thing which must be, and

44

had always been, but which I had not yet noticed. I compared this phenomenon to my afterimages, which at first had astonished me equally, but which I had grown used to without understanding them. I concluded that all things and all persons had their reflection, their double, and I longed to see mine. I called to her a hundred times, telling her to come to me, but she only answered, "Come, do come!" and retired or approached as I did. I called to her in the apartment; she no longer replied. I went to the other end of the terrace; she was dumb. But when called to from anywhere between the center of the terrace and the end closest to the church, she spoke to me, tender and anxious. My double seemed to hover in the air or perch on the wall, but how could I reach or see her?

All this was cut short by my mother's arrival. Far from asking her about what was exciting me, I hid it from her. Perhaps I wanted to find the answer myself; perhaps I'd been disappointed in some other phantasm after explanations had robbed it of its secret charm. I breathed not a word about this new prodigy, and for several days, forgetting my ballets, I suffered my rabbit to sleep in peace and the cheval glass to reflect the motionless worthies in the pictures. I waited until I was alone to repeat my experiment; but one day my mother returned and discovered the secret of my love for the terrace. Now there was no going back; I asked her where was the body who repeated all my words, and she told me, "It's your echo."

Happily for me, she did not explain what an echo was—perhaps she'd never cared to find out. She told me it was a "voice in the air," and so the unknown kept its poetry for me. For a few more days I continued to toss words to the wind. The voice in the air astonished me no longer, but it charmed me still; I was content to name it, and to cry, "Good morning, Echo!"

I had been told that a little brother or sister would soon come, and for several days I had seen my mother stretched out on a chaise longue. One day I was sent out to play on the terrace and the glass doors to the apartment were closed behind me. I heard not the faintest groan, for my mother bore bodily pain bravely and gave birth promptly. I was separated from her for a few minutes only; then my father called me in and showed me a tiny infant. I barely noticed it. My mother was lying on a sofa, her face so pale and her features so tense that I was slow to recognize her. Then a great fear seized me and I ran weeping to kiss her. I wanted her to talk to me, to return my caresses, and when I was taken from her again so she could rest, I grieved a long while, thinking she would die and that her dying was being kept from me. I went back out on the terrace and wept, and no one could interest me in my newborn brother.

This poor baby's eyes were of a singular light blue. After a few days my mother began to worry about the paleness of his pupils, and I heard my father and others utter the words "crystalline lens." After a fortnight it was clear that the child was blind, but no one would tell my mother, hopes being timidly aired that the baby's eyes would improve. She let herself be comforted, and the impaired infant was dandled with all the joy the poor thing would have given had his life not been a sore trial to his parents. My mother nursed him, but scarcely two weeks passed before we had to set off once again—this time for France, through a Spain put to fire and sword.

LETTER
from my father to his mother

Madrid, June 12, 1808

After long sufferings, Sophie has given birth this morning to a bouncing boy who screeches like a parrot. Both mother and child are in excellent health. Before the month is out the Prince leaves for France, and the Emperor's doctor, who attended Sophie, says she will be fit to travel with her child in twelve days. Aurore is in the pink. I'll bundle up the lot in a four-wheeler I've procured, and we'll set off for Nohant, where I expect to arrive on July 20 and to stay as long as possible. The very thought, my dear Mother, fills me with joy. I am living in sure hopes of our reunion, and the charm of our home, without duties, anxieties or painful distractions! How I have longed for this complete happiness!

I have reserved the child's baptism for Nohant. What a fine opportunity to set the belfry pealing and the village dancing! The mayor himself shall inscribe my son in the numbers of the French; for I would bar that he ever have anything to unravel with the Castilian notaries and priests.

I cannot conceive that my two latest letters were censored. They were so silly that they would have found grace in the eyes of the severest police. I described for you an African saber I had acquired. There were two pages of explanations and citations. You shall see this marvel, as well as the indomitable Leopardo of Andalusia, upon whom I shall engage Deschartres to cut a caper—after mustering all the mattresses of his tenants to pad the ring!

Farewell, my dearest mother. Sophie shares my impatience to embrace you. Aurore would leave this moment, and were it possible, we should already be on our way.

This letter, so glad and gay and hopeful, is the last that my grandmother ever received from her son. The reader will soon see what doom befell his hopes, and how few days he would have to savor his reunion with the objects of his affection. The reader will also see that my father's jest about the "indomitable" Leopardo bears a ghastly construction.

It was Ferdinand of Asturias, then currying favor with Murat and his staff, who had given this terrible horse to my father following a mission that they had accomplished together at Aranjuez. It was a deadly gift which my mother, as if by presentiment, distrusted and feared. Yet she could not persuade my father to get rid of the beast, though he admitted that Leopardo was the only horse he couldn't mount without an uncanny feeling. My mother claimed that Ferdinand had given him the horse in hopes that it would kill him. (She also claimed that the surgeon who had delivered her son in Madrid had blinded the child out of hatred for the French. She imagined that in the exhaustion following her travail she had seen this surgeon press his thumbs against the infant's eyes, hissing, "This one shall never see the sun of Spain!" Possibly my poor mother was under a hallucination; yet considering where matters stood, it is equally possible that some such deed was done when the surgeon was alone with her and believed that she could not see or hear him; but far be it from me to answer for so terrible an accusation.)

It was during the first fortnight of July that we departed. Murat was about to mount the throne of Naples. My father had a leave. I do not know if he accompanied Murat to the frontier or even if he traveled with us. I remember that we were in a carriage and I believe that we were following Murat's baggage train, but I have no memory of my father's presence before Bayonne.

What I do remember is the sickness, thirst, devouring heat and fever that oppressed me all during this journey. We advanced slowly alongside the columns of the army. I recall now that my father was with us, because once, as we were following a narrow road in the mountains, we saw a huge snake that stretched almost full across it, like a black line. My father called a halt, ran ahead and slashed it in two with his saber. My mother, afraid as usual, had tried in vain to restrain him.

Yet another occurrence causes me to think that he was often elsewhere, notably with Murat. This event must have been quite striking to be etched still in my memory. One evening my mother and I saw from a window that the sky, still lit by the setting sun, was streaked with crossfire. "Look," said my mother. "It's a battle, and perhaps your father's in it." I had no idea what a battle was. I imagined an immense fireworks display, something merry and triumphal, some festival or joust. The noise of the cannon and the great curves of fire delighted me. I watched all this as if it were a play on the boulevard, while eating a green apple.

Presently our carriage was requisitioned to carry wounded men or persons more precious than ourselves, and we did a stretch in a wagon, together with field baggage, victualers and ailing soldiers. We skirted the battlefield the next day or the day after, and I saw a vast plain covered with formless debris. The air was foul, and my mother hid her face. We did not pass close enough to those horrible objects for me to see what they were, and I asked why so many rags had been sown there. Once the wheel caught something which broke with a strange crunch. My mother held me down in the wagon to keep me from seeing; it was a corpse. I soon saw others scattered on the road, but I was too ill to be keenly affected by this spectacle.

Along with the fever I soon felt another sort of suffering, which also affected all the ailing soldiers with whom we were traveling: it was hunger, an extreme, unhealthy, almost animal hunger. These poor people, so full of care for us, had infected me with an illness which explains this hunger, and which no dame of society would admit to having caught. But when my mother grieved to see my little brother and myself in this condition, the soldiers and the victualers only laughed and said it was the "true baptism of all the children of the cartridge pouch," and meant lifelong immunity for her children. The itch, to call a spade a spade, had started with me, then infected my brother and my mother.

In a few hours, then, our lot had changed indeed. It was no longer the palace of Madrid, with its gilded beds, its Oriental carpets, its silk curtains; it was filthy baggage carts, burning villages, cities under bombardment, roads covered with corpses, ditches where we searched for a trickle of water, only to see blood rise suddenly to the surface. It was above all the horrible hunger and an ominous want of provisions. My mother bore all this with courage, but she could not overcome her disgust for raw onions, green lemons and sunflower seeds (all of which I gobbled heartily). What food for a woman nursing her infant!

We came upon a French camp and at the entrance to a tent saw a group of soldiers eating soup with great gusto; my mother begged them to let me eat from their mess kettle. The good men held me up and smiled tenderly as I ate my fill. I thought the soup was delicious, but when it was half consumed, a soldier said shyly to my mother, "We'd pray you to eat also, but perhaps you couldn't— the taste's a bit strong." My mother peered into the kettle. There was bread there, and a fatty bouillon, but some black wicks floated on the surface: it was a soup made of candle ends.

I remember Burgos, and a town—perhaps the same—where the adventures of the Cid were painted alfresco on the walls. I also remember a superb cathedral, where the menfolk prayed with their hat on one knee while the other rested on a "kneeler" upon the floor. Lastly I remember Vitoria, and a maidservant whose long black hair streamed down her back: it was crawling with lice. I had a few comfortable days at the Spanish frontier; the weather had freshened, the fever and want had ceased. We had regained our carriage for the last leg of the journey; the inns were clean; and there were beds and all sorts of good things to eat, including cakes and cheeses. My mother made my toilette at Fontarabia, and a bath did me a power of good. She washed me as usual, but as I left the tub she plastered me with sulfur from top to toe, and made me swallow pellets of sulfur ground in butter and sugar. That taste and that odor, which I endured for two months, have given me a great repugnance for anything that recalls them.

Apparently we found familiar faces at the frontier, for I remember a large dinner with courtesies that bored me to tears; I'd regained my faculties and my eye for the things around me. Heaven knows what seized my mother to want to return to Bordeaux by sea. Perhaps she was aching with carriage fatigue; perhaps her medical intuition, which she always trusted, told her that the sea air would cure her children and herself of the poison of poor Spain. Apparently

the weather was fine and the ocean calm, for it was a fresh impru-
dence to venture out in a boat along the Gascon coast, in the ever
rough Bay of Biscay. Whatever the reason, a pointed barge was
rented, our carriage was lowered into it, and we left as if on an
outing. I do not know where we embarked, nor who they were
who lavished favors on us all the way to the shore: for I got a big
bouquet of roses, which I kept the whole crossing to preserve me
from the odor of sulfur.

We hugged the shore, for how long I do not know; I had fallen
back into my heavy slumber, and I recall nothing after the departure
but the arrival itself. As we neared our destination, a gust blew us
off the coast, unnerving the pilot and his two mates. My mother
began to quail again, and my father took the helm; but as we at
last entered the Gironde estuary, we struck a shoal and water poured
into the hull. We pointed hard to shore, but the hull was filling
fast and the boat was visibly foundering. Seizing her children, my
mother climbed into our carriage; my father reassured her that we
had time to disembark before the boat would be engulfed. Yet the
deck was already awash, and I saw him take off his jacket in case
he might have to sling his children to his back.

At last we touched land, or rather a high stone sea wall topped
by a boathouse. Behind this boathouse were some dwellings, and
several men came to our rescue. It was none too soon: the carriage
was foundering with the boat, and they tossed us a ladder just in
time. My father, having conveyed us to safety, reboarded the barge
to rescue first our belongings, then the carriage, and finally the
boat itself. I was struck by his courage and strength. Even the boat-
men admired the mettle of this young officer who, after rescuing
his family, refused to take leave of the master before saving his
ship.

Three

Arrival in Nohant.—My grandmother.—Hippolyte.—Deschartres.—My brother's death.—My father's death.—The revenant.—Ursule.—An affair of honor.—First notions of riches and poverty.—Portrait of my mother.

WE REACHED Nohant in late August. I was running a fever again but was no longer hungry. The itch was making the rounds: Cecilia, a little Spanish maid whom we'd engaged on the way, also began to feel its symptoms and avoided touching me. My mother was nearly recovered by now, but my poor little brother, though his rash had disappeared, was even more ill and exhausted than I. We were two torpid, burning masses of flesh; I knew no more than he about what had happened after the shipwreck in the Gironde estuary.

I regained consciousness when we drove into the courtyard of Nohant. It was hardly as beautiful as the palace in Madrid, but it had much the same effect on me, for any large house seems very grand to a child reared in little rooms.

This was not the first time I saw my grandmother, but I have no memory of her before that day. Though only five feet tall, she seemed to tower over me. Her pink-and-white face; her air of authority; her low-waisted brown silk dresses, which she had made her uniform, and which she refused to alter to conform to the Empire style; her blond wig curled upon her forehead, and her round bonnet with its lace cockade at the side—all these made her seem unlike anyone I had ever seen.

This was the first time my mother and I were received at Nohant. After embracing my father, my grandmother turned to my mother, but my mother held her off.

"You mustn't touch me or the children," she said. "You don't know what troubles we've been through—we're all sick."

My father, optimistic as always, merely laughed. "Only think," he said, lifting me into my grandmother's arms. "These children have broken out in a few pimples, and Sophie here, with her lively imagination, actually thinks they have the itch!"

"Well, itch or no," said my grandmother, pressing me to her bosom, "I'll attend to this one. It's plain the children are ill; they both have a high fever. And you, my daughter, run along with your little son and get some rest. You've just made a forced march beyond endurance. I'll look after the girl. You can't possibly manage two children in the state you're in."

Then, despite her delicacy and elegance, the excellent woman carried me to her room, and without the slightest distaste for my condition, laid me on her bed. That bed and that room seemed to me like paradise. Persian silk with a bold floral pattern covered the walls, and all the furniture was Louis Quinze. The bed, in the form of a chariot with pendants at the corner posts, had a double canopy with any number of scalloped valances, and the pillows and bedclothes were wonderfully delicate and sumptuous. I did not dare regard this dainty place as my home, for I was aware of the disgust I must arouse, which filled me with shame. But I was nursed and caressed so much that I soon forgot it.

The first person I saw after my grandmother was a big boy of nine years who came in and tossed an enormous bouquet right in my face with a teasing but friendly expression.

"That's Hippolyte," said my grandmother. "Give each other a kiss, children." We kissed, but without curiosity, and I spent many years with him before I knew he was my brother. He was the child of "the rustic cottage."

My father led him to my mother, who admired him and kissed him. "Now he's mine too, just as Caroline is yours," she said. And we were brought up together, sometimes under her eye, sometimes under my grandmother's.

That day I saw Deschartres for the first time. He wore knee breeches with white hose and yellow garters, a very long and very square nut-brown morning coat, and a pleated cap. He came in and examined me solemnly. Since he was a very good doctor, everyone had to believe him when he diagnosed scabies. But he said that it had already run its course, and that my fever came only from fatigue. He suggested to my parents that to avoid alarming the household they should deny that we had the itch, and declared before the servants that we had a harmless rash. Indeed, only two other children caught it; they were immediately treated and recovered promptly—from what, they never knew.

After two hours of rest in my grandmother's bed, in her cheerful and well-aired room, where I no longer heard the vexing drone of the Spanish mosquitoes, I felt so well that I went down to romp in the garden with Hippolyte. I recall that he held my hand carefully, thinking I might fall at each step; I was piqued that he thought me such a *little* girl, and I soon proved to him that I was a resolute tomboy. That set him at ease, and he showed me several amusing new games, one of which he called "making liver pies à la mud." We took fine sand or leaf mold, watered it, and kneaded and trimmed it into pies on large slate tiles. Then, on the sly, he thrust them in the oven. He was already a practical joker, and it delighted him when the kitchen maids came to take out the bread and biscuits, flew into a rage and, cursing, flung our outlandish, blackened "liver pies" out the window.

Cunning is not in my nature, and I was not a sly little girl. Though wayward and domineering—because spoiled by my father—I couldn't scheme or hide my thoughts. Hippolyte soon saw my weak spot, and to punish me for my freaks and tantrums began to tease me cruelly. He stole my dolls and buried them in the garden, then marked them with a cross and made me dig them up. He hanged them upside down in the trees and tortured them in endless ways that I was simple enough to weep over. Often I hated him, but I've never held grudges, and when he asked me to play with him I couldn't resist.

The big garden and the fresh air of Nohant soon restored my health. Yet my mother still crammed me with sulfur, a treatment to which I submitted only because her word was law. I hated that sulfur, and I told her to cover my eyes and pinch my nose if she wanted me to swallow it. Then, to get rid of its taste, I sought out acidic foods. My mother, who had her own brand of instinctual— or perhaps merely prejudicial—medicine, believed that children sense what foods they require. Seeing me gnaw on green fruit, she gave me lemons, and I began to crave them so greatly that I ate them skin, seeds and all. My fierce hunger was gone, and these lemons were all I ate for five days. My grandmother was alarmed by this diet, but Deschartres, observing that I was improving by leaps and bounds, agreed with my mother that nature had made me sense what would cure me.

But while I was improving by the minute, my little brother, Louis, was rapidly withering away. The itch had gone, but the fever gnawed him still. He was livid, and his poor lackluster eyes expressed indescribable sadness. Watching him suffer, I began to love him. Till then I had barely noticed him, but when he lay on my mother's lap, so languid and feeble that she hardly dared touch him, I shared her sorrow, and vaguely understood what worry is—that feeling which is so unnatural for children.

My mother blamed herself for her baby's deterioration. Afraid that her milk would poison him, she struggled to regain her health so that she might nurse him again. She spent every day outdoors, with the child lying in the shade beside her upon a bed of cushions and carefully arranged shawls. Deschartres advised her to take plenty of exercise that she might work up an appetite and by eating good food restore the quality of her milk. She at once began a little garden in a corner of the large garden at Nohant.

On Friday, September 8, the poor little blind boy, after long moans upon my mother's lap, went cold; nothing could warm him. Deschartres came and took him from my mother's arms. His life had been short and sad, but he himself had never been conscious of it.

The next day he was buried. My mother hid her tears from me, and Hippolyte was told to keep me in the garden all day. Only vaguely did I grasp what was happening in the house. Apparently my father was keenly affected, for this child, despite its impairment, was as dear to him as his others.

After midnight my mother and father retired to their room and wept. Then a strange scene took place which my mother recounted to me some twenty years later. Grief-stricken, and overwrought by certain things my grandmother had been telling him, my father said to my mother:

"My poor Sophie, this trip to Spain has been our undoing. When you wrote that you wanted to join me there, and I begged you not to, you thought you discerned there a proof of infidelity or cooling off on my part; and I, too, had the presentiment of some woe. But you were big with child; how could you have been so foolhardy as to brave so much continual danger, deprivation and disease? It's a miracle you survived; it's a miracle Aurore's still living! Perhaps if our poor baby had been born in Paris he would not have been blind at all. The doctor in Madrid told me that the child's position in your womb, with its fists pressed against its eyes, and the long pressure of your cramped limbs in the carriage, prevented its eyes from developing."

"Now you reproach me," said my mother, "but you're too late. I'm already in despair. As for that surgeon, he was a liar and a scoundrel. I wasn't dreaming when I saw him put out my baby's eyes."

They grieved together for some time, and my mother, who was weeping and could not sleep, grew more and more frantic. She refused to believe that her son had died of undernourishment and fatigue, claiming that he had been on the road to recovery the day before, and that he had only had a sudden fit of nerves.

"And now," she said, sobbing, "he's in the ground, poor dear! How terrible it is to bury someone you love, to lose a child you were so recently caressing with such tenderness! They snatch him from you, nail him inside a coffin, throw him in a hole and cover him with earth, just as if . . . as if they were afraid he'd get out! Oh, it's horrible! I should never have let them tear my baby away; I should have kept him and had him embalmed!"

"And when you think," said my father, "that they often bury people who aren't even dead! Oh, yes, you are right—this Christian custom of burying corpses is the savagest thing in the world!"

"Savages, savages—*we* are the savages!" cried my mother. "Didn't you tell me that the so-called savages lay out their dead on wattle or hang their shriveled corpses from the branches of trees? I'd rather see my baby hanging cradled in one of the trees in the garden than think he'll rot in the ground. And then," she added, struck by my father's observation, "what if he isn't dead? What if he isn't? What if they mistook a fit of nerves for death pangs? What if Monsieur Deschartres was wrong? Because when you think of it, it was he who took him from me and forbade me to rub him, saying I was only hastening his death. Oh, he's a hard man, your Deschartres; he frightens me, and I don't dare disobey him! But maybe he's just a quacksalver who can't tell a coma from death! There, now I'm mad with worry! I'd give anything to see my baby again—living or dead!"

At first my father dismissed this thought, but soon it infected him too. He consulted his watch.

"There's no time to lose," he said. "I must have that child. Quiet now, don't wake a soul. You'll have him in an hour."

He got up, dressed, went softly outside, fetched a spade and ran to the cemetery, which is separated from our garden by a wall. He found the plot of freshly shifted earth and began to dig. It was dark, he had no lantern, and he could not see clearly enough to make out the coffin he was uncovering. By the time he had freed it he was astounded by how long he had worked, and he realized it was too big to be the child's. It was the coffin of a man of our village who had died a few days before. He had to dig again, beside it, and there he found the little coffin. But in struggling to lift it he braced his foot against that of the poor peasant, and the big coffin, pushed partway into the gap he had dug beside it, was levered up on end and struck his shoulder, knocking him into the ditch. Afterward he told my mother that for an instant he felt inexpressible anguish to find himself felled by a dead man and lying in the earth upon the remains of his son. He was brave and not given to superstition; but terror gripped him, and a cold sweat broke out on his brow. Eight days later he was to take his place beside that peasant, in the same earth he had heaved up to wrench back the body of his son.

He quickly got hold of himself and repaired the disorder so cleverly that no one ever suspected what had happened. He carried the little coffin back to my mother, and they opened it. The poor child was quite dead, but my mother took pleasure in making its final toilette, which she had been unable to do in her first grief. Now, uplifted and seemingly revived by her tears, she rubbed the little body with scent, swaddled it in her best linen, and put it back in its cradle, that she might have the sad illusion of watching it sleep once again.

She kept it hidden in her room all the next day, but by nightfall her hopes had vanished. My father wrote the child's name and the dates of its birth and death on a piece of paper, which he placed between two panes of glass and closed up with sealing wax all around.

Strange precautions, taken with apparent coolness, under the sway of an exalted sorrow! . . . When the inscription was placed in the coffin, my mother covered the child with rose petals, and the coffin was nailed up again and carried into the garden, to the ground my mother had broken, and buried at the foot of the old pear tree.

The very next day my mother returned with fervor to her gardening. My father helped her. The others were amazed to see them take up this childish amusement in the midst of their sorrow. Only my parents knew why they loved that patch of ground. They planted beautiful asters, which, as I write, have been blooming for over a month. At the foot of the pear tree they raised a mound of turf with a spiral path that I might climb to the top and sit there. And how often I was to play or work there, without ever suspecting it was a tomb! Round about were pretty sinuous paths, bordered by grass, flower beds and benches; it was a perfect child's garden, which my father, my mother, Hippolyte and I created as if by magic, working doggedly for five or six days. Those days were my father's last, perhaps the most peaceful he had yet tasted, surely the tenderest in their sadness. He brought load after load of earth and turf in a wheelbarrow, in which he sat us, Hippolyte and me, on return trips, happy just to look at us, and making as if to dump us to see us shriek and laugh.

When the little mortuary garden was nearly finished, my father urged my grandmother to have the walls around the large garden torn down. As soon as she consented, he set to work at the head of the laborers; I can see him still, standing in a cloud of dust with an iron pick in his hand, pulling down the old walls, which fell almost of themselves with a frightening crash.

But the laborers finished the task without him. On Friday, September 17, he mounted his terrible horse to visit some friends in La Châtre. He dined and spent the evening there. They observed that he was forcing his wonted gaiety, and that now and then he seemed gloomy and distracted. The recent death of his child weighed upon his soul, but he generously tried not to infect his friends with his sadness.

My mother was still prone to jealousy, especially, as often happens with this disease, of people she did not know. She grew resentful when he failed to return early as he'd promised, and she was simple enough to reveal her distress to my grandmother. She'd already confessed to her that she was a jealous woman, and my grandmother had tried to reassure her. My grandmother had never known passion, and so my mother's suspicions seemed most unfair to her. She must have shown the hot-tempered Sophie some sympathy—after all, she herself was a very jealous mother—but she also intimidated her with her solemnity. She even scolded her, always in gentle, measured tones, but with a certain coolness which diminished her rather than soothed her.

That evening she crammed her with humble pie. She told her that her jealousy tortured Maurice; that he would come to revile her; that she would banish all happiness from their home and that he would seek it elsewhere. My mother wept, but after several attempted mutinies gave in and promised to retire calmly rather than wait for her husband on the highway, where she would probably take sick anyway, being weak with sorrow and fatigue. Falling ill, in the midst of these moral agitations, she might court calamities which would blight her beauty and youthful appearance. The last consideration struck her more keenly than all my grandmother's philosophy: she wanted to be beautiful to please her husband. She went to bed and fell asleep like a reasonable person. Poor woman; she was to be rudely awakened.

Toward midnight my grandmother herself grew worried, but said nothing to Deschartres, with whom she had prolonged a game of piquet in hopes of kissing her son good night before turning in. At last midnight struck, and she had just retired when she thought she heard a strange bustle in the house. Deschartres had been summoned by Saint-Jean, our coachman, and had gone out as quietly as possible. Several open doors, the confusion of her maid, who had seen Deschartres being mysteriously called and had sensed something dreadful in Saint-Jean's expression and above all her own anxiety suddenly panicked my grandmother. The night was dark and rainy, and as I have said, my grandmother, though handsome and strongly built, had—either because her legs were weak or because her upbringing had been too soft—never been one for walking. Whenever she took a slow turn about the garden, for instance, she was overcome for the rest of the day. She had taken a walk only once in her life, to surprise her son in Passy upon her release from prison during the Terror; but she walked again on September 17, 1808, to fetch his corpse at one league's distance from the house upon the road into La Châtre. She went out alone, as she was, in her little sloe-black shoes, and without a shawl. It had taken her a short time to discover the cause of the commotion which had alarmed her in the house, and so Deschartres arrived before her. He was already beside my poor father, and had closed his eyes.

Here is how the fatal accident had happened.

On the way out of the town, a hundred feet past the bridge which marks its limit, the road turns. There, at the foot of the thirteenth poplar, a mound of stones and rubbish had been left earlier that day. My father had spurred Leopardo to a gallop at the end of the bridge. Weber, also on horseback, was following. Reaching the bend, Leopardo struck the pile of stones in the darkness. He did not fall, but startled, and stung by the spur, he reared so abruptly that the rider was unseated and thrown two lengths to the rear. "Here, Weber! . . . I am dead!" was all that Weber heard. He found his master on his back. He had no visible wounds, but his neck was broken. I think he was carried to a nearby inn, and help came quickly from the town. Meanwhile the terrified Weber galloped off to fetch Deschartres. It was too late; my father had had no time to suffer, but only enough to know that death was seizing him just as his career at last stretched bright before him; just as a painful emotional conflict of eight years was ending, allowing him to be happy, with his mother, wife and children reconciled and under one roof.

My grandmother ran to the spot and fell stifled on the body of her son. Saint-Jean had hastened to hitch up the horses, and presently he arrived to collect Deschartres, the corpse and my grandmother, who could not be parted from her son. It was Deschartres who later told me of that night of despair—my grandmother could never bring herself to speak of it. He said that during the drive home he had suffered all that the human soul can bear without breaking. The poor mother, half swooning on the body of her son, gave only a sound like a death rattle.

I do not know what happened then, before my mother heard the terrible news. At six in the morning I was already up; my mother had just dressed in a skirt and white blouse, and she was combing her hair. I can see her still, at the moment when Deschartres came in without knocking, his face so pale and grief-stricken that my mother understood at once.

"Maurice!" she cried. "Where is he?"

Deschartres was not crying, but his jaw was clenched, and he just managed to stammer a few words.

"He fell. . . . No, stay, think of your daughter. . . . Yes, it's serious, very serious. . . ."

And making an effort which might seem brutal, but which came without forethought, he said in a voice I shall never forget, "He is dead!" Then he gave a convulsive laugh, sat down, and burst into tears.

My mother fell on the chair beside the bed. I see her livid face, her long black hair disheveled on her breast, her bare arms, which I covered with kisses; I hear her heartrending cries. But she was deaf to mine, and did not feel my caresses.

"The child," said Deschartres. "You must live for her."

I don't remember what happened then. Doubtless the wailing and the tears soon exhausted me: childhood has no strength for suffering. The extreme pain and the horror numbed me and deprived me of any sense of what was happening about me. My memory skips several days, until I was given mourning to wear. The black color disturbed me, and I cried when I had to put it on. Though I had already worn the customary black dress and veil of Spain, I had never had black stockings, and it was these that terrified me. I claimed they were drawing "Death's legs" on me, and my mother had to show me that she was wearing them too. That same day I saw my grandmother, Deschartres, Hippolyte and the whole household in mourning. It had to be explained to me that my father had died, and I asked my mother a question which caused her great pain: "Mama, is Papa still dead today?"

The house was plunged in gloom and sorrow, and the village with it; for all who knew my father loved him. His death sowed a sort of terror in the vicinity, and even those who had not known him were shocked by the catastrophe.

Hippolyte was very shaken by the spectacle of death, from which he had not been screened so carefully as I. He still did not know that my father was also his. He, too, was grief-stricken, but the image of death added terror to his grief, and he did nothing but weep and scream all night. The servants, confounding regret with superstition, claimed to have seen my father walking about in the house after his death. Saint-Jean's elderly wife swore she had seen him cross the passage at midnight and go downstairs. He was in full uniform, she said, and walked slowly and seemed to see no one. He had passed her without a glance or a word. A housemaid had seen him too, in the antechamber of my mother's apartment. This large room was bare, awaiting a billiard table, and it contained only a few chairs and a table. Crossing it one evening, she had seen him sitting there with his head in his hands. What is true is that some domestic thief tried to avail himself of the terror of our folk, because a white phantom prowled the courtyard for several nights. Hippolyte saw him and took sick with fright. Deschartres saw him also, and aimed a musket at him. He didn't come back.

Happily for me, I was watched over carefully, and heard nothing of this nonsense. For me death had none of the hideousness which superstitious fancy has loaned it. My grandmother separated me for several days from Hippolyte, who was beside himself, and who was also too wild a playmate for me. But she was disturbed that I was so often alone, and alarmed by the blank, contented passivity into which I sank in her care. I was lost in daydreams, which were a physical need of mine, a fact she could not grasp. It seems that I sat for hours on a stool at her feet or at my mother's, silent, glassy-eyed, open-mouthed, with my arms dangling, and looking sometimes like an idiot.

"She's often like that," said my mother. "She's not being contrary; it's her nature. You may be sure she's always meditating on something. She used to babble when she daydreamed, though nowadays she doesn't say a word. But as her poor father used to say, it's not that she isn't thinking."

"Yes, I believe she is," said my grandmother. "But it's unhealthy for children to daydream so much. I saw her father enter such trances when he was a child, and eventually he fell into a decline. The child should be distracted, shaken out of herself. We must beware, or *our* sorrows will make *her* die. She senses them, even if she doesn't understand them. My daughter, you, too, must find some distraction, if only a bodily one. You're robust, you need exercise. Why don't you take up your gardening again? Then the child will fancy it too."

My mother obeyed, but I doubt that she put much effort into her work. She wept so much that she contracted frightful headaches, which stayed with her for twenty years, prostrating her almost weekly.

My grandmother, still concerned that I was alone so often, looked about for a child of my own age for me to play with. Mlle. Julie, her chambermaid, proposed to bring her niece, who was only six months older than I, and soon little Ursule was dressed in mourning and brought to Nohant. She spent several years with me there; afterward she was put in domestic training. She served as our house-keeper for a time after my marriage, and then she herself married. She still lives in La Châtre; we have never lost sight of each other, and our friendship, tempered by age, is now forty years old.

I shall often have occasion to speak of Ursule, and I shall begin be saying that she was a boon to my health and spirits following our family disaster. The Lord was good enough to give me a playmate who though poor was not servile. The rich man's daughter—and compared to Ursule I was a princess—will always abuse her station, and when her less fortunate playmate offers no resistance, the little despot will gladly take up the lash, as in the days of barons and serfs. I was very spoiled. Only Clotilde had stood up to me; but for several months I'd had no occasion to see her or any of my peers. I was alone with my mother, who, however, did not exactly spoil me, for she had a sharp tongue and a quick hand, and followed the maxim: Chastise where you love. But to wage constant war against a child's whims during those days of mourning was beyond her. Both she and my grandmother needed to fondle and indulge me if only to lessen their pain, and I naturally took advantage of this. Besides, the voyage to Spain, and the suffering I had witnessed there, had left me in a state of excitation. Thus I was very irritable, and not really myself. I had one caprice after another, and came out of my mysterious trances only to demand the impossible. I asked for the birds in the garden, and when this request met with laughter I rolled on the ground with rage; I asked Weber to lift me onto his horse (not Leopardo, who had been sold soon enough), but of course I was not allowed near a horse. My thwarted desires began to torture me. My grandmother said that these urgent whims gave proof of imagination, and that she only wished to coax that imagination out of its derangement. But that proved long and hard.

After my initial joy at Ursule's arrival—for I sensed that she was a brave and intelligent child—the urge to domineer returned, and I tried to force all my wishes on her. In the middle of some game she liked, I would insist that we play something I liked better, but as soon as we switched, and she, too, began to prefer it, I would tire of it. Or I would force her to sit still and "meditate" with me; and if I could have made her get a headache, such as I myself often had, I would have demanded that she keep me company in that too. Indeed, I was the most sullen, wretched and petulant child imaginable.

But Ursule, thank heaven, would not be enslaved. She was cheerful and energetic, and so talkative that she was tagged Miss Mag-piety, a nickname that stuck. She had (and has) plenty of wit, and her long speeches often set my grandmother laughing through her tears. At first the latter feared that I might tyrannize Ursule; but no one could have stood up to me better, and when I played pull and scratch she replied with kick and bite. She still remembers one of our great battles. It seems we had a serious account to settle, and as neither would yield, we agreed to have it out. It was a sharp tussle, whose wounds we both bore; but when dinner was announced in the midst of it, we knew we would have to appear downstairs, and left off, equals now in our fear of a scolding. We were alone in my mother's room, and we quickly washed the droplets of blood off our faces and did each other's hair, kind in the face of the common danger. Then we went downstairs, asking each other on the way "if it showed." All the bitterness was gone, and Ursule proposed that we kiss and make up, which we did gladly, like two old soldiers after an affair of honor. I do not know if this was our last fight, but it is certain that we were equals forever after, in peace and in war, and we loved each other so much that we could not bear to be apart for an instant. Ursule took meals with us, as she has ever since. She slept in our room too, often with me in the big bed. My mother was very fond of her, and when she had her migraines Ursule would stroke her forehead at length with her cool hands. I was a bit jealous that she could render my mother this service, but my own hands were always hot, either from our games or from the after effects of my fever, and I only made her headaches worse.

We stayed at Nohant two or three years without my grandmother's ever thinking of returning to Paris, and without my mother's ever finding out what was expected of her. My grandmother wanted my upbringing entrusted to her. Of course, my mother could not abandon Caroline, who boarded at a school and who would soon require sustained attention, but she could not accept a permanent separation from either of her daughters. My uncle de Beaumont spent a summer at Nohant to convince my mother to leave me behind, which he deemed necessary to my grandmother's and to my own happiness: for even with my grandmother adding as much as she could to my mother's means, the latter still had only two thousand five hundred pounds a year of her own, which was hardly enough to provide her two children with a brilliant education. My grandmother became more attached to me each day—not, to be sure, on account of my crotchety little personality, but because of my striking resemblance to my father. My voice, my features, my habits, my tastes—everything about me reminded her of her son as a boy, to such a degree that sometimes when she watched me play she seemed to succumb to an illusion, and called me "Maurice" and referred to me as "my son."

She was bent on developing my mind, of which she had a high opinion. Indeed, I managed to understand everything she said, but only because she explained it all so clearly. I also showed some musical ability, which has never been sufficiently cultivated, but which charmed her because it reminded her of her son's boyhood; and she became a young mother again when she gave me lessons.

Often my mother would wonder out loud in my presence: "Wouldn't my child be happier here than with me? I don't know A from B, and I shouldn't be able to teach her anything for very long. Besides, if her grandmother doesn't have her here and grows cool to her, she may reduce her fortune. But then, are money and talent enough to make her happy?"

Even I grasped this logic, and when she discussed my future with my uncle de Beaumont, who warmly urged her to yield, I was all ears, though I didn't show it. Thus I formed a great contempt for money before I knew what it was—I had a sort of vague fear of the wealth that threatened me.

Yet this wealth was not so much: one day it would come, all told, to about twelve thousand francs a year. But relatively that was a lot, and it terrified me because it was linked to my being separated from my mother. Once alone with her, I covered her with kisses and begged her "not to give me away to my grandmother for money." Of course, I loved my grandmama—she always spoke to me so sweetly—but this affection could not match the passion I was beginning to have for my mother. This passion was to rule my life until circumstances made me waver between my two mothers, each jealous of the other over me, as they had been over my father.

The time came when, savagely torn between two affections compatible in principle, I fell victim by turns to each of these easily wounded women, and to my own sensitive nature as well, which they failed to treat gently enough. Until the age of four—that is, until the journey to Spain—I had cherished my mother instinctively but unconsciously. I was not aware that I had affections, and I lived, as little children and primitive peoples live, in the imagination. The life of the heart awoke in me when my blind baby brother was born, when I saw how my mother suffered. Her despair after my father's death developed this sense still more, and I had just come under the spell of my love for her when the idea of a separation suddenly surprised me in the middle of my golden age.

I say "golden age" because it was Ursulette's favorite expression. I don't know where she'd picked it up, but she used it whenever she was trying to bring me to reason (for she already shared my distress and, more by reason of her character than because of the six or eight months she had over me, understood the real world better). "How fine it is, all the same," she would say whenever I wept over parting with my mother and staying with my grandmother, "to have a big house, and a big garden to stroll in, and carriages, and dresses, and good things to eat every day. Know where it all comes from? From richness. You mustn't cry, you know, because with your grandmama you'll always have golden age and you'll always have richness. When I go to see Mama in La Châtre, she says I've given myself airs at Nohant and like to play gentlewoman. 'Phooey,' I say, 'I'm in my golden age. I'm helping myself to richness while I can.'"

But Ursule's reasoning did not console me. Mlle. Julie, her aunt and my grandmother's maid, who was fond of me and shared Ursule's point of view, asked me one day if I "wanted to go back to my attic and eat beans." This expression revolted me, for the attic and beans seemed to me the essence of happiness and dignity. But I outrun myself; I was perhaps seven or eight when the question of wealth was framed for me in this way. Before relating the outcome of my mother's inner struggle over my future, I want to sketch the two or three years we spent at Nohant after my father's death. I cannot recount these events in their proper order; I can offer only the rough and somewhat confused picture my memories present.

First I must tell how my grandmother and my mother got on: for they looked unalike, had been reared very differently, and had different habits. Indeed, they embodied the two extremes of our sex: the one fair, grave and dignified, a true Saxon noblewoman full of refinement, ease and protective good will; the other dark, intense, awkward and shy with people of fashion, but also quick to explode—a Spanish temperament, jealous, passionate, irascible, weak, spiteful and tender at once. It was with mortal repugnance that these two creatures, poles apart in nature and in rank, had accepted each other; and while my father lived they contended for his heart too strenuously not to hate each other just a bit. After his death grief drew them together, and their efforts to love each other bore fruit. My grandmother could not understand my mother's keen passions and violent instincts, but she was alive to her grace, intelligence and heartfelt impulses. She had often observed her with a sort of curiosity, wondering why my father loved her so greatly; but at Nohant she discovered for herself the power and magnetism of this untutored spirit. For my mother was a brilliant artist, but one who had remained merely potential for lack of training. I don't know what she would have done best, because she had a marvelous talent for all handicrafts and arts. She'd never studied, and knew nothing; my grandmother chided her for her barbarous spelling, and told her that she must correct it. So she began not to study grammar—it was too late for that—but to read attentively, and soon she could write almost correctly, and in a style so simple and pretty that my grandmother, who knew what style was, admired her letters. She couldn't read music, but she had a voice of unmatched lightness and freshness, and my grandmother, a fine musician herself, loved to hear her sing, and remarked upon her natural phrasing. Then, to fill the long country days after my father's death, she took up drawing though she'd never touched chalk. She worked, as always, by instinct, and after cleverly copying several engravings she began to make portraits in pen and wash, which were very accurate, and which always had a simple grace and charm. Her embroidery was a trifle clumsy, but she worked so fast that she made my grandmother a dress of cambric muslin, embroidered from top to bottom (for such was the fashion), in a few days. She made all our dresses and hats, the latter no miracle since she had been a milliner for years; but everything was designed and executed with unequaled speed, taste and freshness. What she began in the morning would be ready the next day, even if she had to spend the night on it, and she set about the slightest things with an absorption which seemed miraculous to my grandmother, who was lackadaisical, and awkward at handiwork, like all the great ladies of her day. My mother washed, ironed and let out all our clothes more nimbly than the best workwoman in the trade. I never saw her busy herself with any of the useless, costly fancy work that rich ladies like to do. She did not do little purses, little screens, or any of that sort of trumpery, which costs more to make than to buy at a shop; but to our thrifty household she was worth ten seamstresses. She was always ready for anything. Had my grandmother broken her sewing box, my mother would stay in her room for the day and at dinner bring her a new one made out of clothboard: she would cut, assemble, paste, decorate . . . and there it was, an elegant little masterpiece. And so it was with everything. Was the spinet awry, my mother—though ignorant of both its fingering and mechanics—would restring it, paste the ivories back and tune it by ear. She'd try her hand at anything and bring it off. She'd have made shoes, furniture, locks, if she'd had to. "She's a fairy," said my grandmother; and there was something to it. No task was too poetic, vulgar or taxing for her; but there was one thing she had a horror of, and that was objects which had no use. "These," she would say in a low voice, "are old countesses' toys."

Her talents were magnificent. She had so much natural wit that when she wasn't frozen by her timidity, which became extreme in the presence of certain people, it fairly sparkled. I've never heard anyone so cutting as she could be, and it was best to keep on her good side. When she felt at ease she used the incisive, humorous and picturesque jargon of the true "child of Paris," which is unlike any other language on earth; and into it came lightning flashes of poetry, of things felt and seen in a way that would have been spoiled by self-consciousness. She was not vain of her intelligence, and indeed did not suspect she had any. She was sure of her beauty but not proud of it, and used to say ingenuously that she was never jealous of the beauty of others because she had received a fair share on that score. But she was tormented by what she supposed to be the superior intelligence and education of women of fashion, and their appeal to my father. This reveals her modesty: for nineteen out of twenty of the women I've known, whatever their station, would have seemed like idiots beside her.

And yet for all this, it must be said: she was the most difficult woman who has ever lived. I managed to handle her in her last years, but not without suffering. She had the world's shortest temper, and to calm her one had to pretend to be irritated. For gentleness and patience exasperated her, silence maddened her, and she was for many years unfair to me, or so I felt, precisely because I respected her too much. I could never really lose my temper with her, because her outbursts wounded me without much offending me; I saw her as an *enfant terrible* who was eating herself alive, and I suffered too much from the hurt she did herself to worry over what she thought she was doing to me. But I took it upon myself to talk to her rather severely, and her soul, which had been so tender toward me in my childhood, gave in at last.

Yet I must paint her warts and all, this estranged woman; for no one would understand the mingled sympathy and disgust, trust and fear, that she always excited in my grandmother, and long did in me, if I did not tell all her strengths and weaknesses. She was a woman of contrasts, and it was for this reason that she was so greatly loved and hated, and so greatly loved and hated herself. In some ways I am very like her, though less harsh and blunt. I am her imprint, but eroded by nature and altered by education. I have not her grudges nor her flights of fancy, but when I turn from a bad to a good impulse I deserve less credit than she, for my spite has never turned to fury nor my estrangement to hate. To move from one such extreme to another, to adore what one has cursed and to caress what one has broken, requires rare strength. I have seen her practically draw blood, then suddenly admit she was going too far, dissolve in tears, and pick up to adore what she had just dashed at her feet.

Penurious on her own account, she was prodigal toward others. She would haggle over trifles, then suddenly feel guilty and offer too much. Her simplicity was admirable. Sometimes, when she was damning her enemies, Pierret would enlarge upon her curses, either to exhaust her store of spite the sooner, or else because he simply saw things through her eyes. Suddenly she would change her tune: "Nonsense, Pierret!" she would say. "You're raving. Don't you see that I'm angry, that I'm saying unfair things, that in a minute I'll feel wretched that I said them?"

Often enough, I was the object of those curses; if she thought she saw something to complain of in my conduct, she would shower me with terrible, and I daresay utterly unwarranted, reproaches. But if Pierret or someone else agreed, she would cry, "Liar! My daughter is a jewel, the best daughter in the world. Try as you may, I'll love her more than you."

She was sly as a fox and then all at once innocent as a child. She lied with the best will in the world, unaware what she was doing. Her imagination and her hot blood easily overcame her, and she would accuse you of the ghastliest misdeeds, then suddenly stop. "Why, that's not true, what I just said. . . . No, not a bit of it, not a word. . . . I dreamed it!"

Four

*My mother.—My grandmother.—Deschartres.—Deschartres's no-
tions of medicine.—Hieroglyphics.—First readings.—Fairy tales,
myths.—The nymph and the bacchante.—First study and impressions of music.—The green screen.—First separation from my
mother.—The donkey.—My fright at the age and the imposing
mien of my grandmother.*

I BELIEVE I have accurately portrayed my mother's character, but
I cannot continue my life story without giving the best account I
can of that character's decisive influence upon my own.

It took time for me to assess a nature so unique and paradoxical,
especially in that we rarely lived together after my early childhood.
In my first years I knew only her love, an immense love that she
later admitted having resisted in order to resign herself to our separation; but her love was of a different sort than mine. Mine was ten-
derer, hers more passionate; yet she would scold me sharply for
some piece of mischief which she in her distraction had long let
go by, and for which I consequently felt no guilt. I always gave in
to her, and she used to say I was the fondest creature in the world,
which I was—with her. An impossible child with others, I obeyed
her because I liked to. She was my sibyl, she had given me my

first notions of life, and they suited my natural mental needs. But children forget, they get muddled, they do things they shouldn't and never intended to: then she would berate me and hit me as if I'd disobeyed her on purpose, and I loved her so much that her anger drove me to despair. In those days I never imagined she could be unjust; I never felt bitter or resentful. Indeed, whenever she saw she'd gone too far she would pick me up and cry and caress me. She'd even say she'd been wrong, and was afraid she'd hurt me; and I was so happy to win back her tenderness that I begged her to forgive herself for the blows she'd given me.

How odd the mind is! If my grandmother had been a fraction so harsh with me, I'd have risen up at once. I was much more afraid of her, and a word from her made me go pale; but I would not have forgiven her the least unfairness, while all my mother's injustices went unnoticed, and even increased my love.

I must say that my mother's and my grandmother's natural animosity toward each other was never more than half vanquished, or rather was indeed vanquished, but only for spells which were invariably followed by sharp turnabouts. When apart they still hated each other and could not keep from maligning each other. But neither could they help enjoying each other's company, for each had a winning charm complementary to the other's. This situation may be attributed to the store of justice that both had, and also to their great intelligence, which forbade them to slight each other's virtues. My grandmother's prejudices resided not in her mind but in the company she kept. She had a soft spot for certain people, and she let them air opinions which, in her heart of hearts, she did not share. She allowed her elderly friends to slur my absent mother, and seemed eager to apologize for having welcomed her into her inner circle and treated her like a daughter. Then, when the two were together again, my grandmother would forget the ill she had just spoken of her, and show her a warmth and trust which I witnessed time after time. But cool and staid though my grandmother seemed, she was also pliant; she needed to be loved, and even slight attentions touched her and made her grateful.

How many times did I not hear her say, "There is much that is lofty in Sophie's nature, she is charming, and her conduct is unimpeachable. She is so generous she would give her shirt to a pauper. She is liberal as a great lady, and simple as a child." But at other

71

times, calling up all her old maternal jealousy, and feeling it live on and attach to the one who had caused it, she would say, "She's a devil, a madwoman. My son never loved her; she just dominated him and made him unhappy. She's not even sad he died." She made countless charges of this sort, which, though unfounded, soothed her secret and incurable bitterness.

My mother acted in precisely the same way. When favorable winds prevailed she would say, "What a fine woman! She's still lovely as an angel, and she knows everything. She's so gentle and well-bred that even if she nettles you sometimes, before you can get angry she says something that makes you want to kiss her. If only one could get rid of her old countesses, she'd be adorable."

But when the storm lowered in my mother's impetuous soul, the tune changed. Then her old mother-in-law was a prude and a hypocrite; she was dry and pitiless; she was stuck in the Old Regime; and so on. Then it was woe to any of her venerable lady friends who might provoke a scene with their comments. The old countesses were like the ten plagues to my mother, and she would demolish them with such deft cuts that even my grandmother, most often a casualty herself, would begin to laugh.

Deschartres—there's no denying it—was the main hindrance to their complete reconciliation. As far as my mother went, he refused to make the best of a bad job, but leaped at each chance to chafe the old sores. It was the story of his life. Always harsh and unkind to those he treasured, how could he have been otherwise to those he hated? He could not forgive my mother for having supplanted the influence that he claimed he should rightfully have exercised upon the soul of his dear Maurice. He would contradict or bait her on any pretext, then repent and try to repair his blunders with absurd fawning. Sometimes it seemed he was in love with her; and who's to say he wasn't? Oh, but he'd have eaten you alive if you'd suggested it, because he flattered himself that he was above all human weaknesses. Besides, my mother bristled at his advances, and made him pay for his wrongs with such cruel sarcasm that his old hatred only flared anew, fanned by all the spite of the latest row.

Just when they seemed on a better footing, with Deschartres doing his best to be less surly—he tried to be teasing and sweet, though God only knows how he managed it!—my mother would start galling him again, and he would fly off the handle and become crude and

72

offensive, until my grandmother had to dress him down and shut him up.

They played cards in the evening, the three of them, and Deschartres, who thought he was first-rate at all games and played them all abominably, always lost. I remember one evening when, exasperated by his steady losses to my mother—who had no strategies but very good hunches—he threw up his cards, shouting, "I should throw them in your face, you play so badly and win so often!" My mother saw red, got up, and was about to reply when my grandmama said in her grand calm way and in her sweet voice:

"Deschartres! If you do anything of the sort, I shall box your ears."

This threat of boxing, and of boxing ears at that, made in so mild a way, and by one whose lovely hands were half palsied and so weak they could hardly hold a few playing cards, was the funniest thing imaginable. My mother went into a fit of the giggles and, unable to stop, fell back in her chair. There was nothing she could add to the abashment of the poor goggle-eyed tutor.

But this episode took place considerably after my father's death. Long years passed in that house of mourning before a grownup was heard to laugh.

During these years a calm and orderly life, a well-being I'd never known, and a pure air whose like I'd rarely filled my lungs with gave me by degrees a robust health. As my nervousness subsided, my temper evened and my spirits rose. Everyone saw that I was no worse that any other child; and besides, commonly children are cranky only because they suffer without feeling free to say so.

And indeed, I had been disgusted by the medicaments of the day, of which such free use was made that I refrained from complaining of my little aches and pains. I recall that I often came near fainting at play, and resisted with a stoicism that I should probably not exhibit today. But my only other choice was to be given up to Deschartres's physic and become the victim of his system, which was to give emetics for everything! Though a clever surgeon, he knew nothing about internal medicine, and he applied that damnable emetic to every ill. It was his cure-all. Was I pale, did my head ache, then it was bile, and quick! the emetic—which made me retch horridly and left me exhausted for several days. My mother, on the other hand, believed in worms, still a great concern of medicine in those days. All children had worms, and were continually plied with vermifuge, a horrid black medicine which made them nauseous and took away the appetite. Then, to restore the appetite, rhubarb was spooned in. What is more, if a gnat bit me, my mother thought it was the itch again, and sulfur was once more mixed with all my food. In brief, I was perpetually drugged, and my generation must have been tough indeed to survive the cures of those who were trying to preserve it.

I learned to write toward the age of five. My mother had me do big pages of "pothooks and hangers," but as she herself wrote like a spider, I would have scrawled up plenty of paper before learning to write my name if I myself had not been keen to express my thoughts with signs. Weary of copying the alphabet every day and penning downstrokes and upstrokes in staring capitals, I was impatient to write whole sentences, and during my ample free time I practiced by writing letters to Ursule, Hippolyte, and my mother. But I didn't show them, for fear I'd be forbidden to "spoil my hand" at this exercise. I soon managed to create my own orthography. It was very simple and full of hieroglyphs. My grandmother came upon one of these letters and thought it very funny. She said that it was a wonder how I'd expressed my ideas with such barbarous methods, and she advised my mother to let me scribble on my own as much as I wanted. She rightly held that much time is wasted in trying to teach children a fine hand, and that during this time they are never even told what writing is for. So I was left to my own devices, and when my exercises were done I reverted to my natural system. For a long time I printed, copying typefaces; I don't recall how I came to use cursive, but I do remember that I imitated my mother, who was learning spelling by observing printed words. I counted the number of letters in each word, and by some instinct I eventually learned the chief rules. When Deschartres later taught me grammar, it took only two or three months; for each lesson was only the confirmation of what I had already observed and applied.

At seven or eight, then, I could spell; not well—I still don't— but as correctly as most literate people.

Teaching myself to write, I came to understand what I was reading. Practicing forced me to do so; I already knew how to read but without grasping what most of the words meant. Each day this revelation found a wider scope, until I was able to read a fairy story all by myself.

And how delightful that was! I loved them so, and my mother, weighed down by grief, had given up telling me them. At Nohant I found Mme. d'Aulnoy's and Perrault's tales in an old edition which became my chief joy for five or six years. Oh, what hours I spent with "The Bluebird," "Tom Thumb," "The Donkey's Skin," "Belle-belle or the Lucky Knight," "Serpentin Vert," "Babiole" and "The Beneficent Mouse." I've never read them since, but I could tell each tale straight through, and I don't think anything in all one's intellectual life can be compared to these first delights of the imagination.

I also began to read my short Greek mythology, which I liked insofar as it resembled fairy tales. But there were myths which pleased me less, for in all myths the symbols are gruesome in their poetry, and I preferred the happy endings of my fairy tales. Yet the nymphs, the zephyrs, Echo, all the figurations of the smiling mysteries of nature turned my mind toward poetry, and I was not yet such a freethinker that I did not sometimes hope to surprise the sylphs and dryads in their woods and meadows.

There was a wallpaper in our room that often possessed my thoughts. The background, very thick and deep green, was varnished, and stretched upon canvas backings. This way of placing panels along the wall gave the mice thoroughfare, and in the evenings, behind these panels, scenes of the other world took place: ragtag steeplechases, furtive scratchings and highly mysterious little shrieks. It was not these that attracted me most; rather the decorative border which girdled each panel. These borders were a foot wide, and represented a trained vine whose leaves parted at intervals to disclose a series of medallions wherein I saw sileni and bacchantes laughing, drinking and dancing. Above each of the doors was a larger medallion with a little figure in it, and I thought these figures were superb. They were not alike. The one I saw on wakening every morning was a nymph or dancing Flora. She wore pale blue and a crown of roses, and she was wafting a garland of flowers. She pleased me hugely, and my first glance each morning went to her. She seemed to smile at me and beckon me to rise and run to her and frolic in her company.

Across from her there was another such figure, which I saw from

75

my writing table and when I said my prayers before going to bed; but this one wore a different expression: she did not laugh or dance. She was a glum bacchante. Her tunic was green, her crown was a vine shoot, and her outstretched arm rested upon a staff. Perhaps these two figures represented Spring and Autumn. In any case, the two little presences, each about a foot high, struck me vividly. Each, perhaps, was as banal as the other, but to me they offered the perfect contrast of gladness and grief, kindness and severity. The glum bacchante always alarmed me—I had read how Orpheus was torn apart by cruel ladies like her—and in the evening, when the guttering candlelight flickered along her extended arm and the staff, I thought I spied the head of the divine songster impaled upon a javelin.

My bed was placed against the wall in such a way that I could not see this figure which so oppressed me. As no one suspected my dislike for her, at the onset of winter my mother moved my bed over toward the fireplace, so that my back was now to my beloved nymph and I was facing the fearful maenad. I wasn't about to call attention to my fear—indeed, I was beginning to be ashamed of it—but when the she-devil stared me out of countenance and threatened me with her motionless arm, I hid my head under the covers so I wouldn't have to see her while I was trying to fall asleep. But even that was no good; in the dead of night she glided off her medallion, slid down the door jamb, became a "real live person," and walked across to the other door, where she tried to wrench the pretty nymph off her medallion. The latter gave a heartrending cry, but the bacchante was pitiless. She scratched and tore the paper until the nymph stepped off it and fled to the middle of the room. The other pursued her, and when the poor disheveled nymph rushed to my bed and hid under the canopy, the furious bacchante dashed at me and lunged at the two of us with her staff, which had become a sharp spear; and at each stab I felt real pain.

I cried, I struggled, my mother came to my rescue; but though I was wakeful enough to see my mother getting up, I was also asleep enough still to see the bacchante. The real and the chimerical were before my eyes at once. I distinctly saw the bacchante shrink and draw away as my mother came near, until she was as tiny as she had been in her medallion; then she climbed up the doorjamb like a mouse and took up her station between the vine leaves, where she assumed her usual pose and her glum look.

I fell asleep again, and at once the mad creature returned to her old ways. She ran to the end of the border, calling the sileni and bacchantes who were feasting or disporting in the medallions, and forcing them to dance with her and to destroy all the furniture in the room.

Slowly my dream became muddled, and I grew almost fond of it. Upon wakening next morning I saw the bacchante instead of the nymph, and forgetting that my bed had been moved, I thought for an instant that the two little figures had returned to the wrong medallions; but this illusion was dispelled by the sun's first rays, and I thought no more of the matter for the rest of the day.

But that evening my anxieties returned; and so it went for a long time. While the day lasted I did not take the two colored wallpaper figures seriously, but the first shadows of night troubled my brain, and I dared not remain alone in the room. I said not a word about it, for my grandmother made fun of sissies and I was afraid that someone would tell her about my silly fears; but not until I was eight did I begin to face the bacchante calmly before falling asleep.

At about the same period my grandmother began to teach me music. Despite her half-palsied hands and her hoarse voice, she still sang admirably, and the few chords of accompaniment she managed to play were always so inventive and bold in harmony that when she went into her room, closed the door and took up some old opera score in secret, I was truly ecstatic if she let me stay with her. I would sprawl under the old spinet—perhaps Brillant, her favorite dog, would share a yard of carpet with me—and I was so spellbound by that quavering voice and the tinkle of the old spinet that I could have spent the rest of my life there. What she made, despite the frailty of her voice and of her instrument, was fine music, exquisitely felt and understood. I've heard plenty of singing since then, coming out of magificent throats; but though I've heard louder, I've never heard better. She had read much of the music of the masters, and had known both Gluck and Piccini without taking sides, saying that each was good in his own way, and that one should not compare them but appreciate each for his own merits. She knew by heart airs of Leo, Hasse and Durante, which I never heard anybody sing but her, and whose names I don't know, but which I would recognize if I heard them again. These airs were simple, grand ideas, calm and classic forms. She had seen through the fashions of her youth, and disliked what we today call the rococo. Her taste was pure, serious, severe.

She taught me the principles of music, and so clearly that it did not seem like counting the stars. Later I had teachers, and I no longer grasped a thing of these principles and grew sick of studying music, which I thought I was ill fitted for. But since then I've realized it was these teachers' fault more than my own, and that if my grandmother had been my sole instructress I'd have been a musician, for I have the ear for it, and I understand beauty; which, in this art more than any other, moves me and carries me away.

I was still at the age when fairy princesses and kings were my chief passion, for in my childhood dreams these figures were all grace and beauty and kindness. I loved their luxe and adornments, but only because they were fairy things: those kings had nothing in common with the kings of this world. Besides, those kings were very cavalierly treated by the genii whenever they made mischief, and were subject to a justice more severe than that of people.

Ah, the fairies and genii! Where did they live, those creatures who did as they pleased and who, with one wave of a magic wand, could whisk you into a world of marvels? My mother never wanted to say they didn't exist, and now I am infinitely grateful to her. My grandmother would have had a ready reply if I'd ever put to her such a question. Reared on Rousseau and Voltaire, she'd have leveled the whole enchanted house of my imagination without pity or remorse. But my mother was different. She did not confirm or deny anything. Reason came to me in good time, and presently I knew that my fancies would never come true; but if the door of hope was no longer open, neither was it locked, and I was allowed to poke around it, and to peek through the cracks. I could still daydream, and never wasted a chance to do so.

On winter evenings my mother would read to us from Berquin, from *Veillées du château* by Mme. de Genlis, or from other books which were about the house but which I do not remember. At first I would listen closely. I sat at my mother's feet, before the fire, and between myself and the fire was an old screen fitted with green taffeta. Seen through this threadbare taffeta, the fire became a constellation whose brilliance I could increase by blinking, and so, by degrees, I would lose the trend of what my mother was reading, and her voice would lull me into a sort of slumber wherein I could not follow any train of thought; pictures crowded before me and fastened on the green screen; there were woods, meadows, streams, towns of a strange and gigantic architecture such as I still see in dreams; and enchanted palaces with gardens the like of which have never been seen, with myriads of blue and gold and purple birds which fluttered in the flowers and let me catch them as easily as you would pick a rose. There were green roses, black and violet roses, and best of all, blue roses. I also saw forests, brightly lit, and jets of water, and mysterious abysses, and Chinese footbridges, and trees laden with golden fruit and gemstones. Indeed, the whole fantastic world of my fairy tales became palpable, and I wandered there in ravishment. I closed my eyes, and still I saw the vision; but when I opened them I had to search for it again upon the screen. I do not know what brainwork of mine had affixed the vision there rather than elsewhere; but it is certain that I saw marvels on that screen. One day these apparitions became so real that I was almost afraid, and asked my mother if she did not see them too. I claimed the screen showed high blue mountains; and she bounced me on her knee to bring me home.

We had a donkey at the house, the finest I have ever known; I don't know if he'd been naughty in his youth like all his fellows, but by then he was old, very old, and he had no crotchets or complaints. He walked with a grave and measured gait, and venerated as much for his great age as for services rendered, he was never punished or scolded. Yet if he was the world's most irreproachable donkey, he was also the happiest and most respected. Ursule and I were often put in his panniers, and we traveled at his flanks without his ever dreaming of lightening his load. Once back from these walks, our donkey would return to his wonted freedom; for he knew neither leader nor hayrack. Straying about the courtyards, the village or the lawn, he was left wholly to his own devices. He never did anything wrong, and made discreet use of the facilities. Often he was seized with a desire to enter the house, and he would go into the dining room or even into my grandmother's apartment, wherein she found him one day, sniffing at a box of iris powder with a serious, thoughtful look. He had even learned to open our doors, which shut with a latch only, according to an ancient system in use hereabouts, and as he knew the whole ground floor perfectly, he always made for my grandmother, knowing she would give him a treat. He did not care a fig if you laughed at him; he was above such jibes, and had a philosophical air about him that was all his own. The only thing wrong with him was that he was unemployed, and consequently lonely and bored. One night, finding the washroom door open, he climbed a stair of seven or eight steps, crossed the kitchen and the passage beyond it, nosed up two or three latches, and arrived at my grandmother's bedroom; finding it bolted, he began to scratch with his hoof to tell her he was there. Puzzled by this noise, my grandmother thought a thief must be trying to force her door. She rang for her maid, who ran to her without a candle and tumbled over the donkey with a piercing shriek.

At last the family arrangements were concluded, and my mother signed a contract leaving me to my grandmother, who wanted absolute control of my upbringing. I had shown such a warm dislike for this contract that no one said a thing to me about it when it was signed. It was agreed upon that I should be weaned away from my mother so gradually that I would not notice it; and as she was impatient to see Caroline again, the first step was that she left for Paris without me.

Since I was to go to Paris a fortnight later with my grandmother, and since I already saw that the carriage and baggage were being made ready, her departure did not frighten or hurt me. I was told that in Paris I would live very near my mama, and see her every day. Yet I felt a sort of terror to find myself alone in that house, which began to seem as big as it had during the first days I had spent there. Though I was apart from her only a fortnight, that fortnight is clearer in my memory than the three years which followed, and which she spent with me. For the truth is, only suffering makes a child aware of itself.

Actually, nothing remarkable happened during those two weeks. My grandmother saw that I was downcast and made an effort to distract me with work. She gave me my lessons and proved much more indulgent than my mother toward my writing exercises and fable recitations. Gone were the scoldings, gone the punishments. Of these she had aways been sparing, and now, wanting to be loved, she gave me even more praise, encouragement and sweets than usual. By all rights this should have been very pleasant for me, for my mother was unbending, and without pity for my laziness and monkeyshines; but a child's heart is a little world as odd and inconsistent as an adult's. So it was that I found my grandmother more severe and more frightening in her patience than my mother in her exasperation. Until then I had loved her, and had shown with my caresses that I trusted her. But from then on—and until long after—I felt cold and reserved toward her. Her caresses only pained me and made me feel like crying, because they reminded me of Mama's more fervent squeezes. And besides, I wasn't really with her all the time, in continual closeness and warmth. No, respect was required, and respect, for me, was like ice. The terror that my mother sometimes caused me was nothing but a passing moment of pain; the next moment I would be on her lap again, climbing all over her; whereas what I gave my grandmama was merely cere-monial caresses. She kissed me solemnly, as if to reward me for good conduct; and she was so eager for me to learn to "bear myself well," and to cast off my inveterate sloppiness—which my mother had never much troubled to correct—that she ended by forgetting that I was, after all, a child. I wasn't to roll on the ground anymore, or to laugh so loud, or to talk our broad Berrichon dialect. I had to stand like a ramrod, wear gloves, and be seen and not heard—unless it was to whisper in a corner with Ursulette. My every natural spurt of energy was curbed—gently, of course, but insistently. She never scolded me, but when she was irked she called me "little miss," and that was enough. "Little miss, you're sitting like a hunch-back," "Little miss, you're walking like a peasant girl," "Little miss, you've lost your gloves again," "Little miss, you're too big for that now." Too big! I was seven! No one had ever said I was big. This idea, that I'd suddenly grown big since my mother's departure, frightened the wits out of me. And then, I had to learn all sorts of manners that I thought were just plain silly. I had to drop a curtsy to anyone who came by. I wasn't to set foot in the kitchen anymore, and was certainly not to "thou" the servants, so they might lose the habit of "thouing" me. Moreover, I wasn't to call my grandmama "thou"; I wasn't even to call her "you"; no, I had to use the third person: "Does my grandmama wish to let me out in the garden?"

The excellent woman was certainly right to want to instill in me a deep respect for herself and for the highly civilized code of behav-ior that she wished to impose upon me. She was taking possession of me, and she found herself with a difficult and cranky child on her hands. She had seen my mother deal forcefully with me, and she thought that instead of quieting my unhealthy outbursts she merely excited my senses, and so subdued me without reforming me. She may well have been right. A child whose nervous system has been jolted too hard is soon on the rampage again, precisely because it has been curbed too abruptly. My grandmother was aware that by quelling me with calm but sedulous warnings, she would bend me, without struggles or tears, to an instinctual obedience so that eventually I would lose all thoughts of resistance. And indeed, it took her only a few days. Though it had never occured to me to revolt against her, I had scarcely refrained from rising up against others in her presence. But as soon as she took possession of me, I felt that if I did anything naughty in her presence I would incur her blame. This blame was expressed very politely, but very coldly, and it chilled me to the bone. It did such violence to my instincts that I began to shudder convulsively; this alarmed her, but she did not grasp its cause.

She had achieved her goal, which was, first and foremost, to make me respond to discipline, and she was amazed she had succeeded so fast. "My heavens," she said, "how good-natured the child's become!" And she plumed herself on having transformed me so easily with a system just the reverse of the one used by my mother, who was alternately my tyrant and my slave.

But my dear grandmama soon found cause for even greater surprise. For she craved not only pious respect but also passionate love. She recalled her son's childhood, and fondly hoped she was about to enjoy it again with me. Alas! That was not in her power, nor in mine. She failed to take account of the number of generations between us, and of how much older she was than I. Nature cannot be fooled; and despite my grandmother's infinite kindness and invaluable help in bringing me up, an aged and infirm ancestress cannot be a mother, and an old woman who nannies a tot flouts nature at every moment. God knew what He was doing when He put an end to the power of maternity at a certain age. The little being who embarks on life needs another who is still young and full of sap. My grandmother's solemn ways were like iron in my soul. Her dark and scented room gave me headaches and fits of yawning. She was afraid of heat, of cold, of drafts, of a sunbeam.

Whenever she said, "Run along now and play quietly," I felt she was shutting me up with her in a shoebox. She would give me etchings to look at, but I didn't see a thing; I was dizzy; a dog barking outside, a bird singing in the garden, would make me tremble. I wanted to be that dog, that bird! And when I was in the garden with her I was chained to her petticoats by the dutiful feelings she had instilled in me, though she never forced me to do anything. She could scarcely walk, so I was always close by, ready to pick up her snuffbox or her glove which she often dropped and which she could not stoop to retrieve; for I have never seen a weaker or more languid body; yet since she was fat and fresh and perfectly well, her inability to move drove me to distraction. A hundred times I had seen my mother on her bed like a dead woman, prostrated by fierce headaches, her cheeks pale and her jaws clenched; and this drove me to despair; but my grandmother's lackadaisical paralysis was something which I could not understand, and which sometimes seemed self-willed. Indeed, it must have been, at least at the outset; it was the fault of her early upbringing. She, too, had lived too long in a shoebox, and her blood had lost its pulse; whenever she was bled not a drop came out, so dead was it in her veins. I was horribly afraid of becoming like her, and when I was beside her, and she ordered me not to fidget or shout, I felt that she was asking me to be dead.

In brief, all my instincts revolted against this difference in her constitution, and I never really loved my grandmother until I could reason. Until then, I confess, I had for her a sort of veneration conjoined with an irresistible physical repulsion. Of course, the poor woman noticed my coldness, and tried to overcome it with reproaches, but they only worsened it by making me aware of a feeling I had not been conscious of till then. She suffered deeply, and perhaps I, unable to defend myself, suffered even more. But once my mental powers had developed, I was powerfully drawn to her, and she owned she had been wrong to think me stubborn and ungrateful.

Five

Journey to Paris.—The big berlin.—The forest of Orléans and the hangings there.—My grandmother's apartment in Paris.— Walks with my mother.—The Chinese bob.—My sister.—My first violent sorrow.—The black doll.—Illness, and a vision in delirium.—Rose and Julie.—My grandmother's maternal diplomacy.— I'm "'ome" again.—My uncle's Sunday dinners.—His snuff boxes.—Mme. de La Marlière.—Mme. de Pardaillan.—Mme. de Ferrière and her lovely arms.—Mme. de Bérenger and her wig.— Mme. de Maleteste and her dog.—The abbés.—False graces.—The shabby-genteel literature of today.

IT MUST HAVE BEEN early in the winter of 1810–1811 that we left for Paris, for Napoleon had just marched triumphally into Vienna; he had married Marie Louise during my first stay at Nohant. I recall the two spots in the garden where I heard my family discuss these events. I bade Ursule good-bye; the poor child was very upset, but we were to see each other soon, upon my return, and besides, I was so happy to be off to see my mother that I was well nigh indifferent to anything else. For the first time I had experienced a separation, and had got some notion of the passing of time: I had counted each day and hour that went by while I was apart from the object of my love. But I loved Hippolyte too, despite his teasing, and he

84

also had cried at being left alone for the first time in the big house. I was sorry for him; I would have wanted him to come; but really I had wept for myself, and thought only of my mother. My grandmother, who spent all her time observing me, said to Deschartres in a low voice (children hear everything), "This child is not as sensitive as I thought."

At that time you needed three or four days to reach Paris. Although my grandmother traveled post, she could not spend the night on the road, and when she had made twenty-five leagues by day in her big berlin she was exhausted. This coach was a real rolling house. Everyone knows how with many bundles, provisions and conveniences of all sorts elderly people, especially the more refined, cumber themselves upon a journey. This vehicle's countless compartments were stuffed with victuals, tidbits, scent bottles, playing cards, books, guide books, money and whatnot. We could have been a month upon the road. My grandmother and her chambermaid, packed in with quilts and pillows, half-reclined in the rear; I took the front seat, and though I was quite comfy there, I found it hard to contain my exuberance in such a little space without kicking whoever was facing me. I had become very frisky in the free life of Nohant, and so had begun to enjoy perfect health; but soon the Paris air, which has never agreed with me, made me feel sickly and dull.

But the trip did not bore me. It was the first time I had traveled without being lulled into a heavy slumber by the rolling of the carriage, as in my early childhood, and all the new sights kept my eyes open and my mind alert.

To cross the forest of Orléans is nothing today, but in my childhood it was still something redoubtable. Great trees overhung the road for two-hour stretches, and carriages were ofttimes halted by brigands, who composed one of the traveler's unavoidable concerns. The postilions had to hurry through these stretches before nightfall; but despite our efforts, night overtook my grandmother and me in just such a place during this first journey. Not one to scare easily, she did all that prudence commanded; if fate foiled her precautions, she would face it with admirable determination. Her chambermaid was not so cool, but she was careful to keep her fears to herself, and the two of them merely conversed, with great philosophy, upon the subject of their apprehensions. For some reason the thought of brigands did not scare me; but I was petrified when I heard my grandmother say to Mlle. Julie: "Nowadays holdups are infrequent here, and the forest is well pruned by the roadsides in comparison with the way it was before the Revolution. Then it was just a dense thicket, and there were no ditches, so that one was attacked without knowing by whom, and without time to cock a gun. I was lucky enough never to be attacked on my trips to Châteauroux, yet Monsieur Dupin and all his servants armed themselves to the teeth to get through this death trap. Robberies and murders were common, and the authorities had a singular way of reckoning them up, and of warning the travelers: whenever brigands were captured, tried and sentenced, they were hanged from the trees along the road, at the same spot where they had committed their crime; so that here, for instance, on each side of the road, and at rather short intervals, one saw corpses swinging from the branches, and occasional gusts would blow them directly before one's eyes. If one made the trip often, one grew to recognize all the hanged men, and each year one could count the new ones—which proves, by the bye, that hanging never deterred a soul. Well, I recall one winter when I saw a tall woman whose body stayed intact a very long time, and whose long black hair streamed upon the breeze, while the crows fluttered about her and disputed her flesh. It was a horrid spectacle, and a contagion which pursued one as far as the city walls."

Perhaps my grandmother thought I was sleeping during this dreadful speech. But I was dumb with horror and cold sweat covered my limbs. It was the first time that I pictured death as something frightful. Those hanging corpses! those trees! those crows! that floating hair! They caused such horrible images to pass through my brain that my teeth chattered with fright. I did not worry about being attacked or killed in the forest, but I could already see those bodies swinging in the branches of the old oaks, and I pictured them in the most frightening detail. This terror stayed with me until long afterward, and every time we crossed the forest, until I was fifteen or sixteen, it again descended upon me, and just as keenly and as painfully—which shows that real torments are nothing compared with what our fancies offer.

We arrived in Paris at a pretty apartment in the Rue Neuve-des-Mathurins; from the windows we could see all the vast park across the street. My grandmother's rooms were full of furniture from before the Revolution; these pieces were what she had salvaged from the shipwreck, yet all were still comfortable and fresh in color. Her own room was hung and upholstered with a sky-blue damask; there were rugs everywhere, and a blazing fire in every fireplace.

I'd never had it so easy, and I was amazed by every aspect of this studied luxury, which Nohant could hardly match. But I needed none of it. I had been reared in that dingy room in the Rue Grande-Batelière, with its old wainscot and its tiled floors, and I got no pleasure from such comforts. Indeed, my grandmother had hoped that I would show a keener interest in them; but I came to life and began to smile only when my mother was with me. She came every day, and my passion for her grew with each meeting. I almost devoured her with my kisses, and the poor woman, seeing how this pained my grandmother, was obliged to contain me, and to refrain from showing too much emotion. We were allowed to go out together—indeed, we had to (though this hardly helped wean me from her), for my grandmother never went out on foot. She could not get along without Mlle. Julie, who was herself clumsy, absent-minded and near-sighted, and who would have lost me in the street, or let me be run over by a wagon; so I could not have gone out at all if my mother had not taken me every day on her lengthy rounds. Everything, when seen through my mother's eyes, was beautiful. The new quarters of town were an enchanted place; the Chinese baths, with their hideous rocaille decorations and their stupid apes, were the very palace of faerie; the performing dogs who danced in the boulevards, the toy shops, the print-sellers and the bird-sellers—they were the stuff of my delight, and my mother, stopping before anything that caught my fancy, took pleasure in whatever I did and doubled my joy by sharing it.

My grandmother's power of discernment was more schooled, and of a natural loftiness. She wanted to form my taste, and trained her discriminating judgment upon any object that attracted me. "That figure is out of scale," she would say. "That color chord pains the eye." "That composition—those words—that music—that style of dress—is in bad taste." But this I would understand only in the course of time. My mother, simpler and less captious, communicated her impressions to me directly. Almost any product of art or industry pleased her, if only it had a beguiling form and fresh colors, and what did not please her still amused her. She had a taste for the new: the latest fashion always seemed the best she'd ever seen. And besides, everything became her; there wasn't a stitch that could make her look ugly or ungainly, despite the quips of my grandmother, who stayed faithful (and with reason) to the long-waisted, roomy skirts of the Directory.

My mother, caught up in the mode of the day, thought it was a shame the way my grandmama dressed—like a "sweet little old lady," she said. My grandmother's slightly worn but still fresh quilted morning coats were cut down to my size, so that I almost always wore dark "tents" that fell straight to my thighs. In those days your belt was supposed to pass under your armpits, so I looked a fright. But I felt freer. My brown hair had grown very long and hung about my shoulders, and if anyone wiped my head with a wet sponge it frizzled naturally almost at once. At length my mother pestered my grandmama into yielding her my poor head, so she could dress my hair *à la chinoise*.

This can only be described as the most freakish coiffure ever devised and it was certainly invented for women without foreheads. They combed your hair upright till it was at right angles to your scalp, and then they wrung this pigtail till it lodged tightly against your skull, so that your head resembled a ball topped by a smaller ball of hair. You looked like a brioche or a pilgrim's gourd. It was hideous, but worse still was the torture of having your hair drawn the wrong way; for it took a week of racking pain and insomnia for it to take this forced set, and they bound it so tightly to train it that the skin on your brow was stretched upward, and the corners of your eyes slanted like the eyes on the faces in a Chinese fan.

I submitted dumbly to this torture, for all that I didn't care a rap if I was ugly or beautiful, if I followed the fashion or protested its excesses. My mother liked it, I pleased her, and so I suffered with stoical courage. My grandmama said I looked a fright; she was appalled; but she thought it unseemly to quarrel over such trifles. Besides, my mother was obliging her by causing me to tone down my adoration of her.

In the beginning this seemed easy. Since my mother took me out every day, and dined or spent the evening with me often, I was scarcely apart from her, except in sleep; but one occurrence for which I thought my grandmama was decidedly to blame soon rekindled my preference for my mother.

Caroline had not seen me since my departure for Spain, and it seems that my grandmother had ordained that my mother break forever the bond between my sister and myself. Why this aversion for such an open-hearted and strictly reared child, who had been a model of self-denial all her life? I cannot say; even today I cannot explain it to myself. Why, at the moment when the mother was taken in and accepted, was the daughter reviled and banished? Behind it all lay a prejudice, unaccountable in one who could rise above the prejudices of her circle whenever she escaped certain influences unworthy of her mind and heart. Caroline had been born long before my father had met my mother; my father had loved her like a daughter, and she had been the even-tempered and obliging playmate of my first years. She was a pretty and gentle child, and I cannot see that her companionship posed any threat to me, nor any reason why I should have blushed to declare before the whole world that she was my sister, unless it be a sin to have no noble blood, and to come, in all likelihood, from the popular classes; for I never knew what rank Caroline's father occupied in society, and presume he was of the same humble and obscure origin as my mother. But wasn't I also the daughter of Sophie Delaborde, the granddaughter of a bird-seller, and the great-granddaughter of Goodwife Cloquard? How could anyone have cherished hopes of making me forget that I came from the People, while persuading me that my sibling was inferior to me only because she did not have the dubious honor of counting the King of Poland and Marshal Saxe among her paternal ancestors? What madness! what silliness! And when a high-minded person of mature years acts silly in front of a child, how much time, and how many efforts and examples, are not required to rub out that bad impression?

Well, my grandmother performed this feat; for that bad impression, though never rubbed out, was nonetheless overlaid by the treasures of tenderness that her soul lavished upon me. But if there had not been some deep explanation for all that she suffered in nurturing my love for her, I would have been a monster. Thus I am obliged to relate her initial transgression, though now that I know how stubborn the aristocracy is, the fault seems nowise her own, but rather to weigh wholly against the circles in which she had always lived, and which, despite her noble heart and lofty power of reason, she was never able to quit altogether.

She had required, then, that my sister be estranged from me, and since I had left her at the age of four, I was probably on the way to forgetting her. Indeed, this would have happened already, had not my mother continued to mention her to me; nevertheless, my affection for her had not had time to grow very keen before my departure for Spain, and I doubt that it would ever have reawakened if violent efforts had not been made to destroy it, and if a little family scene had not affected me terribly.

Caroline was twelve. She boarded at a school, and each time she came to see our mother she begged her to take her to my grandmother's to see me, or else to bring me to see her. Somehow my mother stalled her off, neither wanting nor being able to explain her incomprehensible exclusion. But the poor child, quite bewildered and unable to contain her eagerness to embrace me, listened only to her heart; taking advantage of an evening when our mama was dining with my uncle de Beaumont, she persuaded my mother's concierge to take her to our rooms, where she arrived bursting with joy and impatience. She was a bit afraid of my grandmother, whom she had never seen; but perhaps she thought that she, too, was dining at my uncle's, or perhaps she had simply decided to run the gauntlet to see me.

It was about seven or eight o'clock. I was all alone, playing mournfully on the parlor rug, when I heard someone stirring in the next room. My maid half-opened the door and called me in a low tone. My grandmother appeared to be drowsing in her easy chair; but she was a light sleeper. Without knowing why my maid had called me, I tiptoed to the door. Just then my grandmama turned around and said sternly:

"Where, little miss, are you going so mysteriously?"

"I don't know, Grandma. My maid called me."

"Rose! Come in this instant. What do you want? Why are you calling the child behind my back?"

The maid flushed, demurred, then blurted out:

"Oh, Madame, Mademoiselle Caroline is here!"

This pure, sweet name produced an extraordinary effect upon my grandmother. She thought that my mother had openly mutinied, or else decided to deceive her, and that Caroline or the maid had clumsily revealed this deception. She spoke sharply and dryly, which she rarely did.

"The child must leave at once," she said, "and let her never call here again! She knows very well that she must not see my granddaughter. My granddaughter no longer knows her; *I* do not know her. And you, Rose, if you ever try to slip her in here again, I'll dismiss you on the spot!"

Terrified, Rose vanished. I was upset and frightened. I felt something like grief, and was very sorry that I had caused my grandmother such anger, for I sensed that it was unnatural with her, and that it was making her suffer. My shock at seeing her in this state caused me to forget all about Caroline, whom I remembered only vaguely anyway. But all at once, after an exchange of whispers behind the door, I heard a stifled, piteous sob, a cry out of the depths of a soul, which pierced my own soul and stirred the voice of my blood. It was Caroline; she was weeping; and she went away dismayed, crushed, humiliated, wounded in her natural self-esteem and in her innocent love for me.

Directly the image of my sister quickened in my memory, I saw her as she had been in the Rue Grande-Batelière and in Chaillot: tallish, slender, gentle, modest, obliging, a willing slave to my whims, singing me lullabies, telling me fairy tales. . . . I dissolved in tears and rushed to the door, but it was too late; she was gone. My maid was crying too, and she took me in her arms, urging me to hide my grief from my grandmother lest the blame fall upon her. My grandmother called me back and tried to take me on her lap to talk to me and calm me down; but fleeing her caresses, I slipped away and threw myself on the floor in a corner, shrieking, "Mama! I want to go back to my mama! I won't stay here anymore, I won't, I won't!"

Mlle. Julie appeared in turn and tried to talk sense into me. She assured me that my grandmother, whom I refused to look at, was becoming sick on my account:

"You're hurting your grandmama, who loves you, who worships you, who lives for your sake!" But I wouldn't listen; I only screamed despairingly for my mother and sister. I was so out of breath and so feverish that she gave up trying to get me to say good night to my grandmama. I was put to bed, and all night I sighed and moaned in my sleep.

Doubtless my grandmother had a bad night too. Since then I've learned how kind and tender she really was, and I know the pain she felt when she believed herself obliged to hurt others. But her dignity forbade her to show it, and it was only by devious favors and pampering that she tried to make me forget.

When I awoke I found a doll upon my bed. I had coveted this doll the day before when I had seen it with my mother in a toyshop, and I had sung its praises to my grandmother when I returned for dinner. The doll was a little Negress who seemed to be laughing uproariously, her white teeth and bright eyes agleam in her black face. She was round and shapely, with a dress of pink crepe fringed with silver. She had seemed so bizarre, so fanciful, so wonderful; and that morning, before I had wakened, my poor grandmother had sent for the doll to indulge my craze and to beguile my sorrow. And indeed, my first reaction was one of intense delight; I took the little darling in my arms; her laughter made me laugh, and I kissed her as a young mother kisses a newborn babe. But while I was looking at her and rocking her in my arms, my memories of the night before revived. I thought of my mother, my sister, my grandmother's unkindness, and I threw the doll across the room. The poor Negress only laughed the more, and I picked her up and caressed her again and washed her with my tears, giving myself over to the illusion of maternal love, which my own aggrieved filial love had brought to a keener pitch. Then suddenly the world swam; I dropped the doll and began to vomit up bile, greatly alarming my maids.

I do not know what happened during the next few days. I had measles with a high fever. I was probably about to come down with them anyway, but all the excitement and suffering must have precipitated or intensified them. I was quite dangerously ill, and one night I had a vision which oppressed me terribly. A lamp had been left guttering in my room; my two maids were asleep, but my eyes were open and my head on fire. Yet apparently my thoughts were clear, and as I fixed my gaze upon this lamp I was well aware what it was. A large fungus had formed upon the wick, and the candle snuff which issued from it cast a tremulous shadow on the ceiling. Suddenly this "stranger" took on a distinct shape: a little man was dancing in the flame. By degrees he slipped out of it and began to whirl around it, and as he whirled he grew and grew, until he was the size of a real live man, and he grew again until he was a giant who trod rapidly upon the floor, and his long, disheveled hair whipped about the ceiling with the stealth of a bat.

When my fever subsided, and I was being kept in bed only out of caution, I heard Mlle. Julie and Rose discussing my illness in low tones, and wondering what had made it so grave.

Rose had been in my mother's service when my father was still alive, and my mother had been satisfied with her loyalty and with several good qualities of hers. Finding her in Paris without a position, and desirous of seeing me attended to by an honest woman, my mother had persuaded my grandmother to engage her to look after me, to take me walking and to keep me busy. Rose was a strong, red-haired girl, bold and energetic, and built like a boy. She bestrode horses and galloped like a demon, leaping ditches and sometimes even falling and cutting her head; but nothing depressed her spirits. On the road she was a precious asset to my grandmother because she never forgot a thing; she foresaw every eventuality, blocked the wheels with her wooden shoes, prodded the postilion if he dozed off, repaired the traces, and would readily have put on top boots and led the horses. Hers was a powerful nature; she was a real draywoman from Brie, where she had been brought up in the fields.

Rose was full of heart and devotion, but she had one cruel fault, which I got to know very well, and which came of her fiery blood and high animal spirits: she was brutal and violent. As she loved me very much, having cared for me during my infancy, my mother thought she had procured me a friend, and indeed, she adored me; but she had bullying ways and fits of temper that were to oppress me and to make of my early youth a sort of martyrdom.

Yet I've forgiven her everything, and oddly enough, despite my natural independence and the sufferings she inflicted upon me, I never really hated her. The reason is that she was sincere, with a core of generosity too, and above all she loved my mother, and my mother always loved her.

It was just the opposite with Mlle. Julie. She was mild, polite, never raised her voice, and showed angelic patience in everything; but she was devious, and that is one fault I've never been able to bear. I don't mind saying she was a girl of high mentality. Though barely literate, having grown up in the little town of La Châtre without learning a thing, she had filled the long evenings of Nohant by reading every book she could get her hands on. First it was novels; then history books; finally philosophy. She knew her Voltaire better than my grandmother herself, and I used to see her carrying about Rousseau's *Social Contract,* of which she had a remarkably good understanding. Every memoir since creation was devoured and digested by that cold, level and solemn head. She was, like some old diplomat, an authority on all the court intrigues under Louis XIV, Louis XV, the empress Catherine, Maria Theresa and Frederick the Great; and if you were hard put to recall some family connection between a peer of Old France and one of the great families of Europe, you would simply turn to her, and it would already have formed upon her lips.

I shall have much to say of her; for she made me suffer greatly, and her role in my life as my grandmother's police spy and informer made me a great deal unhappier than all the brutalization of Rose's well-intentioned naggings and beatings; but I have no bitter plaint to make against either of them. They did what they could for my physical and moral upbringing, each according to the system she thought best. (I grant that I found Julie particularly unpleasant because she hated my mother. Here she thought to evince her devotion to her mistress, though on that score she did her much more harm than good.) In fine, we had in our house "my mother's party," represented by Rose, Ursule, and me; and "my grandmother's party," represented by Deschartres and Julie.

I must say to the credit of Grandmama's two waiting maids that this difference of opinion did not prevent them from being very thick, and that Rose, without ever abandoning the defense of her first mistress, always professed great respect and even great devotion for her second. They nursed my grandmother until her dying day with unimpeachable zeal; they closed her eyes. So I have forgiven them all the troubles and tears they caused me, Rose in her fierce solicitude for my person, Julie in her abusive sway over my grandmother.

Now then, I believe I left them whispering in my room (and what family secrets didn't I learn from them, which I'd much preferred not to have known so young!). That particular morning they were saying:

JULIE: Now you see how foolish Aurore is to adore her mother so. She hasn't come once since the child took sick.

ROSE: Her mother's been by every day for word of her. She wouldn't come upstairs because she's miffed at Madame over Caroline.

JULIE: All the same, she could have looked in on her daughter without going in to Madame. She told Monsieur de Beaumont she was afraid of catching the measles. She fears for her skin.

ROSE: Poppycock, Julie. She's just afraid she'll bring the measles to Caroline; do both her daughters have to be sick at once? I'd have thought one sufficed.

This explanation soothed me, and quieted my yearning to embrace my mother. The next day she came up as far as the threshold of my room, and called good morning.

"Oh, my darling Mama! But don't come in; I don't want Caroline to catch the measles."

"There!" said my mother to somebody in the passage. "You see, she knows her mama! She doesn't accuse me. They can do what they please; they'll never stop her from loving me."

As the reader has gathered, there were about my two mothers people who continually tattled and so envenomed their disputes. More and more, my poor little heart was the pawn of their rivalry. The object of a perpetual jealous tug of war, I began to form my own prejudices just as surely as I ached with the pain that I was causing.

As soon as I was well enough to go out again, my grandmother bundled me up carefully and took me in a carriage to my mother's rooms on the Rue Duphot, where I had not yet been since my return to Paris. The apartment was small, dark, low and poorly furnished; the stewpot was simmering over the fire in the sitting room. Everything was very clean, but it hardly smacked of wealth or extravagance. My mother was so often reproached with cluttering up my father's life and sinking him into debt that I am delighted to find her such a thrifty soul, almost miserly on her own account, in all my recollections.

Caroline opened the door, looking pretty as an angel with her little snub nose. She was bigger for her age than I was for mine, and her skin was less brown, her features more delicate; she wore a guarded look, a bit cool and sarcastic. She was at home, so she handled my grandmother with aplomb. She kissed me passionately and pestered me with questions, caressing me the while.

"Sit down, Madame Dupin," she said, calmly and proudly drawing up a chair. "I shall send for Mama, who is calling upon the neighbor." And after summoning the concierge, who ran errands for them in the absence of a maid, she went back to the fire, where she sat down, took me upon her lap and began again to question and caress me without another word to the great lady who had so cruelly insulted her.

No doubt my grandmother had prepared some kind and dignified statement to reassure her and to heal her wound, for she had expected to find her timid and frightened, or sullen, and to have to submit to a torrent of tears or reproaches; but seeing that none of this had come to pass, she began, I think, to feel rather surprised and ill at ease, for I noticed that she was taking plenty of snuff, pinch after pinch.

Presently my mother arrived. She kissed me passionately and said good morning to my grandmother with a hot, dry look. The latter saw that she had better meet the coming storm head on.

"My daughter," she said, with all the calmness and dignity she could muster, "when you sent Caroline to my home, you misunderstood, I believe, my intentions regarding the mutual relation which must exist between her and Aurore. I have never dreamed to thwart my granddaughter in her affections. I shall not stand in her way if she wishes to visit you and to see Caroline here. We'd best sort out the whole thing to avoid future misunderstandings."

She could not have got out of it more wisely, or more fairly or adroitly. But she had not always been so fair. It's quite certain she had ordained that I should never see Caroline, even at my mother's, and had forced my mother to promise that she would never bring me to her home during our walks, a promise which the latter had faithfully kept. But it's also certain that when she saw that in my heart I remembered Caroline better and was more attached to her than she had thought, she gave up her resolution for a bad, indeed an impossible, job. Yet having made this concession, she still reserved the right not to receive a person whose presence she found disagreeable. Her shrewd and tidy explanation precluded all recriminations; and my mother, sensing this, let her anger wane.

"Well, Mother," she said, "this is welcome news." And they readily changed the topic. My mother had come in like a lion, and as usual she was astounded, as she confronted the flexible, polite firmness of her mother-in-law, to find herself going out like a lamb.

In a few moments my grandmother stood up to go about her calls, and asked my mother to keep me until she should return. This was one more delicate concession, and its aim was to show that she did not claim the right to cramp or to oversee our effusions. Pierret arrived in time to escort her to her cab. My grandmother had a certain regard for him because of the great devotion he had shown my father. She always greeted him warmly, and Pierret was not among those who tried to whip up my mother against her. On the contrary, he had made it his chief business to calm her and to urge her to be on a good footing with my grandmother. But he visited the latter very rarely. It made him too fidgety to spend a half hour without lighting a cigar, making funny faces or introducing each sentence with his favorite oath: "Tarnation!"

What joy I felt to be back with what seemed my real, my only family! How dear my mother seemed, how adorable my sister! How funny and obliging Pierret was! And that little apartment, so poor and ugly in comparison with my grandmother's "padded salons" (so I called them in mockery)—why, in one instant it became the promised land of my dreams! I explored all its nooks and crannies, I beheld the slightest objects with love: the little alabaster clock, the vases of paper flowers already yellowed under their bell jars, the woolen balls that Caroline had embroidered with chenille in her boarding school, and finally my mother's little foot warmer—a proletarian furnishing banished from smart homes, and the old Delphic tripod of my first improvisations in the Rue Grande-Batelière. How I loved it all!

"I'm home!" I said. "I'm home, I'm home, I'm home!" I thought I'd never tire of saying it. "There I'm at my grandmama's. Here I'm home!"

"Tarnation!" said Pierret. "She'd better not say 'ome at Madame Dupin's or she'll say we give 'er speech lessons at the 'aymarket!" And he burst out laughing, for he laughed at just about anything, and my mother began to mimic him, and I shouted, " 'Ome! 'Ome! What fun we have at 'ome!"

Caroline made "rabbits" for me with her fingers, and with a cat's cradle, showed me all those figures and designs that children call "bed," "boat," "scissors," "saw," etc. All my grandmama's fine dolls and picture books seemed like nothing compared with these games that reminded me of my childhood; for though still a child, I already had an earlier childhood, a past, behind me, with its own memories and regrets—a whole finished life that I would never get back again.

I felt hungry. Of course, we didn't have cakes or preserves at " 'ome," just the classic stewpot for every meal. In a trice it was off the fire and on the table. And with what delight I fingered my old earthen bowl! Never had I eaten with such gusto. I was like a traveler returned after long ordeals, who relishes every detail of his little home.

My grandmother came to fetch me, and I felt a lump in my throat. But I knew that I musn't abuse her generosity. Laughing, I followed her out, but my eyes were full of tears.

Nor did my mother want to take advantage of my grandmother's concession, and she brought me to her home only on Sundays. Sunday was Caroline's holiday: she still boarded out, or perhaps she had aready started to learn the trade of music engraving, which she worked at until her marriage with much industry and some slight gain.

Those happy and impatiently awaited Sundays passed as in a trance. Then, at five o'clock, Caroline went to dine with my aunt Maréchal, while Mama and I joined my grandmother at my uncle de Beaumont's house.

It was an old and very pleasant family custom, this weekly dinner which always brought the same guests together. It has been virtually lost in the helter-skelter life of today. It was simply the most pleasant and the easiest way for people of leisure and of regular habits to meet. My great-uncle had for a cook a *cordon bleu* who, never before having plied his trade outside a palace staff of consummate skill and taste, invested a vast capital of self-esteem in pleasing his master. My great-uncle and his housekeeper, Mme. Bourdieu, brought an enlightened supervision to these important undertakings. On the stroke of five we would arrive, my mother and I, to find my grandmother and my great-uncle already seated about the hearth in vast armchairs placed directly across from one another, and between them Mme. de La Marlière, her feet resting upon the andirons and her disarranged skirt disclosing two thin legs shod with daggerlike shoes.

Mme. de La Marlière was an old and intimate friend of the late

Countess of Provence (wife of the man who later became Louis XVIII). Her husband, General de La Marlière, had died upon the scaffold. This lady, often mentioned in my father's letters, was very kindhearted and gay, expansive, prosy, obliging, devoted, noisy, tart and a bit cynical-sounding. She was not at all pious when I saw her, and poked fun at priests, if no one else was at hand, without the slightest compunction. At the Restoration she became devout, and she lived until the age of ninety-eight, I believe, in the odor of sanctity. She was, in sum, an excellent woman, quite without prejudices when I knew her, and I doubt that she ever became bigoted or intolerant. Anyway, she hadn't the right, considering how little heed she'd paid to spiritual matters during the first three quarters of her life! She was very kind to me, and as she was the only one of my grandmother's friends who had nothing against my mother, I showed her more trust and friendship than I did to any of the others. Yet I admit that she was really not to my liking. Her clear voice, her southern accent, her odd getups, her sharp chin which bruised my cheeks whenever she kissed me, and especially the gross, burlesque idiom she employed, hindered me from taking her seriously, or from deriving any pleasure from her pampering.

Mme. Bourdieu lightly came and went from kitchen to parlor and back; she could not have been much older than forty. She was a stout brunette, unmistakably of the South. She came from Dax, and had an even heavier Gascon accent than Mme. de La Marlière, who liked to behave like a child, and call my uncle "Papa." My Mother called him "Papa" too, which had the odd effect of making him seem younger than she.

My uncle, though a light eater, was a gourmand, but his gourmandise was as sober and tasteful as his surroundings, not at all gaudy or showy; it smacked, moreover—a vain point, this—of a certain positivism. It was amusing to hear him expound his culinary theories, for he oscillated between a gravity and a logic which had sorted well with the matter of political economy or philosophy, and a kind of witty, comical indignation.

"Nothing is so foolish," he would say in a playful tone, his gross words offset by his elegant pronunciation, "than to ruin oneself for one's maw. It doesn't cost a penny more to get a tasty omelet than to be served, under the sacred name of omelet, an old burned dish-rag. The root and essence is to know what an omelet *is;* and once a housekeeper has grasped *that,* I should prefer her in my kitchen to some pretentious savant who has himself called Monsieur by his scullery boys, and who christens a joint of carrion with pompous appellations."

All during dinner the conversation turned upon the grub. I have offered the foregoing so that the reader may form a good picture of the sort of classic old church canon my great-uncle was: I wager there are very few left of his type. My grandmother, who though a light eater was very fond of delicacies, also had scientific theories on how to make a vanilla custard or a soufflé. Often my great-uncle would have words with Mme. Bourdieu because she had put too many or too few lumps of nutmeg in the sauce; my mother laughed at their quarrels. Only old Marlière dispensed with such table talk, because she ate like an ogress. As for me, these long dinners—served, discoursed upon, analyzed and savored with such deep seriousness—bored me to death and I excused myself from time to time to go play with the old poodle, Babet, who spent her days making little poodles and giving them suck in a corner of the dining room.

The evenings were just as tedious. My mother had to fetch a deck of cards and make a fourth with the elder folk, which did not amuse her much, since my great-uncle was a first-rate player and never got angry, as Deschartres did. Anyway, old Marlière always won because she cheated. She even owned that cardplaying without cheating bored her, and that that was why she refused to play for stakes.*

In the meanwhile that kind soul Mme. Bourdieu would be trying to amuse me. She would help me build houses of cards or little structures out of dominoes. My great-uncle, who was a teasing sort, would occasionally turn around and blow hard, or nudge our little

* Since then I have made an observation which seems sad to me: that most women cheat at cards and are dishonest where stakes are involved. I have noticed this trait even in rich, pious and respected women. I must mention it because it is the case, and because to draw attention to an evil is to fight it. I wonder if this instinct of duplicity, which may be observed even in girls who do not play for stakes, comes from an inborn need to deceive, or rather from a ruthless, nervous desire to escape the laws of chance. I prefer to think merely that the moral education of women is incomplete. There are two sorts of honor in society: the honor of men bears upon the gallantry and loyalty observed in money transactions; that of women attaches to modesty and marital fidelity. If I should venture here to tell the men that a bit of chastity and fidelity would do them no harm, they would surely just shrug. But do they deny that an honest woman—who would also be, in a fuller sense of the term, a *gentleman*—would have redoubled claim upon their trust and respect?

table with his elbow. And he would say to Mme. Bourdieu (who was called Victoire like my mother): "Victoire, you're dulling the child's mind. Show her something more interesting. How about my snuffboxes, for instance?" And so we would open a little chest, and I would be allowed to examine a whole collection of a dozen or so utterly lovely snuffboxes painted with charming miniatures. These miniatures were portraits of pretty ladies scantily clad as nymphs, goddesses or shepherdesses. Today I know why my great-uncle had so many such ladies on his snuffboxes! But by then he had got over his interest in them, and found them useful only to beguile the eyes of a baby. So give your portraits to the abbés!—but happily this is no longer the fashion.

Sometimes my grandmother took me to Mme. de La Marlière's, but the latter gave no dinners, for she had very slender means. She lived in a small apartment three flights up at 6 Rue Villedot, which I think she occupied from the days of the Directory straight through to her death in 1841 or '42. Her furnishings, though much less fine than my great-uncle's, were remarkable in that everything matched. I don't think they had undergone the slightest alteration since the era of Louis Seize, of which they were a perfect little collection.

Mme. de La Marlière was then very thick with Mme. de Junot, Duchess of Abrantès, who has left some interesting memoirs, and who died very miserably after a life of pleasures and disasters. She devoted, as I recall, a page to Mme. de La Marlière, where she talked her up. But then, friendship must be permitted such inaccuracies! Anyway, this old friend of the Countess of Provence and of Mme. de Junot and of my grandmother did have more virtues than faults—enough, indeed, to win pardon for a few failings and foibles.

Among my grandmother's other friends was a Mme. de Pardaillan, whom she rightly preferred to all the others. She was a sweet little old lady who had been very pretty and who still was neat, dainty and spry beneath her wrinkles. She had no more wit or education than the other ladies of her day, for of all whom I have just mentioned, my grandmother was the only one with good grammar and correct spelling. Mme. de La Marlière, though funny and piquant after her fashion, wrote the way our cooks no longer write; but Mme. de Pardaillan, having never had any sort of pretension, and never aiming to be witty, was never boring. Her judgments showed great common sense, and she formed her principles and opinions in her heart, without worrying about other people. I think that she never said a nasty word in her life, and what is more, that she never even cherished a bitter or hostile thought; hers was an angelic nature, calm, yet sensitive and loving—a loyal soul, maternal to everyone, pious but not fanatical, and tolerant not out of indifference but out of tenderness and modesty. I really don't know that she had any faults; she was one of the two or three people I've met in my life in whom I was unable to detect a single one.

Though her mind did not appear to shine, I think that her thoughts had some depth. She had got the habit of calling me "poor child," and one day when we were alone I felt emboldened to ask why. She drew me close and kissed me, and said in a voice full of emotion:

"Always be kind, poor child, for that will be your only happiness in this life."

Her prophetic powers impressed me.

"Will I be unhappy, then?" I asked.

"Yes," she answered, "Everyone is doomed to unhappiness. But you will have more of it than others; and remember what I say, because you will have a lot to forgive."

"But why *should* I forgive?" I asked.

"Because in forgiving you will find the only happiness you will ever have."

Did she have some secret sorrow that made her talk like that to everyone? I think not; indeed, I think *she* was happy, for her whole family adored her; yet I also rather think that she must have suffered some heartbreak in her youth, which she never revealed to a soul; or was it merely that with her noble heart, she saw how much I loved my mother, and how much I was to suffer in that love?

There was also a Mme. de Bérenger and a Mme. de Ferrières; both were so infatuated with their titles that I wouldn't know which to hold up as the model of vanity and dowager airs. They were really the most perfect "old countesses" my mother could have found to sport with.

They had both been very beautiful, and very virtuous too, which only added to their haughtiness and stiffness. Mme. de Ferrières was still "well preserved," and she let one know it. Her arms were always bare under her muff, even in the mornings, and no matter how cold it was. These arms were terribly white and pasty, and I always beheld them with astonishment, baffled by this display of faded coquetry. Those "lovely" sixty-year-old arms were so flaccid that when she rested them on a table they seemed to turn into pools, which rather disgusted me. I've never understood this need for nudity in old women, especially in those who have lived a chaste life. But perhaps Mme. de Ferrières had always dressed that way, and simply did not care to give it up.

Like her, Mme. de Bérenger was not the favorite of any princess of the Old (or the new) Regime.* She regarded herself as too high and mighty for that, and would readily have told you that it was not for her to pay court to others, but to hold court herself. I don't remember whose daughter she was, but her husband claimed descent from Berenger, a Goth king of Italy; for this reason he and his wife regarded themselves as the top link in the great chain of being, ". . . And like a dung heap looked down upon creation."

They had had heaps of money, and still had plenty, though they enjoyed claiming that "that dreadful Revolution" had "ruined" them. Mme. de Bérenger did not show an inch of arm, but she was enchanted by her waist. She wore her corset so tight that two chambermaids had to thrust their knees in the small of her back while they laced it up. She may once have been as beautiful as people said, but you'd never have known it, especially with the coiffure she wore, which consisted of a tiny blond wig frizzed à l'enfant or à la Titus. Nothing could have been so ugly or ridiculous as this old woman pretending that this short, fair, crimped hair was her own, especially in that Mme. de Bérenger was very brown-skinned and had oversize features. Evenings, the blood went to her head, and she could not stand the warmth under her wig; she took it off to play cards with my grandmother, and sat there in a black headband, which made her look like an old priest; but if a caller was announced, she would scramble for her wig, which was often on the floor, or in her pocket, or on her armchair beneath her rump. Well, you may guess what curious folds those locks of frizzed hair had taken; and since in her haste she often put it on inside out, or backward, she offered a whole series of caricatures in which it was hard indeed to discern the beauty of bygone years.

There were others whose names I hardly recall; and there was

* Mme. de Pardaillan was the friend of the Dowager Duchess of Orléans.

a Mme. de Troussebois, whose chin touched her nose; a Mme. de Jassaud, who had a mummy's face; and the youngest in the gallery was a blond church canoness who had a rather fine head upon a deformed dwarf body. Although she was a maiden, she had the privilege of calling herself "Madame" and of bearing the ribbon of an order across her hump, for she had sixteen quarterings of the escutcheon. There was also a Baroness d'Hasfeld, or d'Hazefeld, who had the figure and the manners of an old top sergeant; and finally, a Mme. Thing, the only lady who had "no name at all" and who, just for that reason, had nothing laughable about her. Oh, there was another—I don't know what she was called—who had a big purple lip that was always swollen, split and chapped, and whose kisses I shunned.

There was also a certain Mme. de Maleteste, who was still rather young, and who had married an old, poor and whiny man, merely to bear the name of the Malatestas of Italy; the name is scarcely beautiful, since it means quite simply "bad head," or better still, "nasty head." By a singular coincidence, this lady had a perpetual headache, and as her name was pronounced Mal-tête, "headache," I sincerely believed that it was a nickname she had been given on account of her illness and her endless complaining. And so, one day, I asked her what her real name was. Stupefied, she answered that I knew very well.

"But I don't," I replied. "Headache is not a name."

"I beg your pardon, miss," she answered proudly. "It's a very fine and very great name."

"Fiddlesticks," I said. "You ought to get angry when they call you names like that."

"May *you* have such a name!" she said with an emphatic nod.

"Thank you," I said, "but I like mine better."

And the other ladies, who were not overfond of her, probably because she was the youngest, hid their tittering behind their fans. My grandmother silenced them, and Mme. de Maleteste retired several minutes later, in high dudgeon over an impertinence whose cutting edge I had not suspected.

There were men too: the abbé de Pernon, a gentle and excellent man, without a trace of religion about him, who always wore a light-gray suit and whose face was covered with big chick peas; the abbé d'Andrezel, who wore a spencer over his coats; and de

Vinci, a knight with a nervous tic which, by a continual contraction of the eyebrows and the frontal muscles, set his wig atremble and, in five minutes, pulled it off his skull and onto his nose. Just as it was quitting his head and falling into his plate, he would catch it and push it far back on his skull, so it would have a long way to travel before it fell off again. There were two or three other old men, whose names escape me but which may perchance come to my mind in some other connection.

Mme. de Maleteste had a horrid dog called Azor; today this is the classic name for a hall portress's dog, but all men "praise newborn gauds," and in those days "Azor" would have seemed charming had it not been borne by an old and conspicuously filthy dog. Not that he wasn't lovingly washed and combed, but his greed had brought very sorry results, and his mistress had a craze for taking him wherever she went, insisting he was too sad when left at home. Mme. de La Marlière, on the other hand, despised pets, and I admit that my tenderness for animals did extend to my finding it cruel when she aimed, with her long, daggerlike shoes, copious kicks at Azor de Maleteste, as she called him. Then Mme. de Maleteste would get into a huff, and let fly with a whole battery of dry, stinging quips. But Mme. de La Marlière, who was not at all malicious, only quick-witted and sharp-tongued, never got angry, but only provoked her the more with her crude jokes.

Something that amazed me as much as Mme. de Maleteste's name was the title "abbé," which I noticed was given to gentlemen who dressed like everybody else and had no religious customs or gravity of manner. These bachelors, who went to the theater, and gobbled fowl upon Good Friday, struck me as peculiar beings, whose place in the scheme of things eluded me; and like one of Gavarni's *Enfants Terribles,* I would ask them embarrassing questions. I recall that one day I said to the abbé d'Andrezel: "See here, if you're not a priest, where's your wife? And if you are a priest, where's your habit?" This *mot* was regarded as ever so witty and cutting, but I had not intended it thus; I had merely put my finger on a sore without realizing it. This was not the last time that I did: I have, in thoughtless or silly moments, asked questions or made remarks that other people thought very profound or stinging.

A certain conventional grace was an article of such importance in the life of the men and women of the old high society that our actors, however long they study, must strain to depict that grace today. I knew some of those gracious old creatures, and I must declare that despite their old admirers of both sexes, I never saw anything more ridiculous and unpleasing. I infinitely prefer a laborer at his plow, a woodcutter chopping up a tree, a washerwoman raising her basket to her head, a child rolling on the ground with its companions. It is beautifully built animals who are models of grace. Who teaches the horse his grand, swanlike airs, his proud stances, his broad and supple movements? Who teaches the bird his indescribably dainty ways, and who the kid his dances and inimitable leaps? Phooey on that old grace which consists in artfully pinching snuff, affectedly wearing an embroidered jacket or a train, rattling a sword or plying a fan! The beautiful ladies of Spain handle the last-named toy with indescribable grace, we are told; it is an art with them. So much I concede; but that art is in their nature. So do Spanish peasant girls dance the bolero better than our Opéra chorus; but their grace comes only of their beautiful lineaments, which bear it in instinctual form.

Grace, as it was understood before the Revolution—that is, false grace—was the torment of my childhood. I was taken to task for everything, and didn't make a gesture that wasn't judged. This made me chafe continually, and often I thought: "I wish I were an ox or an ass! They'd let me walk in my own gait, and browse as I saw fit, instead of turning me into a performing dog, and teaching me to walk upon my hind legs and to present my paw."

Well, sweet are the uses of adversity; and I suppose that it is to the disgust which this perpetual hectoring gave me for all affectation that I owe my faithfulness to my natural thoughts and feelings. I hate the false, the stilted, the mannered, and I spot them even when they have been cleverly lacquered with false simplicity. I see no beauty or goodness except in what is true and simple, and the older I get, the more I think I am right to require these qualities above all others in the character of men, in the work of the spirit and in the ventures of our common life.

Besides, it wasn't hard to see that this so-called grace, no matter how pretty and seductive, was a certificate of clumsiness and physical weakness. All those lovely ladies and fine gentlemen who were so adept at walking upon carpets and bowing or curtseying couldn't take three steps on God's good earth without collapsing of fatigue.

They couldn't open a door; they hadn't the strength to lay a fagot on the fire. They needed servants to pull up a chair; they couldn't go out or come in alone. What would they have done with their grace, without valets to act as arms, hands and legs? I think of my mother, who with hands and feet far daintier than theirs, did two or three leagues each morning in the country before breakfast, and lifted big stones and pushed the wheelbarrow as easily as she handled a needle or a piece of chalk. I'd rather have been a scullery maid than one of those ancient marquises whom I observed each day in an atmosphere of old musk!

O writers of today, you who never cease inveighing against the coarseness of our age, and weeping over faded frills and laces; you who have created, in these days of constitutional monarchy and bourgeois democracy, a peruked and powdered literature in the image of the Trianon nymphs: I salute you for never having spent a moment of your happy childhood in the ruined purlieus of the old *bon ton!* Ungrateful wretches, you have never known what it is to be bored to death; and now you deny the present and the future, kneeling beside the urn of a charming past which you have known only on canvas!

Six

Back to Nohant.—A year of happiness.—Childhood pranks.—The false Deschartres.—M. Gogault and M. Loubens.—The family quarrel festers.—I begin to experience unhappiness.—A talk with my mother.—My entreaties, her promises, her departure.—First night of sleeplessness and despair.—The empty room.—First disappointment.—Brutality of my maid.—This tyranny fosters certain moral traits in me.—My mother returns to Nohant.—I forgive my maid.—Energy and languor of adolescence.—Deschartres makes me sick of Latin.—My heart is broken.

WITH THE COMING of spring we packed to return to the country. I was in sore need of it. Because of too much comfort, or because of the Paris air, which has never agreed with me, I had fallen into a visible decline again. It was unthinkable to separate me from my mother; since I could not yet muster any will to resignation or blind obedience, I would likely have died of such a separation. So my grandmama invited my mother to return to Nohant with us. As I worried so much about this that the others began to worry too, it was decided that my mother herself would bring me, and that Rose would come with us. My grandmother would go by herself, with Julie. The big berlin had been sold, and because of straitened finances it had not been replaced, except with a brougham with two seats.

That part of the year 1811 which I spent at Nohant was one of the rare times in my life when I was completely happy. I had been similarly happy in the Rue Grande-Batelière, although we had had neither big rooms nor a big garden. Madrid had been an upsetting and painful ordeal for me; the poor health in which I had returned, the unexpected catastrophe of my father's death, and the struggle between my two mothers, with all that it did to acquaint me with fear and sorrow—these had provided an apprenticeship in unhappiness and suffering. But the spring of 1811 was cloudless, and the proof thereof is that that year left me with no memories. I know only that Ursule spent it with me, and that my mother had fewer headaches than before; and if she was at all at odds with my grandmama, it was so well hidden that I forgot she ever had been or could be. Indeed, this was probably the time when they got on best, for my mother was not one to hide her feelings. Such efforts exceeded her strength, and when she was angry even the presence of her children could not induce her to restrain herself.

There was also more gaiety in the house. Time does not heal all wounds, but there are some that it can soothe. Almost every day I saw one or the other of my two mothers weeping furtively, but their very tears proved that they were not always mourning. Sorrow at its greatest intensity has no climax; it acts upon us in a permanent climax, so to speak.

Toward the age of seven I came under Deschartres's tutelage. For a considerable period I had no reason to complain of how he treated me, for he was as patient and mild with me in those first years as he was harsh and brutal with Hippolyte. Consequently I made rapid strides, for he explained things quite clearly and succinctly when he was calm; but when put out of temper he grew muddled and botched his explanations, and his anger made him stammer unintelligibly. He browbeat and bullied poor Hippolyte horribly, despite his facility and excellent memory. He seemed unaware that the boy's robust nature required exercise and was only exasperated by too long lessons. Yet despite my affection for my brother, I must concede that he was an impossible child. He thought only of smashing, destroying and teasing, and of playing practical jokes upon everybody.

One day he threw burning firebrands in the fireplace under the pretext of a "sacrifice to the gods of the nether world," and the house caught fire. Another day he put gunpowder in a big log; it exploded in the hearth and sent the contents of the stewpot flying all over the kitchen. He called this "studying volcanic theory." He tied saucepans to dogs' tails and enjoyed watching their ungainly flight through the garden and their howls of terror. He also "shod the cats," that is, glued nutshells on their paws and tossed them on frozen ponds or varnished floors to see them slip about—all to the sound of his appalling oaths. Sometimes he said he was Calchas, the high priest of the Greeks, and under the pretext of sacrificing Iphigenia upon the kitchen table, took up a knife destined for less illustrious victims, and slashing every which way, wounded himself or others.

Occasionally I took part in his misdeeds, though within the bounds of my less stormy temperament. One day we saw a hog slaughtered in the poultry yard, and Hippolyte got the idea of massacring the garden cucumbers in the same way. He stuck a splinter of wood in the end of each cucumber for a neck, and pressing the unfortunate vegetables with his foot, forced out all the juice. Ursule collected it in an old flowerpot "to make blood sausage," while, off to the side, I solemnly kindled an imaginary fire, as we had seen the butcher do, to "grill the pork." This game was so much fun that we picked all the cucumbers, starting "with the fattest" and working down to the least ripe. We promptly laid waste to several rows on which the gardener had lavished much care. The reader may well imagine his distress upon discovering this carnage, with Hippolyte standing amid the corpses like mad Ajax slaughtering the flocks of the Greek army. The gardener complained, and we were punished; but that did not bring the cucumbers back to life, and we had none to eat that year.

Another of our naughty delights was to make what the children of our village called "dog traps." A "dog trap" was a hole in a lane or garden path, lightly filled with moist earth. We covered it with twigs, on which we laid slate tiles and a light layer of soil or dry leaves, and when the trap was finished we hid in the bushes and watched until the first comer sank into the mud, cursing the abominable urchins who'd "invented theirselves" such tricks. One day we snared Deschartres. As usual, he was wearing a pair of elegant stockings, white and ribbed, knee breeches and pretty nankeen gaiters, for he was vain of his foot and calf; he was always well scrubbed, and he chose his shoes with care. He walked (like all pedants, even if they are not pedagogues—it's one of their trademarks) like a goose, with his feet turned out. We followed him to secure a good view. All at once the earth gave way, and he found himself over his ankles in a yellow glaze perfectly qualified to dye his stockings. Hippolyte feigned surprise, so that all Deschartres's fury fell upon Ursule and me; but we were well out of reach before he had fished out his shoes.

Since Deschartres beat my poor brother cruelly, but was content with offering inane remarks to us little girls, Hippolyte, Ursule and I agreed that the two of us would take the most blame, to put him off the track: and we even prearranged a little act which met with success for a while. Hippolyte always had the first line: "Oh, the ninnies!" he would cry as he broke a chair or made a dog howl in Deschartres's hearing. "Must you, little girls?" And he would vanish just as Deschartres's nose appeared against the windowpane; but to the latter's astonishment, no little girls were anywhere to be seen.

One day when Deschartres had gone to sell cattle at the fair— for agriculture and the stewardship of our farms were his principal occupation—Hippolyte, having conceived to prepare his lessons in the Great Man's room, got it into his head to play the Great Man himself. Scarcely had he put on his big sporting jacket, which came down to his heels, and donned his pleated cap, when he found himself strutting up and down the room with his feet turned out and his hands clasped behind his back. He tried to imitate the tutor's way of speaking, went over to the blackboard, drew a few figures with chalk, began a demonstration, got angry, stammered, and denounced his pupil for a "crass ignoramus" and an "oaf"; and finally, satisfied with his talent for mimicry, he opened the window and abused the gardener for his way of pruning the trees; he criticized, chided, insulted and threatened him, all in Deschartres's style of speech, and in his usual barking voice. Either because he played the part well, or because the gardener was far off, the latter, who was in any case a simple and credulous fellow, was taken in and began to mumble a reply. All at once he was astonished to notice, a few feet away, the real Deschartres, who witnessed the entire scene without missing a word or a gesture of his double. As he was hidden by the trees, the hapless Hippolyte did not see him.

Deschartres, who had returned from the fair sooner than expected, went quietly up to his room and abruptly opened the door just as the little rascal was shouting at an imaginary Hippolyte:

"You're utterly unprepared! You write like a spider and spell like a chimney sweep! [Bim, bam!] That's for your ears, little beast that you are!" At that moment the scene became double; and while the false Deschartres beat the imaginary Hippolyte, the true Deschartres beat the real Hippolyte.

M. Gogault, our dancing master, was a dancer at the Opéra. He made a screech upon his pocket violin, and twisted our legs to teach us the turnout. Sometimes Deschartres would also attend the lesson, and expand upon the dancing master's opinion that we danced "like bears and parrots." But my brother and I hated Deschartres's pretentious gait, and found M. Gogault merely absurd when he entered the room like Zephir upon the verge of an entrechat; so as soon as he was gone, we turned our feet in; and just as he had dislocated our hips to force us into first position, so we dislocated them in the opposite direction for fear of being permanently deformed. We called this secret corrective "sixth position."

Hippolyte was frightfully clumsy and lumpish, and M. Gogault declared that never had such a dray horse "passed through his hands." When he changed positions, he shook the whole house, and his battements brought down the walls. When told to "hold his head" without craning his neck, he grasped his chin with one hand and held it that way while dancing. Even the dancing master could not keep from laughing, but Deschartres gave vent to the most profound and vehement indignation over the pupil, who had thought merely to signal his good intentions.

Our writing master's name was M. Loubens. A professor of high aspirations, he could spoil the best hand with his system. He insisted upon correct body and arm posture, as if handwriting were a choreographed dumb show; but indeed, all our lessons only reflected the sort of education that my grandmother wanted to give us: we were to acquire "grace" in everything. M. Loubens had invented divers engines of torture to force his pupils to keep their heads erect, their elbows out, and three extended fingers on the quill, while the little finger, also extended, bore the "burden" of the hand along the paper. As this sort of movement and muscle tension is just what the natural nimbleness and suppleness of children are least likely to admit, he had invented:

1. for the head, a sort of diadem in whalebone;
2. for the body and shoulders, a belt which was attached to the diadem in back by means of a strap;
3. for the elbow, a wooden bar which was screwed to the table;
4. for the right pointer, a brass ring welded to a smaller ring through which the pen was inserted;
5. for the positioning of the right hand and the little finger, a sort of boxwood plowshare, with finger slots, and moving upon casters.

If you add these tools, which M. Loubens insisted were indispensable to the study of handwriting, to the necessary rulers, paper, pens and pencils, all of which were worthless if not supplied by the professor, you will see that he was doing a brisk trade, and one which somewhat offset the modesty of the fees generally received for writing lessons.

At first these inventions caused us plenty of giggles, but after five minutes of practice we saw that they were torture: our fingers ossified, our right arms stiffened, the diadem gave us headaches. But nobody listened to our complaints, and we were not to be quit of M. Loubens until he had succeeded in making our writing absolutely illegible.

My mother returned to spend a month with us, but was obliged to depart again to help Caroline leave her boarding school. It was then that I realized I would be seeing less and less of her at Nohant. My grandmother spoke of spending the winter there, and I fell into the lowest spirits I had ever known. My mother tried to cheer me, but she could no longer deceive me, for I was old enough to see the limits to our mutual relation. The acceptance of Caroline into the family would have settled everything: yet it was just this point upon which my grandmother refused to yield.

My mother was again very unhappy at Nohant; she felt constrained, spiritually stifled, and she was always bottling up her anger. My stubbornness in openly preferring her to my grandmother (I did not know how to pretend, though that would have been in everybody's interest) had embittered the latter against her. And it must be said that my poor grandmother's declining health had altered much in her character. She had daylong moods I had never seen before. She became overly irritable, and sometimes addressed me so curtly that I felt crushed. Mlle. Julie had gained an extraordinary and deplorable sway over her mind, receiving all her confidences and exacerbating all her displeasures, doubtless with the best of intentions, but thoughtlessly and unfairly.

My mother would have borne all this for my sake, had she not been anxious about her other daughter. This I understood; I did not want Caroline to be sacrificed for me. She complained about her mother's yearly absences, and sobbed and accused her of favoring me.

Thus we were all unhappy, and I, innocent cause of all this domestic bitterness, felt the pain even more acutely than the others.

When I saw my mother begin to pack, I was terror-stricken. On that day she happened to be very irritated by something Julie had said, and when she remarked that she could no longer endure the rule of a chambermaid become more mistress of the house than her own mistress, I thought that she would never return; and guessing that even if she did her visits would be few and far between, I groveled at her feet and implored her to take me with her. If she did not I would run away, I said, and walk by myself from Nohant to Paris to be with her.

She took me on her lap and tried to explain her situation.

"Your grandmother," she said, "may well reduce me to fifteen hundred francs if I take you away."

"Fifteen hundred!" I cried. "But that's plenty, plenty for all three of us."

"No," she said, "it isn't. It isn't even enough for Caroline and me. Your sister's tuitional fees and allowance run to half as much, and with what remains to me now I can barely buy food and clothing. You'd know that if you knew anything about money. If I take you with me, and lose a thousand francs a year, we'd be so poor you couldn't bear it. You'd want your Nohant back, and every sou of your fifteen thousand francs."

"Never!" I shouted. "Maybe we'd be poor, but we'd be together. We'd never leave each other, we'd work, we'd live in a garret and eat beans, like Mademoiselle Julie says; what's wrong in that? Oh, we'd be happy! Nobody could thwart our love!"

I was so determined, so fervent, so desperate, that she was shaken.

"What you say may well be true," she replied with the simplicity of a child, of the generous child she was. "It's years since I thought money brought happiness, and I'm sure if I had you with me in

Paris I'd be far happier in my poverty than I am here, where I want for nothing and yet am sick at heart. But it's not me I'm thinking of, it's you; I'm afraid that one day you'd blame me for having deprived you of a good education and marriage, and a big fortune"

"Ha! A good education," I cried. "Grandmama just wants to make me into a wooden doll. And why should I want to marry some codger who'd go red in the face when you called, and have you turned out? As for the fortune, I'd be paying for it with my happiness, and it would make me a bad daughter. I'd rather die than have any of it. Oh, I do want to love my grandmother, I do want to take care of her, and play grabouche and lotto with her when she's in her moods; but I don't want to live with her! I don't want her chateau, I don't want her money; I don't need it. Let her give it to Hippolyte or Ursule; or how about Julie—you know how she *loves* Julie! I just want to be poor with you. No child is happy without her mother!"

I don't know what else I said, but I suppose I was eloquent after my fashion, because my mother seemed swayed.

"Listen," she said, "you don't know what penniless young girls go through. I'll not have you and Caroline suffering the way I did when I was fourteen and an orphan without a crust to eat; if I happened to die, you'd be in a pretty fix. Oh, I suppose your grandmother might take *you* back, but she'd never take in your sister, and what would become of her then? But look, there's a way out for all of us. We can always have money if we work; and anyway, I don't see why I don't work. It's not as if I didn't know how; yet here I am, living on my income like a fine lady! I'll tell you what: I'll try to open a millinery shop. I make better hats and headwear than the old hens who gussy up your grandmother in those lopsided rag bundles of theirs, which cost the earth. I don't think I'll set up in Paris—no, that'd cost too much—but if I save for a few months, and borrow a small sum, which Pierret or my sister would surely put up, I can open a shop in Orléans, where I've worked before. Your sister's handy, you are too, and believe me, you'll learn that trade quicker than Monsieur Deschartres's Latin and Greek. Why, the three of us would do splendidly! Things sell briskly in Orléans, but it's not dear there. Of course, we're not princesses, we'll scrounge like we did in the Rue Grande-Batelière; and who knows, maybe

Ursule could even join us after a while! We'll save, and stint ourselves, and in a few years I'll give you a dowry of eight or ten thousand, and you'll marry an honest workingman who'll make you happier than any king's son ever could. Because you'd never feel at home in society, don't you know; they'd never let you forget that you're my daughter and that your granddad was a bird-seller. They'd have you blushing every minute, and if you were stupid enough to give yourself airs, you'd never forgive yourself for being half rabble. Well, I see you're all for it—but keep mum now. I have to be off, but I'll stay a few days in Orléans to look about and see what shops are available. Then I'll get everything ready in Paris, and write you secretly through Ursule or Catherine, and come and pick you up. I'll announce my decision to your grandmama, and I won't take no for an answer: I'm your mother, and nobody can take away my right over you! Oh, she'll be furious, she'll cut off my allowance, but I won't care a rap. We'll move in over our little shop, and when she goes down the main street of Orléans in her big carriage, she'll see the letters, big as my arm: WIDOW DUPIN, MILLINERY."

This lovely project turned my head. It almost gave me a fit of nerves. I leaped out the room shouting and laughing, and at the same time I was crying. My poor mother obviously meant what she said, and believed she would be steadfast; she would never have poisoned the carefreeness, or rather the resignation, of my youth with a mere dream; for indeed, this dream seized my imagination, and for a long time made me agitated and fretful.

After this declaration I put as much zeal into speeding my mother's departure as I had into preventing it. I helped her pack, I was gay, even happy; I had the impression she'd be back to fetch me in a week. My gaiety and exuberance amazed my grandmama at dinner, especially in that I had been weeping so much that my eyelids were almost bloody. The change seemed inexplicable. My mother urged me in a whisper not to give cause for suspicion, and I was so discreet that nobody suspected my intentions, although I had borne them in my heart for four years with every sort of hope and fear. I confided in no one, not even Ursule.

But as night approached (my mother was to leave at the crack of dawn) I grew anxious, and then my anxiety turned to horror. I saw that my mother was not looking at me with that air of shared secrets and reassurance which was necessary to quiet my apprehensions. Instead she seemed sad and distracted. But why, why was she sad, since she was to return so soon, since she was to arrange for our joyful reunion? Children do not doubt what they are promised, nor count the obstacles; but when they see those they trust thrown into doubt, their souls fall into such deep distress that they tremble and bend like poor reeds in the wind.

I was put to bed at nine as usual. My mother promised me that she would not retire without coming in to say good-bye and to renew her pledge; but I was afraid she would not wake me if she thought I was asleep, and so I did not stay in bed, but got up as soon as Rose had tucked me in and gone downstairs to wait with Julie for the hour of my grandmother's night toilette. This toilette dragged on and on. First my grandmother ate something, very slowly; then, while her maids were fussing over a dozen little night bonnets and fichus of linen, silk, wool and wadded quilting for her head and shoulders, she listened to Julie's tattle concerning our family secrets and Rose's report on the goings-on in the house. This continued until two in the morning, and only then did Rose go to bed in the antechamber adjoining my room.

This room gave on a long passage. Almost directly across the passage was the door to my mother's dressing room, through which she usually passed on her way into her bedchamber. Thus I could not fail to intercept her and to plead with her again without Rose surprising us. But we might also be very closely watched that night; and in my terror that I might not be able to pour out my heart to the one I loved, I decided to write her a long letter. It took much dexterity and patience for me to relight my candle without matches, in the embers of the fire; but I succeeded, and tearing a few pages out of my copybook of Latin verbs, I began to write.

I seem to have that letter once again before my eyes; I see my round, childish handwriting; but what was it I wrote? I cannot remember. I know only that I wrote under full fire, pouring out my heart, and that my mother kept my letter for a long time, as a remembrancer; but I have not found it in the papers she left me. My recollection is that no deeper or purer passion was ever expressed more simply, for I literally watered it with my tears, and was forced each moment to retrace the words they had washed away.

How to convey this letter to my mother if Deschartres should accompany her upstairs? At the last moment I decided to tiptoe into my mother's room, which entailed opening and closing several doors directly over Mlle. Julie's room. The house was (and is) frighteningly prone to reverberate, owing to an immense front staircase which vibrates at the faintest whisper; but I succeeded in placing my letter behind a little portrait of my grandfather Dupin de Francueil, which was blocked from view by an open door. It was a pencil drawing in which he was shown, not young, slender and dashing, as in the big pastel in the parlor; not in a dressing jacket of russet taffeta with lozenge-shaped buttons, his hair combed up, a palette upon his forearm, and contemplating a landscape sketched in with rose and a turquoise blue; but old, careworn, in a heavy, square-cut swallowtail, fat, flaccid, bent over a worktable—just as he must have been shortly before his death. I had written upon the outside of my letter: "Put your answer behind this portrait of Grandpa Dupin. I'll find it tomorrow when you are gone." Now I had only to alert my mother to the fact that something was hidden behind the picture; so I hung her nightcap upon it, and in this nightcap I placed a scribbled note: "Shake the portrait."

Having taken these precautions, I returned to bed without making the slightest sound. And there I sat, fearful lest my fatigue undo my determination. I was exhausted by the day's tears and commotions, and with each moment I began to nod off; but roused with a start by my own heartbeats, I would think I heard footfalls in the passage. At last Deschartres's clock struck midnight (his room was divided from mine by a partition only). He came up first—I heard his regular, heavy tread, and his door closing with magisterial slowness. My mother came up a quarter of an hour later, but Rose was with her, to help her pack. I knew Rose would not thwart us, but she had often been scolded for her weakness in such moments, and I felt that I could not trust her. Anyway, I needed to see my mother alone. So I pulled the covers over my head—I was still half dressed—and lay stock still. My mother went by; Rose stayed with her for half an hour, then went to bed. I waited half an hour more, long enough for Rose to fall asleep, and then, braving all, I softly opened my door and went in to my mother.

She was reading my letter; she was weeping. She pressed me to her heart: but she had slipped from the pinnacle of our romantic hopes in a hesitation born of despair. Now she was sure that I would grow used to my grandmother, and blaming herself for having excited me, she prayed me to forget her. Her words were so many cold dagger thrusts to my poor heart. Tenderly I reproached her, and I was so vehement that she again pledged to come back and fetch me within three months, if my grandmama did not take me to Paris the next winter, and if I persisted in my resolve. But this was not enough to reassure me; I wanted her to write an answer to the burning entreaty of my letter. I asked her to leave behind the portrait a letter which I should find after she was gone, a letter I might read in secret every day to give me heart and to nourish my hopes. It was my price for returning to bed. Once back, I tried to warm my icy body in the even colder sheets, but I felt sick. I wanted to sleep, as she had wished me to, if only to forget my anguish for a moment; but I could not. Doubt and despair had entered my soul. I wept so bitterly that my brain ached, and when day broke gloomy and pale, it was the first dawn I had ever seen after a sleepless and sorrowful night.

I heard doors opening, trunks being carried downstairs; but Rose was about, I dared not show her I was awake. Had she seen me, she would have softened; but my love had become romantic in its exaltation, and needed mystery. Yet when the carriage rolled into the courtyard, and I heard my mother's footsteps in the passage, I could not restrain myself; I ran barefoot on the floor, I threw myself into her arms and, losing my head, begged her to take me with her. She reproached me for hurting her; she was already suffering too much from leaving me. I submitted, and went back to bed; but when I heard the last faint rolling of the wheels that were bearing her away, I could not stifle my cries of despair, and even Rose, despite the severity with which she had begun to arm herself, was unable to check her tears over my piteous state.

I rested for several hours, but scarcely had I wakened when I was again beset by sorrow. My heart was broken at the thought that my mother had left, perhaps forever. As soon as I had dressed, I ran into her room and fell upon her unmade bed, kissing the pillow which still bore the imprint of her head. Then I went over to the portrait where I was to find her letter, but just then Rose came in, and I had to choke back my sorrow; not that this girl, whose heart was good, would have blamed me for it, but I felt a sort of sweet pain at hiding my suffering. She began to do the room, taking off the sheets, turning the mattress and closing the blinds.

Half dazed, I sat in a corner and watched her. I felt that my mother had died, and that this room, which she would never enter again, was being given up to a final silence and to darkness.

It was only later that I found a way to slip back unobserved, and I ran straight to the portrait, my heart pounding with hope; but I shook the picture of old Francueil in vain; my mother, unwilling to feed a delusion which she regretted having planted in my mind, had thought best not to reply. This was the final blow. Motionless, stupefied, I spent the rest of my free hour in her room. It had grown suddenly cold, mysterious, mournful. I did not weep—I had no tears left—but I was beginning to suffer from a pain still deeper and more distressing than absence. I said to myself, "My mother does not love me as much as I love her"—an unfair thought in the circumstances, but in substance the revelation of a truth which each passing day was to confirm. My mother had for me, as for all the people she had loved, more passion than tenderness. Large cavities had gradually appeared in her soul, and she was unable to see them herself. Along with her precious love she had abysses of neglect and lassitude. She had suffered too much; she needed not to suffer anymore; whereas I, who still had such strength to expend upon that score, was ready and almost eager for suffering.

Until then Rose had treated me rather gently, considering her natural rashness. This had been bridled by my mother's frequent presence at Nohant; or perhaps she had merely obeyed some instinct, which now began to change (for I am pleased to grant her in all fairness that she never dissembled anything). I think she was like one of those good brood hens who care tenderly for their chicks so long as they sleep beneath her wing, but do not spare them a peck once they have begun to fly and gad about. As I grew taller she gave up pampering me, for, indeed, I no longer needed it; but she began to brutalize me, and that I could have done without. Terribly eager to do my grandmother's bidding, she became her gendarme in the matter of my physical education, which she turned into a sort of torture. If I went out without all sorts of little precautions against catching a cold, I was—I shan't say "scolded"; "struck dumb" is a better expression, only those words being able to convey her furious voice and insulting epithets, which racked my nervous system. Had I a rent in my dress or a broken clog, had I romped in the bushes and got a scratch which might lead my grandmother to suspect that I was not being carefully looked after—then Rose beat me, rather mildly at first, merely to deter me, but with increasing severity, as a systematic repression; and in the end she beat me to show me who was master, and because she'd got the habit of it. If I cried she beat me harder; and if I'd ever had the bad luck to start screaming I think she'd have killed me, for when she was in one of her paroxysms of anger I don't think she even knew who she was. Unpunished herself, she grew harsher and crueler with me each passing day, and in this she abused my kindness; for if I did not have her dismissed (my grandmother would not have forgiven her for raising a finger against me), it was only because I loved her despite her awful temper.

Why did I love this girl so much that I let her batter me? The answer is simple: she loved my mother, she was the only one who ever mentioned her, and always with admiration and tenderness. She had not the intelligence to see the sorrow that consumed me, or to understand that my absent-mindedness, my sloppiness, my sulks, had but one cause; but when I was sick she nursed me tenderly. She had many kind ways of beguiling the time, which I found in no one else, and if I was in any danger she got me out of it with a courage and vigor that recalled my mother's. She would have thrown herself into fire or flood to save me; and she never exposed me to what I most feared, my grandmother's reproaches; rather she protected me from them. She would have lied to spare me my grandmother's blame, and when I saw that some peccadillo of mine was bound to incur either a beating from my maid or a scolding from my grandmother, I always chose the beating.

Yet her blows offended me deeply. Those my mother had given me had never caused me any pain aside from the sorrow of seeing that she was angry at me. Besides, she had long before given up this sort of correction, which she thought useful only with young children. But Rose, proceeding in the opposite fashion, adopted this system at an age when it could only humiliate and demean me, and if it did not make me into a coward, that is only because God had given me a good instinct for dignity. On this score I thank Him with all my heart for what I went through, for I learned early to despise insults and attacks which I have not deserved. With Rose I had a deep conviction of my innocence and her unfairness, for I had no faults that might have provoked her fury. All my mistakes were unwilled, and so trifling that even today I would be unable to understand her rages did I not recall that she was red-haired, and had such hot blood that she wore calico dresses in midwinter and slept with the window open.

Thus I grew accustomed to this humiliating slavery, and in it I found meat for a sort of natural stoicism which I perhaps needed in order to be able to live with my overexcited sensibility. Alone I learned to fortify myself against unhappiness, though here my brother encouraged me somewhat, for in the midst of our escapades he would say with a chuckle; "Tonight we shall be beaten!" Himself horribly beaten by Deschartres, he accepted his fate with mingled hatred and nonchalance. He found his vengeance in parody; as for me, I found mine in my heroism, and in forgiving my maid. I even affected a certain superiority in order to raise my self-esteem in this contest between moral and brute force, and whenever a blow upon my head inflamed my nerves and filled my eyes with tears, I hid to dry them. I'd have blushed to be caught crying.

I would have done better to scream and sob. Rose was actually kindhearted and she would have felt remorse had she but been aware that she was hurting me. But she was so rash and impulsive that it is not unlikely she was unaware of her own violence. One day when she was showing me how to "mark" my stockings, and I was taking three stitches instead of two, she gave me a furious slap.

"You should have removed your thimble to hit my face," I said coldly. "One day you'll break my teeth." She stared at me in genuine amazement, then looked down at her thimble and the mark it had left upon my cheek. She could not believe that it was she who a moment earlier had made that mark. Sometimes she would threaten me with a big clout right after she had unwittingly given it.

I shall not dwell upon this trivial subject; it is enough to say that for three or four years scarcely a day passed that I did not receive, out of the blue, a blow which did not necessarily hurt me, but which, each time, cruelly shocked me and forced me into a tension of my whole moral being. This condition was perhaps not enough to make me unhappy, especially in that I could have put an end to this state of affairs yet never did. But whatever my grounds for complaint, I felt myself to be unhappy, and therefore I was. I even grew used to deriving a sort of bitter satisfaction from my inner unceasing protest against my fate; from my growing stubbornness in loving only a being who was absent and who seemed to abandon me to misery; from my refusing my grandmother the expression of my feelings and thoughts; from criticizing in my mind the up-bringing I was receiving and whose excesses I allowed her to remain ignorant of; and lastly, from regarding myself as a poor waif marked out for slavery, injustice, tedium and eternal unrequited longing.

So let no one continue to ask why I, who might pride myself on something like high birth and appreciate the comforts of affluence, have always turned my solicitude and my familiar sympathy—my intimacy of heart, if I may use such a term—toward the downtrodden. This tendency was produced in me by the force of events, by the pressure of circumstances, well before the study of the truth and my conscience had made it my duty. It is nothing I glory in; and those who think as I do should not commend me for it, any more than those who think otherwise should make of it the ground of a reproach.

What none may dispute who have in good faith read the story of my childhood is that the choice of my opinions has been no whim or artist's caprice, as some have said: it has been the inevitable outcome of my first sufferings, of my most sacred affections, of my very plight in life.

The enemy's sojourn in Paris made life unbearable for those who were not so fanatically of the Royalist party as to lose all love for their country. My mother left Caroline with my aunt, and came to spend the summer at Nohant. I had not seen her for seven or eight months, and the reader can imagine my transports. Rose lost her power over me, and readily reposed from her furors. From the moment my mother arrived, I was often tempted to complain of Rose's mistreatment; but since in her heart Rose was genuinely unaware of her wrongs toward me, and instead of fearing my mother's return rejoiced with all her heart to see "Madame Maurice" again; since she prepared my mother's room with great care, and counted with me the days and hours till her return—since, in brief, she loved her too—I forgave her everything, and not only entombed the secret of her brutality, but even had the courage to deny it when my mother began to be suspicious. I recall that one day her suspicions grew very dark, and I, to my credit, dispelled them.

My brother had conceived the idea of making bird lime. Perhaps he had found the formula in the Great or the Little Albertus Magnus, or in our old manual of necromancy. Whatever the case, one had simply to grind mistletoe; but we succeeded not in making lime but only in spattering our faces, hands and clothes with a greenish paste of dubious hue. My mother was working beside us in the garden, engrossed as usual, and not even thinking to protect herself from our splashing bucket. Suddenly I saw Rose appear at the end of the alley, and my first impulse was to run.

"Well, what ails her?" my mother asked Hippolyte, coming out of her reverie and watching me run off. My brother, who has never cared to make enemies, replied that he did not know; but my mother called me back, and challenged Rose in my presence.

"This isn't the first time I've noticed that the child is terrified of you," she said. "You beat her, don't you?"

"Well, just look at her!" said the red-haired girl, furious to see me so soiled and stained. "How can I keep my patience when I have to spend all my time washing and mending her clothes?"

"Indeed!" my mother retorted. "And do you fancy that I took you on to do anything but wash and mend? Or do you think you should collect a pension, and read Voltaire like Mademoiselle Julie? Well, rid your mind of such notions at once! You're here to wash and mend and let my baby play!"

As soon as my mother and I were alone she questioned me heatedly.

"You go pale and start trembling whenever she looks sternly at you," she said. "Is it that she scolds you too harshly?"

"Yes," I said, "She scolds me too harshly."

"Well, I hope she's never had the ill luck to give you so much as a flick of the finger," she continued, "because if she has, she goes packing tonight!"

The idea that I might bring about the dismissal of this poor girl who despite her rages loved me so much caused me to keep my secret. I said not a word. My mother hotly insisted. I saw that I would have to lie for the first time in my life—and to my mother! But my heart silenced my conscience; I lied; and my mother, still suspicious, and attributing my discretion to fear alone, put my generosity to a sore trial by forcing me to reaffirm several times that I had told her the truth. But I felt no remorse; my lies could hurt only myself.

In the end, she believed me. Rose never knew what I had done for her. Kept at bay by my mother, she grew milder; but later when she and I were alone together, she made me pay dearly for my heart's folly. I was too proud to tell her of it, and as usual I submitted in silence to her blows and abuse.

Amid my endless daydreams, and despite my sad situation, I was developing with extraordinary rapidity. I seemed likely to become tall and robust; between the ages of twelve and thirteen I grew three inches and acquired exceptional strength for my age and sex. But there I stayed; my development stopped just where it often starts in others. I did not surpass my mother in height, but I was always very strong, and capable of enduring, with something akin to masculine strength, long walks and exertions.

My grandmother had finally understood that the only time I was ill was when I was deprived of exercise and fresh air. She had decided to let me romp, and provided that I did not return with scratches upon my person or rents in my clothes, Rose let me run wild. Some irresistible impulse compelled me to aid nature's work, and those two years, for all that I dreamed and wept them through as never before, were years in which I got the most exercise. My body and my mind by turns required boisterous activity and a meditative fever, so to speak. I would devour what books came my way and then suddenly leap through the ground-floor window, if it was nearer than the door, and gambol in the garden or the countryside like a runaway colt. I passionately loved solitude and with equal fervor the company of other children; I had friends and companions everywhere. I knew in what field, what meadow, what path, I would find Fanchon, Pierrot, Liline, Rosette or Sylvain. We rampaged in the ditches, trees and streams. We "tended" the herds, that is, we forgot all about them, and while the goats and sheep feasted on corn in the blade, we did a ragtag dance, or regaled ourselves upon the grass with our pancakes, cheese and corn bread. We did not hesitate to milk the goats and kids, or even the cows and heifers, if they proved willing. We cooked fowl and potatoes in the fire. Wild pears and apples, plums and mulberries, even roots—it was all one to us. But in the fields we were always on the lookout for Rose, for I was not supposed to eat between meals, and if she arrived, armed with a green switch, she struck me and my companions impartially.

Deschartres became much gentler when my brother* was no longer there to enrage him. He was often pleased during lessons, which I now did well at; but my own moods stirred gusts from him on occasion, and he accused me of ill will when really all I had was growing pains. Once or twice he threatened to hit me; and as such threats are already half-done deeds, I kept on my guard, determined not to suffer from him what I was beginning not to suffer from Rose. Usually he was good-humored with me, and infinitely grateful for my quickness at following him when he was clear. But sometimes I was so distracted that one day he hurled a fat Latin dictionary at my head. I think he'd have killed me if I hadn't deftly dodged the projectile. Without a word I gathered up my texts and copybooks, put them in the cabinet and went out for a walk.

The next day he asked me if I had construed my lines.

"No," I said. "I know enough Latin as it is."

He never mentioned it again, and that was the end of Latin. I don't know how he explained the matter to my grandmother, but she never mentioned it either. It may be he was ashamed of having given way to his rage, and was grateful to me for not telling anyone; and at the same time, he saw that my determination not to expose myself to another such rage was irrevocable. This intermezzo did not prevent me from being fond of him; but he remained the sworn enemy of my mother, and I had never been able to stomach his manhandling of Hippolyte. One day when he had beaten him cruelly I had said, "I'm telling Grandma." I was as good as my word. I presume that she severely rebuked him, but for that he bore me no grudge. We were both too frank to fall foul of each other.

He had much of Rose in him, and for this reason they couldn't bear each other. One day when she was sweeping my room and he was passing in the corridor, she emptied her dustpan on his beautiful glossy shoes. "Slattern!" he said. "Scalawag!" she replied. The battle was joined: Rose threw her broom between the tutor's feet as he was going down the stairs and he almost broke his neck. From then on they cordially detested each other, and each day found them engaged in fresh quarrels, which sometimes degenerated into boxing matches. Somewhat later he had less violent but

* Who had joined a regiment of hussars. —Translator.

more bitter disputes with Julie. The cook, too, was at daggers drawn with Rose, and they threw plates at each other's head. Said cook also fought with her old husband, Saint-Jean. Ten valets were engaged in succession because none of them could get on with Rose or Deschartres. Never was house beset with such battling and bawling; such was the sorry effect of my grandmother's excessive weakness. She refused either to part with her servants or to settle their disputes. Deschartres, trying to make peace, only added the storms of his own temper. It all merely sickened me, and increased my love for the fields and the company of my shepherds, who were so sweet, and who lived so harmoniously.

Until then no one, least of all my grandmother, had made any serious charge against my mother. It was easy to see that Deschartres hated her, that Julie maligned her in order to woo my grandmother, so that the latter was often overcome with bitterness and coldness toward her. Julie made dry jokes and unwarranted innuendos, and assumed airs of disdain; and I, in my innocent partiality, ascribed the deep regrets that my father's marriage had left in his family to my mother's low birth and poverty. For all that, my grandmama seemed to feel obliged to respect in me the respect I had for my mother.

But then we quarreled, for three days, and those three days made her suffer so greatly that she apparently sought the quickest, surest means to attach me to herself and to all she had done for me, of which I seemed so unaware; by such means she reckoned upon robbing my heart of the trust and love which drew me to another. She considered awhile, and chose the most fatal of weapons.

I was kneeling, pressed against her bed, and just bringing her hands to my lips, when she said, in a voice I thought strange to her, bitter and heaving:

"Stay, kneel there and listen carefully, for you have never heard what I am about to tell you, and you will never again hear it from my lips. Such things are said once in a life, because they are never forgotten; but if one does not know them, when alas they are true, one fails of one's life—one loses one's soul."

After this preamble, which made me shiver, she told the story of her own life, then that of my father's; then she told the story of my mother's life—that is, what she thought she knew of it, or

127

what, at the least, she understood of it. There I daresay she was without pity or intelligence, for the poor in their life span know something of abandon, of wretchedness, of calamity, which the rich cannot understand, and which they judge as the blind judge color.

All that she said was factually true, and grounded in circumstances whose very details admitted of no doubt. But she could have revealed this terrible story without trying to rob me of my respect and love for my mother, and the story, so told, would have seemed much more authentic. She would have had to tell about the *causes* of my mother's wretchedness: her abandonment and misery from the age of fourteen; the venality of rich men who wait until hunger strikes and then blight innocent girls; and the pitiless rigor of social opinion, which permits neither return nor expiation. She would have had to tell me how my mother had ransomed her past, how she had loved my father faithfully, and how, after his death, she had lived humbly, sad and withdrawn. The last point I had been sure of; but now my grandmother intimated that though I was to know all about my mother's past, I was to be spared her present, and that there was some new secret in my mother's life which I was not to know, and which, were I to insist on living with her, would make me tremble for my future. At last my grandmama, exhausted by her long narration, her voice choked, her eyes wet and red— indeed, she was no longer herself—let the horrid cat out of the bag. My mother, she said, was a "fallen woman," and I a blind child who wished to leap to her doom.

For me at that time this was a nightmare; I was dying; each word was a dagger. I felt the sweat running on my brow, I tried to interrupt, to get up, to run, to reject with horror the dreadful secret; but I could not: my knees were nailed to the floor, my head was riven and bent by that voice which brooded upon me and wasted me like the north wind. My icy hands no longer held the fiery hands of my grandmother; I think that I had mechanically dropped them from my lips in terror.

At last I rose without a word, without entreaty or caress, without thought of being forgiven; I went up to my room. On the stairs, I met Rose.

"Well, is it all over?" she asked.

"Yes, it's over," I said. "Forever and ever and ever." And recalling that the girl had had only kind words for my mother, and sure that she knew all I had just been told, yet was no less attached to her first mistress—then, although she was horrible, although she was my tyrant and almost my executioner, she suddenly seemed my best, my only friend. I hugged her passionately, and running to hide, threw myself on the floor in a convulsion of despair.

I was not stoic enough to stifle my sobs, and Rose, hearing my gasps, ran to help me. I got a grip on myself, and not wanting to act sick, went down at the first call for lunch and forced myself to eat. I was handed my copybooks and pretended to work, but my burning, acrid tears had made my eyelids raw; I had a frightful headache, I no longer thought, no longer lived; I was dead to everything. I no longer knew if I loved or hated anyone, I felt no warmth for anyone, no resentment against a soul; I had a sort of huge internal wound, a searing emptiness in place of my heart. I was aware only of a contempt for the entire universe and of a bitterness toward life and toward whatever it might bring: in brief, I no longer loved myself. If my mother was contemptible, then so was the fruit of her womb. I had sustained a frightful wrong, whose damage might prove irreparable; a being had tried to poison within me the moral springs of life: faith, love, hope.

Seven

MY GRANDMOTHER HAD QUESTIONED a certain Mme. de Pontcarré about the English Convent, where she had been imprisoned briefly during the Revolution. One of Mme. de Pontcarré's nieces had been brought up in the covent and had just left it. My grandmama, who had certain not unpleasant memories of this monastery and of the nuns she had met there, was pleased to learn that the niece had been very well cared for and had received a refined education; it seemed that the girls were good scholars, that the "masters of the polite arts" were renowned, and in sum, that the English Convent merited the vogue it then enjoyed in society, along with its rivals, Sacré-Coeur and the Abbaye-aux-Bois. Mme. de Pontcarré expected to place her own daughter there, which she did the next year. And so my grandmama decided that the English Convent was the very thing, and upon a winter day, I put on a uniform of purple serge, my school clothes were packed in a trunk, and we took a hackney to the Rue des Fossés-Saint-Victor. After we had waited some moments in the parlor, a communicating door was opened, and then was closed behind us. I was encloistered.

This convent is one of the two or three British Catholic communities which moved to Paris during Cromwell's reign. After having been the persecutors, the English Catholics were now cruelly persecuted themselves, and gathered in exile to pray and most especially to beseech God to bring about the conversion of the Protestants. Though the Catholics soon recaptured the throne and revenged themselves upon the Protestants most un-Christianly, several orders of English Catholics remained in France.

The English order of Saint Augustine is the only one still left in Paris, and the only one whose seat has weathered revolution upon revolution. Tradition has it that the Queen of England (Henriette of France, daughter of our own Henri IV and consort of the unhappy Charles I) came often with her son, James II, to pray in the convent's church and to cure of scrofula the poor who thronged her way. A retaining wall divides this convent from the Scottish College. The Irish Seminary is four doors down. All our sisters were English, Scottish or Irish. Some two thirds of the boarders and tenants, as well as many of the priests who came to officiate, were also of these nations. There were hours when all the pupils were forbidden to speak a word of French—the best possible way to learn English quickly—and of course our sisters scarcely used any other. They also followed the custom of their clime, and took tea thrice daily; and they invited those of us who been very good to take it with them.

The cloister and the church were paved with long ledger stones under which reposed the revered remains of English Catholics who had died in exile and had been favored with burial in this sanctuary. Everywhere upon the tombs and walls were epitaphs and pious maxims in English. In the mother superior's room and in her private parlor were large old portraits of English princes and prelates. The face of the lovely and gallant Mary Stuart, thought by our chaste nuns to have been a saint, shone among them like a star. In brief, everything in that house, both of past and of present, was English;

and when you had gone through that iron gate, it seemed you had crossed the Channel.

Before I tell about my life in the convent, perhaps I should briefly describe the place. One's dwelling places have so great an influence upon one's thoughts that it would be hard to dissociate one's reminiscences from them.

The convent, a compound consisting of buildings, courts and gardens, was more a village than a single house. There was nothing of the historical monument about it, nothing of interest to the antiquarian. Since its construction no more than two centuries earlier, so many changes had been made, so many successive additions and rearrangements, that its original character could be discerned only in a few parts. Yet this hodgepodge had its own character, mysterious and bewildering as a labyrinth, and that poetic charm with which monastic folk imbue the commonest things. It took me more than a month to find my way about alone, and despite a thousand furtive explorations, I never knew all its nooks and crannies, all its ins and outs.

The way into the court was guarded by a door with an iron grating which opened, with a great clangor, upon the echoing cloister. This cloister was a quadrangular gallery paved with ledger stones; everywhere were skulls and crossbones and the inscription *Requiescat in pace*. The galleries were vaulted, and lit by wide, full-arched windows which gave on the ambulatory with its traditional well and flower beds. One corner of the cloister opened upon the church and the garden, and one upon the new annex, wherein were found, on the ground floor, the upper-form classroom; on the mezzanine, the nuns' workroom; on the next two floors, the cells; and on the top floor, the dormitory of the lower-form boarders.

The third corner of the cloister led to the kitchens and cellars, and, if one went on, to the lower-form building, which used to communicate with several others, already very old at that time and falling into ruin; but these no longer exist. The whole was a maze of dark corridors, tortuous spiral stairs, and little detached lodgings joined to one another by footworn landings or passages with warped floorboards. These were probably the vestiges of the earliest buildings, and the efforts made to connect these constructions with the newer ones attested either to great impoverishment during the revolutionary period or to great ineptitude on the part of the architects.

There were galleries leading nowhere, and openings one could barely squeeze through, just as in those dreams where you rush through strange buildings which close upon you and suddenly crush you within their narrowing walls. This part of the convent defies logical description; it is enough to say that the use to which these constructions were put was as incongruous as the way in which they had been jumbled together. Here was a tenant's room, there, a pupil's; farther along, a piano room, and down the way a washroom or several empty apartments, perhaps temporarily occupied by friends from across the Channel; and there were odd nooks where resident old maids, and the nuns especially, mysteriously heaped a crowd of objects which seemed dazed to find themselves together: the vestige of some church ornament, a pile of onions, broken chairs, empty bottles, tattered clothes, a cracked bell, etc., etc.

I should describe the convent in a word if I said that all of us, nuns, lay sisters, ordinary tenants, lay teachers and servants, amounted to some five score souls, lodged in the most unlikely and uncomfortable way: some packed together, others too sparsely sown upon a space where ten families might have dwelt at their ease, with a patch of yard for their leisure. Everything was scattered so widely that we lost a quarter of an hour coming and going.

The nuns' cells, however, were tidy, charming and full of those daubs which a prettifying piety must patiently cut out, frame, beribbon and light with candles. In every corner, vines and jasmine hid the walls' decrepitude. The cocks crowed at midnight, just as in the country; the bell rang with a pretty silver sound like a woman's voice; in every passage was a graceful niche with a plump Madonna in the mannered style of the seventeenth century; in the workroom fine English engravings portrayed the gallant figure of Charles I at all the ages of his life, and the rest of the Catholic royalty as well; and even the little lamp which flickered nightly in the cloister, and the heavy doors which closed each evening upon the passages with a solemn clamor and a lugubrious grating of bolts—these and all things had their own mystical and poetic charm, to which, sooner or later, I succumbed.

Now I shall return to my story.

My first impression upon entering the lower form was distressing. About thirty of us were packed into a low, narrow room. A dreadful egg-yellow wallpaper, a dirty, decaying ceiling, filthy benches, desks and stools, a wretched, smoking stove, an odor of coal and poultry yard, an ugly plaster crucifix, a pitted floor—such was the place where we were to spend two thirds of the day, three fourths in winter. And just then it was winter.

Why our sisters, so beautiful, so kindhearted, and endowed with such noble and natural manners, had put at the head of the lower form a person of repellent bearing, countenance and dress, and of speech and character to match, I cannot fathom. Fat, dirty, stooped, bigoted, narrow, irascible, hard even to cruelty, suspicious, vindictive—she at once became the object of my moral and physical disgust, as she was already for all my companions.

There are natures to nobody's liking who keenly sense the aversion they excite, and who can never do good, even if they want to, because they lead others astray by their very sermonizing, and because they are reduced to "working out their own salvation" in isolation— the most sterile and irreligious thing in the world. Mlle. D. was such a nature. But it would be unfair of me not to tell her good points as well as her bad. She was genuinely pious and ruled herself with an iron hand; and she brought to her devotion a grim exaltation which made her intolerant and hateful, but which might have had a grandeur of sorts had she lived in the desert like the anchorites, whose faith she had. With us she became a dragon of rectitude; she derived joy from punishing, voluptuous pleasure from scolding, and in her mouth a rebuke was always an insult and an outrage. She was treacherous in her stern ways, and pretended to go out (which she should never have done during a lesson), just to overhear us speak ill of her and gleefully to catch us in the act of saying what we thought. Then she would punish us in the stupidest and most humiliating way. She forced us to cringe and fawn, and to kiss the ground for what she called our wicked words. This kissing of the ground was indeed a part of convent discipline, but the other nuns accepted a sham and pretended not to see when we kissed a hand as we bent toward the floor; whereas Mlle. D. pushed our heads into the dust, and would have broken them had we resisted.

It was easy to see what emotions lay behind her harshness, what rage she felt at being hated. In the class was a poor little English girl of five or six years, pale, delicate, sickly, a real *chacrot*, as we say in our Berrichon dialect to describe the frailest nestling in the brood. Her name was Mary Eyre, and Mlle. D. did her best to help her out and perhaps even to love her in a motherly way. But there was so little mother love in her mannish and brutish nature that she could not do it. Whenever D. scolded her she struck terror into her, or upset her to the point that she was soon forced, so as not to yield, to beat her or to lock her up. Sometimes she grew human enough to joke or try to play with her: but so might a bear have played with a sparrow. The little one would just keep on raging and screaming, out of sheer contrariness, or out of anger and despair. From dawn to dusk there was a nerve-racking contest, unbearable to watch, between the vicious fat woman and the sullen and unhappy little girl; but it did nothing to lessen the rigors and rages to which we were all in turn subjected.

I had wanted to enter the lower form out of a feeling of modesty not unusual in a child whose family is too vain; but I soon felt humiliated and offended by the rod of this old bogeyman in soiled petticoats. I had not been three days under her eye before I realized that I had to deal with a nature as violent as that of Rose, but without Rose's frankness, affection and core of kindness. The first time her glance lit on me she said, "I should say you are a most dissipated young person," and from that moment on, I was ranked among her blackest sheep: for gaiety sickened her, children's laughter made her grind her teeth, and health, good humor—in a word, youth— all were crimes in her eyes.

The convent routine did not at all agree with me. We were decently fed—something I've never much cared about—but we suffered from the cruelest cold, and winter was very rigorous that year. The early bedtime hour was also as noxious to me as it was unpleasant. I've always liked to stay up late and not to rise early. At Nohant I'd had my way; I read and wrote in the evening in my room, and I wasn't forced to brave the morning chill. My circulation is slow—the word *sang-froid* perfectly describes both my moral and my physical constitution—but I was paralyzed by the cold, especially in the morning. The dormitory, situated in the attic under the roof, was so glacial that I could not fall asleep, and I would lie there sadly all night listening to the hourly bells. At six the servants Marie-Josèphe and Marie-Anne came pitilessly to wake us. To get up and dress by candlelight has always made me wretched. We had to break the ice in the ewers and the cold water did not clean us properly. We had chilblains, and our swollen feet bled in our tight shoes. We went to matins by candlelight and slept on our knees. At seven we breakfasted on a piece of bread and a cup of tea. Only when we finally entered the classroom did we see a faint light breaking in the sky and a little fire in the stove. I myself did not unfreeze till noon; I had frightful colds, and sharp pains in all my members; they plagued me for fifteen years thereafter.

Apathetic, mute, morose, I seemed in class to be the calmest and most submissive pupil. I had but one set-to with the ferocious D., which I shall describe anon. I never talked back, I never got angry, and I do not recall that I had the least crotchet during the three years that I spent at the convent. Thanks to this disposition, I made but one enemy, and that is the reason why I have kept a sort of grudge against D., who forced upon me the feeling most contrary to my nature. I was always liked, even in my most mischievous phase, and even by the sourest of my companions and the severest of the mistresses and nuns. The mother superior told my mother that I was "standing water." Paris had chilled the feverish restlessness which had come over me at Nohant. But none of this stopped me from running on the roofs in December or from spending whole midwinter evenings bareheaded in the garden.

On the eve of my grandmother's departure from Paris, a storm brewed against me in the councils of the mother superior. I liked to write as much as I disliked to talk, and I amused myself by working the pupils' mischief and D.'s severities into a sort of satirical diary which I sent in installments to my grandmother, who was very amused by it; for she did not in the least commend fawning or docility, much less piety. Now, it was a convent rule that each evening we were to leave upon the cabinet in the mother superior's antechamber all the letters that we wished to have posted. Those not addressed to any relation were to be left open; those to our families were to be sealed, and their secrecy was supposed to be respected.

It would have been easy for me to convey my manuscripts to my grandmother using some more reliable go-between, since her servants often came to bring me things and to see how it was with me; but I had absolute faith in my superior's word. She had said to my grandmother in my presence that she never opened letters addressed to a pupil's family. I believed her, I trusted her, I never gave it a second thought. Yet the volume and frequency of my letters soon disquieted the "reverend mother."* She unsealed them without ceremony, read my satires, and suppressed the letters. Three days running she did me this honor without saying a word, just to gain familiarity with my irreverent gazetteering and with D.'s manner of ruling over us. From these letters a woman of heart and intelligence would have learned a useful lesson—would have scolded me, perhaps, but would certainly have dismissed D. But then, a woman of heart would not have set a snare for a child's simple trust, nor invaded a privacy which she herself had authorized. The mother superior preferred to question Mlle. D., who of course failed to recognize herself in my accurate but unflattering portrait. And it was little wonder that her temper, already kindled by my calm air and manner, reached a speedy limit. She called me a "bald-faced liar," a "freethinker," an "informer," a "snake." The mother superior sent for me and caused a frightful row. I sat there like a stone. Then in her benevolence she promised me not to let my grandmother know of my "calumnies" and to keep the secret of my abominable letters. But I saw the matter differently, and I sensed the duplicity of this promise. I replied that I had a draft of my letters, and that my grandmother would receive it; that I would uphold the truth of my assertions before my grandmother and before the "reverend mother" herself; and that since I could no longer put my faith in her word, I would ask to be placed in another convent.

The mother superior was not a wicked woman; but whatever one may think, I have never felt that she was a very good woman. She ordered me out, showering me with threats and insults. She was a person of standing in society, and she knew how to give herself royal airs when the need arose; but she sounded common indeed when she was angry. Perhaps she did not know how rank were the French expressions she was using (I did not yet know enough English for her to address me in her mother tongue). Mlle. D. only dropped her head and closed her eyes, and stood there in the ecstatic attitude of a saint listening to God's own voice, and when she looked at me she affected pitying airs and a compassionate silence. One

---

* Such was her English title.

hour later the mother superior entered the dining hall followed by a train of nuns; she reviewed each table as if making an inspection; then, stopping before me and rolling her big black eyes, which were very fine, she said to me in a solemn voice:

"Practice the truth!"

The next moment I was deafened by questions from my fellow pupils.

"What this all means," I answered, "is that in three days I shall be gone."

I was indignant; but also very sad. I had no desire to change convents. I had formed bonds that I would suffer to see broken so soon. But at this point my grandmother arrived on the scene. The mother superior retired with her behind closed doors, and foreseeing that I would give everything away, thought best to pass my letters on to my grandmama and to present them as a tissue of lies. I suspect that she took quite a beating, and that my grandmother rebuked her sharply for the abuse of confidence she had been forced to divulge. Perhaps my grandmama even took my side and threatened to remove me straightaway. I don't know just what transpired between them, but when I was called into the mother superior's parlor, both were trying to look solemn, and both were very flushed. My grandmother kissed me as usual, and blamed me for nothing except for my laziness and for childishly rioting my time away. Then the mother superior announced that I was to leave the lower form and to enter at once the ranks of the big girls. This good tiding, whereby so many threats cohered into a marked and irreversible improvement in my lot, was nonetheless announced to me in a severe tone. It was to be hoped, now that I was to have no more to do with Mlle. D., that I would stop lampooning her, and that this separation would do us both much good.

The mistress of the upper form, whom we held up to endless ridicule and who was indeed a bit odd in manner, was at heart a very kind person, though even more absent-minded than Mlle. D. Because she gave herself such grandiose airs we called her the Countess. She had rooms off the garden and directly opposite the upper form classroom, with only a kitchen garden between, and even when she was not supervising the class she could glimpse our pranks from her window. But she was much more interested in observing from the classroom window what was happening in her own lodgings; for it was there, upon her sunlit window sill and doorstep, that the sole object of her affections lived, a preening, warbling and nearly featherless gray parrot; and for this sullen creature we reserved our most contemptuous abuse.

In this we were very wrong, for Jacquot deserved our heartfelt gratitude: it was to him we owed our freedom. Because he continually distracted the Countess, she left us to our foolery. Perched upon his swing, and thus in her line of vision, Jacquot would grow bored and begin to screech. At once the Countess would fly to the window, and if a cat was prowling under Jacquot's perch, or if he had broken his chain and gone forth on an airing to the lilac tree, the Countess, forgetting everything, would dash out of the classroom, through the cloister and across the garden, to scold or caress her beloved bird. And meanwhile we were dancing on the tables, or stealing out of class to take, like Jacquot, an airing, but in the cellar or the attic.

The Countess was a youngish spinster in her forties. She was very highborn—a fact she never let us forget—but without any fortune, and, I think, badly educated, for she gave no lessons and was really nothing more than a perfect. She was tiresome and silly, but also decent and kind. Several of us had conceived a dislike for her, and addressed her so rudely that in replying she was forced out of character. For my part, I had cause only to praise her, and I regret having joined the others in mocking her magisterial demeanor, her pretentious speech, her great black hat, which she never took off, her green shawl, in which she gravely wrapped herself, and her slips of the tongue, which we mercilessly snapped up and featured in our conversation, a fact she never noticed. I really should have taken her side, since she often took mine with the nuns. But children are ungrateful—it is, as they say, a pitiless age—and they regard mockery as their inalienable right.

The chief mistress of the upper form was Mme. Eugénie—more correctly, Maria-Eugenia Stonor. She was a tall woman with a fine figure and a noble bearing, graceful even in her gravity. Her face was rosy and wrinkled, like those of most of the nuns who were getting on in years, and would have been pretty but for her haughty and sarcastic expression, which put you off at first meeting. She was not only strict, she was positively choleric, and gave way to personal animosities which made her many irreconcilable enemies. She showed nobody any affection, and I knew of only one boarder who liked her; that boarder was myself.

This affection which I could not help showing the Fierce Lampshade—such was our nickname for her, on account of the eyeshade she wore, her eyes being weak—astonished the whole upper form. Here is how it came to be:

Three days after my promotion to the upper form, I encountered Mlle. D. at the garden door. She glared at me; I stared back with my usual composure. My promotion had been a defeat for her, and she was furious.

"Well, aren't you proud of yourself," she said. "You don't even wish me good morning."

"Good morning, ma'am, how do you do?"

"Very well—but I detect a mocking smile."

"It's in the beholder's eye."

"Don't make free with me! You forget with whom you have to do!"

"No, ma'am, it's simply that I have nothing to do with you—nothing whatever."

"We shall see!" she said, pointing a threatening finger at me. And she marched off.

It was recess; all the girls were playing in the garden. I seized the opportunity to go into the lower-form classroom to retrieve several copybooks that I had left in a side room. This place, where our ink pots, desks and the big clay jars used in washing the floors were stored, also served as a "dark room" or prison for the little girls—for Mary Eyre and company.

I'd been there a few moments, looking for my copybooks, when Mlle. D. appeared like an avenging angel.

"I am delighted to see you here," she said. "You shall now apologize to me for your impertinent smile a moment ago."

"No, ma'am, I was not impertinent, and I will not apologize."

"Then you shall be punished like a little girl, and locked up here until you've come down a peg."

"You haven't the right! I'm not under your thumb anymore."

"Then try to get out!"

"And so I shall!"

And while she stood and gaped, I walked out of the little room straight toward her, and she, flying into a rage, rushed at me, seized me in her arms and forced me back into the "dark room." I have never seen anything so ugly as that fat bigot in a rage. Laughing and struggling, I pushed her up against the wall. She tried to strike me. I raised my fist. I watched her go pale, I felt her grasp weaken, and I remained there with my fist raised over her, certain that I was the stronger and could easily rid myself of her; but for that I had needed either to trip her or to strike her, or at the very least to push her hard, which might still have hurt her. I released her with a smile, and was about to leave, satisfied with having spared her and showed her the superiority of my instincts to her own, when she treacherously took advantage of my generosity and pushed me from the rear with all her strength. My foot caught a great clay jar of water and, together with this jar, I fell into the "dark room," wherein D. locked me with two turns of the latchkey and vanished with a torrent of insults.

My situation was critical. I was literally in a cold bath; the room was very small and the jar enormous; when I had picked myself up, the water still came to my ankles. Yet I could not keep from laughing when I heard D. mutter, "Ah, the wicked, the accursed girl! She has put me quite out of temper. I must go to confession again: I've lost my absolution."

Coolly I climbed up the cabinet shelves to get my feet out of the water, then I ripped a white page from a copybook, found pen and ink, and wrote a note to Mme. Eugénie:

"Madame, I no longer recognize any authority but your own. Mlle. D. has just assaulted me and locked me up. Please come and deliver me."

I waited for someone to come. I think it was Mary Gordon who came, to fetch her own copybook in the "dark room," and seeing my head appear at the transom window, she took fright and turned to flee. I called to her, she recognized me, and I prayed her to take my note to Mme. Eugénie, who would be found in the garden. Presently Mme. Eugénie appeared, followed by Mlle. D. The former took my hand and led me silently away. When we were alone in the cloister I impulsively kissed Mme. Eugénie to thank her. This impulse pleased her: Mme. Eugénie never kissed anybody; nobody even dreamed of kissing Mme. Eugénie. I saw that she was moved, like a woman who had never known affection, and who yet would not be insensible to it. She questioned me very shrewdly, seeming not to listen to my answers, but losing not a word or a facial expression. I told her everything, and she saw it was the truth. She smiled, shook my hand and motioned me back into the garden.

Several days later the Archbishop of Paris came to confirm several pupils who had received first communion but not partaken of any other sacrament. They were placed in seclusion in a common room, of which Mlle D. was to be the guardian and lector. It was she who was to deliver the religious exhortations. I was called in on the same day, but Mlle. D. refused to receive me, and ordered me to be placed in seclusion in whatever room it would please the nuns to choose. It was then that Mme. Eugénie openly took my side.

"Since it appears our Aurore is a leper," she said in her sarcastic way, "you may send her to my cell."

And she led me there straightaway, Mother Alippe following. They remained in the passage while I sat down in the cell, and presently I heard them conversing in English. Perhaps they knew that I would understand most of what they said.

"Well, now," said Mme. Eugénie, "is this child really so hateful? You know her from the lower form."

"She is not in the least hateful," said Mother Alippe. "She is a good girl, and D. is not a good woman. But the child is, well, a 'devil,' as they say. . . . Ah, you laugh; you rather like 'devils,' don't you?"

Mme. Eugénie replied, "Well, since she is so wild, it's not the moment to confirm her. She would not come to communion with the necessary humility. We'll leave her time to compose her spirits, and she shall certainly not remain in contact with a person who bears her a grudge. Do you grant me that the child is mine now, and that even you will no longer have any rights over her?"

"None but the rights of Christian fellowship," replied Mother Alippe. "Mademoiselle D. is entirely in the wrong. Don't worry, she'll not start up again."

Then, if I mistake not, Mme. Eugénie went to find the mother superior, to review with her, and perhaps with Mother Alippe and Mlle. D. as well, what had transpired, and what was to be done. After an hour I received a visit from Mlle. D. Either the mother superior or her confessor had scolded her. She was sweet as honey, and I was astonished by her caressing tone. She told me that my confirmation had been put off till the following year, that I was believed to be unprepared to receive grace, and that Mme. Eugénie would tell me so officially, but that she herself, before going into seclusion with the neophytes, had wished to make it up with me.

"Come," she said, "will you admit that you, too, were wrong, and give me your hand?"

"With all my heart," I said. "Whatever you offer me gently and kindly I shall gladly return."

She kissed me, which gave me no great pleasure, and all was forgotten, and never again did we have any bone of contention.

What gave me the greatest satisfaction as an upper-form pupil was that I at last received a cell. All the other young ladies in the upper form had one; I had remained a long while in the dormitory because the sisters feared I would make mischief at night. In this attic dormitory the girls suffered terribly from the winter cold and summer heat. They slept poorly too, because some moppet always screamed with fright or colic pains in the middle of the night. And then, never to be " 'ome," or even alone by oneself one hour in the day or night, is most unpleasant for dreamers and musers. Communal living is happiness itself for those who love one another—I felt this at the convent and never forgot it—but every thinking being needs her hours of solitude and rumination. Only then can she savor the sweetness of society.

My cell was about ten feet by six. Sitting up in bed, I could touch the sloping attic ceiling with my head. When I opened the door it scraped along the chest of drawers by the window, and to close the door I had to squeeze into the alcove of this window, which was composed of four little square panes and gave upon a projecting rain gutter, which screened me from the court below. But I enjoyed a magnificent prospect. Through the topmost sprays of one of the garden's great chestnut trees I could look out over a large part of Paris. A vast patchwork of nurseries and kitchen gardens stretched away from the convent compound. Had it not been for the blue horizon of the great buildings and houses, I might have thought myself, not quite in the country, but in some huge village. The convent belfry and the low square shape of the cloister served as a sort of repoussoir, and by moonlight this view made an admirable landscape. The big bell rang in my ear, and though in the beginning I had some trouble falling asleep, I soon grew fond of being wakened by its melancholy timbre, and of hearing the distant nightingales resume their interrupted carols.

My furniture consisted of a bed of painted wood, an old chest of drawers, a cane chair, a deceitful throw rug, and a very pretty little harp in the Louis Quinze style, whose strings had once glimmered between my grandmother's lovely arms, and which I sometimes played while singing. I had permission to practice the harp in my room, but this only served as a pretext for me to be idle one hour in the day, and though I never practiced, my hour of solitude and reverie grew precious to me. The sparrows, attracted by the crumbs I scattered, flocked round me unafraid, even venturing in to eat off my bed. Although this mean cell was an oven in summertime, and literally a glacier in winter—the water ran through my disjointed ceiling and froze into icicles—I loved it passionately, and I recall that I was so attached to it that I spontaneously kissed its walls when I left. Today I cannot say what world of daydreams was enclosed within that dusty, wretched little cranny, but it was only there that I could repossess myself. By day I did not meditate, but I watched: I watched the clouds, the branches, the wheeling swallows. By night I listened to the remote and indistinct noises of the great city, which died away like a death rattle upon the rustic murmurs of the suburb. At the crack of dawn the convent was astir again, its own noise proudly rising above this faint clamor. Our cocks began to crow; our bells rang to matins; the blackbirds who lived in the garden rehearsed to repletion their morning phrase; and the nuns' intoning of the office floated up to me through the passages and thousand crevices of that echoing house. In the court directly below me, the hoarse cries of the tradesmen oddly counterpointed the nuns' plainsong; and finally the shrill call of Marie-Josèphe, running from room to room and drawing the screeching bolts, put an end to my auditory contemplation.

I slept little: I've never been able to sleep to full refreshment. But really I didn't much care to sleep, not, that is, until the moment I had to get up. I would dream of Nohant; it had become my paradise; yet I was in no haste to return thither, and when my grandmama decreed that I should have no holiday but must apply myself to my studies during my two remaining years at the convent, I yielded without sadness, so greatly did I fear to suffer the same unhappiness that had caused me to quit Nohant without regrets.

These studies, for whose sake my grandmama had given up the pleasure of seeing me, amounted, more or less, to nothing. In practice they consisted of finishing-school lessons, and since I had become a troublemaker, I no longer bothered with them. Of course, my errant idleness bored me sometimes; but how to rid oneself of such lazy habits once they have taken root!

At last came the time when a great change overtook me. I became devout. It happened all at once, a passion igniting in a soul ignorant of its own resources. I had, so to speak, exhausted my store of idleness, my store of complaisance toward my fellow mischief-makers, as well as my systematic mute rebellion against discipline. The only violent love I had known, filial love, had wearied and wasted me. I adored one nun, Mme. Alicia, but that was a tranquil love, and I craved a burning passion. All my needs were of my heart, and my heart was bored, if one may use such an expression. No concern for my bodily appearance had wakened in me; I had not that immoderate solicitude of one's person that I had seen develop in almost all my classmates. I had to love something outside myself, and I knew of nothing on earth that I might love with all my heart.

We celebrated Mass every morning at seven, and returned to the church at four for a half hour, which the pious girls devoted to prayer or to the reading of some sacred book. The others yawned, drowsed or whispered among themselves as soon as the mistress turned her back. Out of sheer boredom, I picked up a book I had been given but not yet deigned to open: the leaves were still sticking together at their gilt edges. It was a short *Lives of the Saints*. I opened it at random to the curious legend of Saint Simon Stylites, whom Voltaire has made such sport of, and which seems more like the story of some Indian fakir than that of a Christian philosopher. At first this legend made me smile, then its strangeness surprised and intrigued me. I reread it more attentively, and found in it more poetry than absurdity. The next day I read another story, and the day after I devoured several more. The miracles left me incredulous, but the faith, courage and stoicism of the confessors and martyrs seemed wonderful things, and touched a secret chord in me.

Behind the choir stalls was a superb picture by Titian that I had never been able to make out. As it was very murky, and hung too high in a dark corner, one could descry only masses of warm color upon a dark ground. It represented Jesus in the Garden of Olives at the moment when he swoons in the angel's arms. The Savior had fallen on his knees and was stretching out his arm to the angel, who was supporting his dying head. This picture was directly in front of my pew, and from much gazing I had come not so much to understand it as to sense its meaning. There was but one moment in the day when I could see it in detail, and that was only in winter when the declining sun cast a beam upon the angel's red robe and the bare white arm of Christ. For an instant the tremulous image of the window illumined the picture so brightly that it dazzled my eyes, and at that instant, even when I was not yet devout and thought I never would be, I always felt an indefinable tremor.

As I leafed through the *Lives of the Saints,* my glance returned more and more often to the picture; it was summer, the setting sun no longer illumined it at the hour of prayer, but that blinding sight lived on in my mind's eye. Mechanically I questioned the awesome and tumultuous images in my brain, sought the meaning of the Agony in the Garden, the secret of Christ's willing acceptance of such terrible suffering, and then I began to sense something greater and more profound than what the nuns had taught me; I grew deeply sad, and felt somehow cut to the heart by an unknown pity and suffering. Tears welled in my eyes, and furtively I wiped them away, ashamed that I was moved without apparent reason. I wondered if it was not the beauty of the painting; but at that moment I saw it well enough only to remember that it was beautiful.

Another picture, even less visible though less worthy of being seen, showed Saint Augustine under the fig tree with the miraculous ray, on which was written the famous *Tolle, lege,* those mysterious words which Monica's wayward son believed he hears issue from the foliage, and which made him open the Gospels. I looked up the life of Saint Augustine, which I had heard vaguely related at the convent, where this patron saint of the English Austins was held in especial veneration. From this story, which bears the stamp of such sincerity and enthusiasm, I derived deep pleasure. Thence I passed on to Saint Paul, and the words "Why persecutest thou me?" made a terrible impression on me. The little Latin Deschartres had taught me enabled me to understand part of the services, and now I began to listen to them, and to find a simple poetry in the nuns' psalms. Then, all at once, I became quite absorbed in the Catholic religion for a whole week.

It was the *Tolle, lege* which finally caused me to open the Gospels and reread them attentively. My first impression was not especially vivid: the Good Book has not the attraction of novelty, and my grandmother had so successfully contrived to make the miracles seem ridiculous, had so often repeated Voltaire's quips about the demons cast into the herd of swine, and, in sum, had put me so firmly on my guard against any religious enthusiasm, that I spurned it out of habit, and remained untouched when I reread the story of the Agony in the Garden and the Crucifixion.

That evening I shambled wearily out into the cloister in the failing light. The others were in the garden, I was out of sight of the mistresses, on the sly as usual; but I was not plotting any fresh mischief, and had no desire to be with my companions. I was bored. There seemed no mischief left to do. I watched as several nuns and boarders went singly to pray and meditate in the church, as was the custom of the more fervent during the recreation hours. Naturally it occurred to me to empty an ink pot in the holy-water basin: but that had been done; to hang the cat by a paw from the bell rope: old hat. I owned to myself that my disorderly phase was drawing to a close, and that I must enter upon a new one: but what should it be? The devotees, the pious girls—were they happy? No, their devotion was all gloom, and seemed somehow sick. We "devils" invented a thousand vexations for them, a thousand taunts, a thousand causes of pent-up resentment. Their life was torture, an unending contest between losing face and losing zeal. Besides, faith is like love: when you want it you can't find it, and you can find it when you least expect it. I didn't know this then, but what kept me away from religion was precisely the fear of arriving at it through self-seeking calculation.

"Besides," I thought, "wanting it is not getting it. *I've* not got it. I'll never get it. Today I've had my last go at it. I even read in the Book about the Redeemer's life and teachings! I was unmoved. My heart will remain empty."

And as my inner voice chattered on, I watched the pious women hurry ghostlike through the shadows to bare their souls before the God of love and contrition. I grew curious to know in what posture, and with how much sincerity, they would pray in their solitude.

Here was an old hunchbacked tenant hastening dwarfish and deformed through the gloom, more like a witch running to her sabbat than a wise virgin! "Let's see how that little monster squirms in her pew!" I said to myself. "That will be something to make us laugh."

I followed her through the chapter house and reentered the church. It was forbidden to go there at that hour without permission, but that was just why I did so. Indeed, it is singular that the first time I entered a church on an impulse of my own I did so in a spirit of disobedience and mockery.

No sooner had I set foot in the church when I forgot the old hunchback. She trotted away and vanished like a rat in some fissure of the wainscot. I did not peer after her, for the nighttime appearance of the church had struck and charmed me. This church, or rather this chapel, was unremarkable save for its exquisite cleanness. It was a big rectangle without architectural ornament, all freshly whitewashed, and more similar in its simplicity to an Anglican than to a Catholic church. There were, as I have said, several paintings at the rear of the choir. The modest altar was adorned with lovely sconces, flowers freshly cut, and a fine altar cloth. The nave was divided into three parts: the choir, where entered only the priests and, by special permission on holidays, certain persons from outside the convent; the front choir, where sat the boarders, servants and residents; and the rear or gentlewomen's choir, where the nuns sat. This area had a parquet which was waxed every morning, as were the nuns' mirror-bright walnut stalls, ranged in a semicircle against the extremity of the apse. A screen of fine openwork, with a door of the same which was never closed, separated our part of the nave from the nuns' part. On each side of this door heavy fluted wooden columns in a rococo style supported the organ and the bare podium, which together formed a sort of rood loft between the two parts of the church. Thus, contrary to custom, the organ stood alone, almost in the center of the nave, and this position doubled the volume and effect of the voices when we sang motets or other choral music during the high holidays. Our front choir was paved with ledger stones, and on these great slabs might be read the epitaphs of those deans of the convent who had died before the Revolution. Several Church and even lay persons of the time of James II—certain Throckmortons among others—reposed beneath our feet, and it was said that if you went into the church at midnight, all the corpses thrust up their ledger stones with their fleshless skulls and stared at you with burning eyes beseeching prayers.

Despite the darkness, the impression I received was not one of gloom. The church was lit only by the little silver sanctuary lamp, whose white flame was mirrored in the polished marble of the floor, like a star reflected in water. This reflection scattered pale sparks into the corners of the gilded frames, into the chased silver sconces on the altar and the gold plate of the tabernacle. The door at the end of the rear choir was ajar on account of the heat, and the great casement windows giving on the cemetery were open. The fragrance of honeysuckle and jasmine was wafted in by a cool breeze. Lost in the immense night, a star twinkled in a window frame and seemed to regard me attentively. The birds sang. There was a stillness . . . a spell . . . a mystery . . . a gathering of spirit . . . that I had never dreamed could be.

Empty of thought, I gazed about me. One by one the several persons scattered throughout the church softly retired. Only a nun kneeling at the far end of the rear choir remained, and then, having finished her meditation, she crossed the front choir and drew near to light a candle by the sanctuary lamp. Whenever the nuns entered the sanctuary, they made not only their usual deep bow, with knees touching the ground, but quite prostrated themselves before the altar, and remained so for a moment, as if crushed and annihilated before the Holy of Holies. She who came forward at that instant was tall and solemn; she may have been Mme. Eugénie, Mme. Xavier or Mme. Monique; but we could scarcely recognize these ladies in church because they always came veiled, with their figure entirely concealed under a trailing mantle of black ermine.

This grave habiliment, this slow and silent approach, this simple but graceful gesture of drawing the silver lamp toward her while raising her arm to take hold of the ring; the beam that the light threw across her tall black silhouette as she returned the lamp to its place; and her long bow to the ground before retracing her steps to her stall with the same silence and slowness—all this, even to the hidden face of this nun, who seemed a phantom ready to sink into her ledger stone and recline upon her marble couch, produced within me an emotion of mingled terror and ravishment. The poetry of the holy place captivated my fancy, and I lingered on after the nun had read her prayer and retired.

The hour advanced; the prayer bell rang; someone was drawing near to lock the doors. I had forgotten everything. I knew not what was happening within me. I breathed an air of astonishing sweetness, breathing it more by the soul than by the senses. Suddenly all my being began to quake, and a fluttering like a white light passed before my eyes and seemed to envelop me. I thought I heard a voice murmuring in my ear: *Tolle, lege!* I looked around, thinking it was Mme. Alicia's voice. I was alone.

Oh, I harbored no vain illusions, I did not believe it was a miracle. I knew full well I had undergone a sort of hallucination. I was neither exalted nor frightened. I tried neither to heighten nor to escape it. I felt only that faith had taken hold of me by the heart, as I had wished. For this I was so grateful, so ravished, that a torrent of tears flooded my face. I felt that I loved God, that my mind embraced and fully accepted this ideal of justice, tenderness and holiness which I have never doubted since then, but with which I had not yet been in communication. I felt this communication suddenly raised into being, as if an obstacle between the spark of infinite ardor and the dead embers of my soul had been lifted. I saw an endless road stretch before me; I burned to rush forward. I was no longer held in check by any doubts or coolness. The fear that I might later have to urge myself on, to rally my spirit of abandon, was wholly absent. I was of that company who march forward without looking back—who hesitate on the banks of a Rubicon, but on reaching the far side no longer remember the one they have just left.

Eight

My grandmother's illness grows worse.—My grandmother's last days.—Her death.—My unhealthy state of mind.—Suicidal despondency.—The river.—Deschartres's sermon.—Christmas night.—The cemetery.—The next day's vigil.—Arrival of my mother and my aunt.—Strangely altered feelings.—The will is read.—Unlawful clause.—My mother's resistance.—Singularities, grandeurs and agitations of my mother.

WE ARRIVED at Nohant very early in the spring of 1820, in my grandmother's big blue carriage, and I found my little room given up to workmen, who were repapering and repainting; for my grandmama had begun to find my orange wallpaper with its heavy floral design too stale for my young eyes, and wanted to please them with a fresh lilac color. But my chariot-shaped bed had been spared, and its four worm-eaten pendants had once again outlived the vandalism of modern taste.

I was provisionally installed in my mother's large suite. There nothing had changed, and I slept deliciously in her immense bed with its gilded pomegranates, which called up all the tenderness and the reveries of my childhood.

For the first time since our parting, I beheld the sunlight flood into this deserted room, where once I had wept so copiously. The trees were abloom, the nightingales sang, and I heard from afar the stately balladry of the field hands, that essence of all the calm poetry of Berry. Yet my wakening was compounded of joy and sorrow. It was already nine. For the first time in three years I lay abed in the morning, with no angelus bell nor shrill-voiced Marie-Josèphe to tear me from the sweetness of the night's concluding dreams. I could loll an hour more and not risk doing penance. To escape the Rule, to cross the threshold of freedom, is an extraordinary crisis which brings a pleasure not unalloyed to souls grown fond of musing and meditation.

I opened the window and went back to bed. The fragrance of the verdure . . . youth . . . life . . . independence . . . all were borne to me upon the breeze; but with them came misgivings which filled me with anxiety and sadness. I cannot say what caused this unhealthy despondency, which is so unsuited to the fresh thoughts and the health of adolescence. But it gripped me so poignantly that a distinct memory of it has remained with me these many years, although I cannot rightly recall in what train of thoughts, in what memories of the day before, in what apprehensions of the morrow, I came to shed such bitter tears, just when I should have joyfully reclaimed my father's hearth for my own.

And yet how many delights for a boarder out of coop! Instead of a dreary uniform of purple serge, a pretty chambermaid brought me a clean frock of pink gingham. I was free to dress my hair as I pleased, with no Mme. Eugénie to come remarking upon the indecency of bare temples. Breakfast was enlivened by all those tidbits my grandmother loved, and loved to ply me with. The garden was a big bouquet. All the servants and peasants came to fete me. I kissed all the goodwives of the vicinity, who told me how handsome I had become now that I was "grosser" (by which they meant, in their broad speech, that I had filled out). The Berrichon lilt flattered my ear like well-loved music, and I was wonder-struck that no one addressed me any longer in the British drawl and whistle. My old friends the big dogs, who had snarled at me the evening before, now recognized me and pawed me fondly, with that intelligent and simple air which seems to beg your pardon for a moment's loss of memory.

Toward evening Deschartres, in his sporting jacket, big gaiters and pleated cap, returned from some distant fair. It had not yet dawned on him, dear man, that I would have changed and grown during those three years, and when I threw my arms about him he asked where was Aurore. He called me "miss"; and in sum, he did as my dogs, and failed to welcome me until a quarter hour had passed.

Presently Hippolyte came home on leave. At first we made each other shy. He had become a dashing sergeant in the hussars; an *R*-roller; a stallion-tamer; and a Deschartres-baiter—that gentleman suffering him, as he had my father, to tease him, and to cut him down for his horsemanship and for several other failings. After a few days our friendship revived, and as we began to frolic together, we could scarcely believe we'd ever been apart.

It was he who gave me my liking for riding, and this bodily exercise was greatly to affect my character and habits of mind.

The course in horsemanship that he gave me was neither long nor dull. "See here," he said one morning, when I had asked him to give me the first lesson. "I could play pedant, and drive you mad with the instruction manual that I teach at Saumur to conscripts who can't make head or tail of it, and who learn only from riding every day and getting bolder at it. But really it all boils down to one thing: to fall or not to fall; the rest will come of itself. And as fall you must, let's find a nice soft place where you won't get too many bruises." And he took me to a wide meadow where the grass was thick. There, still leading Colette by her halter, he mounted General Pepe.

Pepe was a very handsome colt, grandson of the fatal Leopardo, and upon whom, in my dawning ardor for the Italian revolution, I had bestowed the name of a heroic man who was in later years to be my friend. Colette, whose real name was Mlle. Deschartres, was our tutor's "pupil" and had never been mounted. She was four, and had just been stabled. She seemed so gentle that Hippolyte, after riding her round the meadow several times, hazarded that she would behave herself, and lifted me onto her.

There is a God for madmen and for children. The odds were heavy that Colette and I, the one no less novice than the other, would soon be embroiled, and violently sundered. But the odds were baffled. From that day hence, for fourteen years, we made a galloping pair. She was to win a most honorable pension, and to end her days tranquilly in my service, without a single cloud ever darkening our comradeship.

I cannot say if reflection would have panicked me, but my brother did not leave me time. He gave her a hard crack, and off she galloped in a frenzy, wildly rearing and kicking, but with the utmost good nature.

"Sit up straight!" shouted my brother. "Hold fast to her mane if you must, but don't lose the reins, and hang on! And remember— *to fall or not to fall!*"

I put all my attention and will into not quitting the saddle. Five or six times, half unhorsed, I held on for dear life, and after a quarter hour, dog-tired, disheveled and in seventh heaven, I'd acquired all the self-confidence and presence of mind required for the rest of my equestrian education.

Colette was a topper in her class. She was thin, ugly, tall and gawky when she stood, but she had a mustang's body and eyes fine enough to redeem all her misproportions. In movement, her fire, grace and limberness cohered into beauty. I've ridden magnificent horses, admirably trained, but nowhere have I found the intelligence and agility of my own rustic mare. She has never taken an unsure step, never shied, and would never have thrown me but for my own inattention and carelessness.

She guessed all that one expected of her and I had her mastered in a week. Her instincts melted into mine. Restive and wanton with others, she willingly yielded to my domination. Within a week we were jumping hedges and ditches, climbing forbidding slopes, fording deep streams; and I, the "standing water" of the convent, had now become bolder than a hussar and more robust than a peasant; for a child knows not the meaning of danger, and woman's nervous will outlasts any masculine strength.

My grandmother and I spent the last evenings of February together, reading a part of Chateaubriand's *The Genius of Christianity.* She did not care for the form of this work, and its content seemed to her false; but its numerous quotations prompted admirable judgments upon the masterpieces from which these excerpts were drawn. I found it odd that she had so rarely let me read to her, and was telling her one evening how greatly I savored her instruction, when she cut me short:

"Enough! What you're reading there is so strange I fear I'll fall ill, and hear not what I'm listening to but something else. Oh, why must you talk of corpses and winding sheets, of tombs and tolling bells? If you are improvising, you are very mischievous indeed to fill my mind with such black thoughts."

My mouth fell open. I was horrified. I had just been reading her a cheerful passage about the savannahs of the New World, wherein was nothing of what she thought she had heard. Presently she composed her mind and said, smiling:

"Bless me, I think I fell asleep, and dreamed while you were reading. How weak I've grown! Not only can I not read—I can't even listen. I'm afraid of falling into idleness and tedium. Get out the cards and we'll play grabouche; that should perk me up."

I dealt the cards and managed to cheer her. She was her usual attentive and lucid self. Then, musing for an instant, she collected her thoughts as if to hold final converse; for sure as the day, she felt her soul slipping out of her.

"That marriage," she said, "did not suit you at all, and I'm happy I broke it off."

"What marriage?" I asked.

"Why, haven't I mentioned it? Well, listen: he's immensely rich, but he's fifty, and he has a great saber scar across his face. He's a General of the Empire. I don't know where he happened to see you—perhaps in the convent parlor. You don't recall such a man? . . . Well, at all events, it seems he knows you by sight, and he has asked for your hand, with or without dowry—can you conceive?—but then, whoever fancied that Bonaparte's people shared our little prejudices? Well, so far he has laid down only one condition: that you never see your mother again."

"And of course you refused, didn't you, Mama?"

"Yes," she said, "I did. And here is proof." She handed me a letter, which I hold once again before my eyes, for I have kept it as a memento of that sad evening. It was in the hand of my cousin René de Villeneuve, and was couched in the following terms:

I am inconsolable, dearest Grandmother, that I am so far away from you, unable to commend the proposal made to Aurore. The fifty years offend you; but in fact the gentleman of fifty years seems almost as young as I. He has a good deal of wit, learning, everything required to secure a bond with happiness; for there are plenty of young men, but of their character one cannot be sure, and their future is most uncertain; whereas with this gentleman, rank, fortune, consequence—nothing is wanting. Were I by your side, I would cite several similar matches to sway your mind. The Duke of Caylus, who is sixty, married, now two years ago, Mlle. de La Grange, who was seventeen. She is the happiest of women, and her conduct is unimpeachable, even though she has come out in high society, and has regiments at her feet, for she is lovely as an angel.* She had received a first-rate education, and been taught lofty principles—need I say more? Do not fail to come up to Paris in early March. I warmly urge you to make this journey in the interest of our dear child, etc.

"Mama," I cried in terror, "are we going to Paris?"

"Yes, dear, in a week. But don't worry, I won't hear of this marriage. And it's not the fifty years that offend me, it's the other thing, the stipulation I mentioned. I was so happy with my elderly husband that I don't particularly fear for your happiness with a man of fifty, though I know that you wouldn't agree. . . . No, hush—I know you now, I know your feelings, and I am deeply sorry that I did not always grasp your situation as well as I do today. You love your mother out of duty and religion, just as in your childhood you loved her out of habit and instinct. I thought it my duty to warn you against too much trust, too much abandon. I was perhaps wrong to do so in a moment when I myself was sad and irritated. I saw that you were shattered. I thought, at that moment, that you must learn the truth from me—that it would be harder to accept it from anyone else. If you think that I exaggerated anything, or judged your mother too harshly, forget what I said; I want you to know that despite all the harm she's done me, I give her credit for her good qualities and her conduct since your poor father died. Besides, even if she were, as I sometimes imagined, the lowest of women, I understand that you would still owe her your respect and fidelity. After all, she is your mother! First I feared to see you too rash; then, too devout. But now I have no worries for you. I know you to be pious but tolerant, and careful to preserve your fondness for things of the mind. I almost regret that I cannot take part in your observances; for I see that you draw from them a strength which is not in your nature, and which sometimes has struck me as beyond your years. When you were in the convent, pent up all year round, without holidays, unable to leave for the nine or ten months I spent

---

* Later I became acquainted with the beautiful and truly angelic person in question. She had remarried; her second husband was M. de Rochemur. She told me the whole story of her union with the Duke of Caylus. Ah, dear cousin René, if only you had heard *her* describe the "perfect happiness" of her first union!

here, you wrote me again and again, entreating me not to allow you to go out with the Villeneuves or Madame de Pontcarré. At first I was hurt and jealous, but I was also touched; and now I see that were I to propose to you that you break with your mother in order to marry into society, I should offend your heart and your conscience. So rest easy, and run along to bed. I shall never consider anything of the sort."

I gave my dear grandmother a fervent kiss, and seeing that she was calm and lucid, withdrew to my room, leaving her as usual to the care of her two waiting maids, who put her to bed at midnight, after the two hours of night toilette and leisurely dawdling to which she was accustomed.

I should have realized that the sort of aural hallucination she had undergone while listening to me read, the sudden clarity of her thoughts, even the turnabout that she had made in talking to me about my mother, bespoke a strange moral and bodily condition. To rescind her own decrees, to blame herself for something she had done, to beseech pardon for a mistake in judgment—all this was most contrary to her habits. It was true that her deeds continually belied her words, but this was a fact she did not care to admit, for she held willfully to her stated positions. As I mulled over her last speech, I felt a vague anxiety, and toward midnight I went down to her again, pretending to fetch the book I had forgotten. Her door was closed, and she was already in bed, having fallen asleep a little earlier than usual. Her waiting maids had found nothing odd in her behavior, and I went upstairs quite relieved.

For the last three or four months I had slept very little. Now that I had reentered my grandmother's intimate circle, it became plainer to me with each passing week that I had learned very little in the convent, though not so little as to confirm Deschartres's sincere belief that I was, to use his favorite term, a person of "crass ignorance." My desire not to vex my grandmama, who sometimes reproached me keenly, and understandably, with having caused her to keep me at the convent for three years while I learned nothing, impelled me, more than any real curiosity or self-regard, to study a little. It pained me when she said that a religious education made women brutish, and I began to read in secret, hoping she would credit the nuns for whatever I might teach myself.

That night, I recall, was extraordinarily beautiful. There was a moon, veiled by those little white clouds that Chateaubriand compares to tufts of cotton wool. I hadn't done a stroke of work; I'd opened my window, and was playing Paisiello's *Nina* on the harp. Then I began to shiver, and I went to bed with my thoughts possessed by my grandmother's sweet effusion. At last, in allowing my filial affection free expression, in putting an end to the frightful struggle which had weighed upon my whole life, she had permitted me to breathe for the first time. At last I could let my two rival mothers be intermingled in the same love. At that moment I felt that I loved them equally, and hoped that I might prevail upon them to accept this idea. Then I thought of marriage, of the fifty-year-old man, of the forthcoming trip to Paris, of the "coming-out" that I had narrowly escaped. But none of it frightened me. For the first time, I was optimistic. I had just brought off a victory, and one which seemed decisive, over the great obstacle upon my path. I convinced myself that I had acquired a tender sway over my grandmother which would enable me to stall off her plans for my future; that little by little she would see that future through my eyes, and let me live free and easy at her side; and that after having devoted my youth to her, I could close her eyes without her demanding of me a pledge that I renounce the convent. "I will leave well enough alone," I thought. "There is no point in fretting her with my secret plans. God will protect them." I knew that my fellow pupil Elisa had left the convent, that she had been made to "come out" in high society, that she was resigned to going to balls, and yet that nothing had shaken her resolve. She wrote me that she accepted the ordeal to which her parents had obliged her to submit, but felt stronger in her calling with each passing day, and that we would meet under the veil, perhaps at Cork, should my nationality exclude me from the English community in Paris.

And so I fell asleep in a tranquillity that I had not known for a long time; but at seven Deschartres came in, and directly I opened my eyes I saw all the woe in his.

"Your grandmother is lost, I fear. . . . I do fear she is," he said. "She tried to get up last night and had a fit of apoplexy and is paralyzed. She fell down and could not get up. Julie just found her on the floor, cold, stiff and unconscious. She's in bed now, she's warm and somewhat revived; but she's wholly unaware of her surroundings and cannot move. I've sent for Dr. Decerfz. I'm about to bleed her; come along and help me."

We spent the day nursing her. She recovered her spirits, recalled having fallen, and complained only of the sprains she had sustained. She became aware that a whole side of her, from shoulder to ankle, was "dead," but attributed this numbness to nothing more than the fall. The bleeding enabled her to move somewhat more freely, with our help, and toward evening there was so palpable an improvement that I regained my calm, and the doctor reassured me as he departed; but Deschartres did not share his hopes. She asked him to read her her newspaper after dinner and seemed to hear him, and she even asked for cards, but could not hold them. Presently her speech began to wander, and I shuddered when she querulously demanded to know why we would no longer soothe her by applying the queen of spades to her arm.

"Delirium?" I whispered to Deschartres.

"Worse," he answered, "she has no fever. It is *childhood!*"

This word fell harder upon me than any announcement of death. I was so overcome that I went out and hid in the garden and fell upon my knees. I tried to pray, but could not. The weather was insolently fine and calm. I think I, too, was back in childhood at that moment; I looked mechanically about me, dazed by how full of life the world seemed, while I had only death in my soul; and I ran inside.

"Be strong," said Deschartres, who was always tender at moments of sorrow. "You mustn't get sick now. She needs us!"

She spent the night in soft raving, and slept all the next day until nightfall. This apoplectic slumber was a new danger to combat. The doctor and Deschartres got her out of it successfully; but she woke up blind. The next day she could see, but everything on the right was transposed to the left. Another day she stammered and forgot certain words. At last, after a series of strange phenomena and unforeseen attacks, she began to mend. Her life had been spared for the moment. She had lucid hours. She did not suffer much, but she was paralyzed, and her enfeebled brain did in fact enter upon the second childhood Deschartres had foretold. Her will was gone, but there was no end to her insatiable whims. She had no reflection or courage left. She saw poorly, and heard hardly a thing. In sum, her fine intelligence and her beautiful soul were dead.

My poor invalid was to pass through many different phases. In the spring she grew somewhat better. During the summer we believed for a moment in a radical recovery, for she regained some of her wit, her gaiety, and a degree of recollection. Now she could spend half the day in her armchair, and she dragged herself, with our help, into the dining parlor, where she ate heartily. She sat in the garden in the sunshine, and sometimes had one of us read to her, and even busied herself with her affairs and her will, with solicitude for all her loved ones.

I lived much, thought much, changed much, during those ten months during which my grandmother regained, in her best moments, but the shadow of life.

It was at the approach of autumn that my poor grandmother lost what scant strength she had recovered; she had no memory for immediate things, no savoring of the hours, no desire of any serious distraction. She always slumbered and never slept. The two waiting maids stayed by her day and night. Deschartres, Julie and I spent the day or the night watching over her and tending her by turns. Julie, though very ill herself, showed extreme courage and patience in these tiring functions, for my poor grandmother allowed her scarcely any repose. More demanding with her than with the other servants, she had a need to scold and contradict her, and often Julie was obliged to come to us that we might cause the invalid to give up some dangerous whim.

Wanting to nurse my grandmother, yet at the same time to continue the riding that I felt necessary for my health and education, I had resolved, considering that four hours of sleep did not suffice me, to go to bed only every other night. I do not know if that was a better system, but I soon grew used to it, and felt much less tired observing it than with small doses of sleep. On occasion, it is true, the invalid rang for me at two in the morning, when I was in the full enjoyment of repose. She would ask if it was really two, as the others had already told her. She calmed down only when she saw me, and reassured at last, managed to murmur a few tender words to send me back to bed; but she was likely to be astir again in a quarter of an hour, and then I would give up my sleep for that night and read to her instead.

My health was apparently none the worse for this hard regimen—youth adjusts rapidly to a change of habits—but my mind keenly felt its effects. My thoughts darkened, and by degrees I fell into a melancholia that I no longer had any wish to combat.

And so it came about that at seventeen I willfully withdrew from the society of those about me. The laws of property and inheritance, murderous oppression, the provocation of wars; the privileges of fortune and education; the prejudices of rank, and those of moral intolerance; the childish idleness of people of fashion; the brutishness of avarice; whatever remains of pagan institutions or customs in a self-styled Christian society—all these revolted me so deeply that my soul was prompted to protest against the work of the centuries. I hadn't the notion "progress"—it wasn't popular then, and it hadn't reached me through my reading—so I saw no way out of my anguish, and the idea of working, even in my obscure and closely bounded social environment, to redeem the promises of the future could scarcely occur to me.

Thus melancholy turned to sadness; sadness to grief; and thence, from a distaste for life to a longing for death was but a step. My domestic existence was so dreary and had been rendered so painful, my body was so irritated by an unremitting struggle against exhaustion, and my brain so fatigued by concerns too precocious and readings too absorbing for my age, that I was exposed to a very grave moral sickness: the lure of self-destruction.

I prayed for and received the strength to resist this temptation. It was sometimes so keen, so sudden, so strange, that I was aware a sort of madness had come over me. It became an obsession bordering on monomania; and it was water, as if by a mysterious spell, that had a peculiar attraction for me. Now I rode but by the river, following it in a daze until I came to its deeper reaches, and as if magnetized, I would halt upon the embankment, my head reeling with a febrile gaiety, and I would say to myself, "How easy, how easy it is! Only one step!"

This mania had a sort of strange charm, yet feeling sure of myself, I did not bother to fight it; and soon it had assumed a fearful intensity. Once I had conceived this possibility, I hung transfixed over the current, and I began to ask myself *Yes or No?* often and long enough to risk being hurled by that *Yes* to the bottom of the transparent water which so enthralled me.

Nevertheless, my religion made me look upon suicide as a crime, and thus I vanquished this delirious temptation. I kept myself from going near the river; yet this nervous phenomenon remained so pronounced that I could not touch the lip of a well without a shudder.

Yet I believed myself cured upon that day when, riding with Deschartres to visit a patient, we found ourselves on the banks of the Indre.

"Be careful," he said, unaware of my obsession, "and follow me. The ford is very dangerous; two paces to the side are twenty feet of water."

"I'd rather not cross over," I replied, suddenly seized with a great mistrust of myself. "Go along; I'll ride around and meet you across the bridge by the mill."

But he only laughed.

"Since when have *you* gone weak-kneed?" he asked. "We've forded a hundred times at much worse places and you thought nothing of it. Come now, we're losing time. We must be back at five to feed your grandmama."

Feeling ridiculous, I followed him. But in the middle of the ford a death tremor seized me, my heart leaped, my sight went dim, I heard the fatal *Yes* thundering in my ears, and spurring my horse to the right, I found myself in the deep water, shrieking with laughter and delirious joy.

Had not Colette been the best filly in the world, I'd have been quit of my life, and very innocently too, for on this occasion no conscious thought had entered my head; but Colette, far from drowning, merely began to swim calmly along, bearing me toward the bank. It was Deschartres's cries which brought me to myself; already he had leaped in after me, and now I saw that the clumsy fellow was going to drown. I shouted to him to sit tight, and thought of nothing but hanging on. It is not easy to stay on a swimming horse. The water bears you up, while your own weight seems always about to force the animal under; but I was light, and Colette had uncommon courage and vigor. The most difficult thing was to get from the horse onto the land; the bank was too abrupt. Poor Deschartres had a moment of terrible anxiety, but he did not lose his head, and called to me to grasp a willow stump which happened to be within reach, and to let the animal drown. I managed to get free of the saddle and to save myself; but when I saw my poor Colette's desperate efforts to clamber up the embankment I totally forgot my own predicament, and though I had been swept only a moment before toward my own destruction, now I desponded over the destruction of my mare. I was about to plunge back in the water, to save her, when Deschartres arrived to pull me up, and Colette was clever enough to return to the ford, where his own mare had remained.

Deschartres did not do as the fabled schoolmaster, and give the sermon before saving the child; but the sermon, for all that it followed the rescue, was no less harsh. Sorrow and anxiety could drive him into a fury. He called me an "animal" and a "brute"—all his vocabulary was enlisted! As he had gone livid, and great tears streamed with his abuse, I kissed him and did not answer back; but the scene continued all the way home, and I resolved to tell him the truth, just as one would to a doctor, and to consult him about the death tremor.

I thought he would not understand me, for I myself barely grasped what I was telling him; but he did not seem surprised. "My God!" he cried. "So *that*, too, is hereditary!" And he told me that my father had been prey to such tremors, and made me vow to fight them with a suitable regimen and with "religion," a rare word upon his lips, for it was then, I think, that I first heard him invoke it.

Toward the end of autumn our invalid grew calm, and I hopeful; but Deschartres saw this improvement as a new step toward the dissolution of her being. Yet my grandmother was not so old that recovery was impossible. She was seventy-five, and had been sick but once in her life. Thus her exhaustion was somewhat mysterious. Deschartres ascribed this feebleness to bad circulation in a system of too narrow vessels. But it might more readily have been laid to an absence of will, and to spirits gradually worn away after the frightful sorrow of losing her son.

December was all gloom. She never got up, and spoke rarely. Yet, used to being sad, we were not alarmed. Deschartres conjectured she could survive indefinitely in this limbo. On December 22 she called me out of bed only to give me a knife with a mother-of-pearl handle, and was unable to say why she had thought of it, or why she wanted to see it in my hands. Her thoughts were befogged. Yet once she wakened and said, *"You are losing your best friend."*

They were her last words. A leaden sleep invaded her calm countenance, which was still as fresh and lovely as ever. She did not waken again, and expired with no pain whatever at daybreak, to the sound of the Christmas bells.

At first we shed no tears, Deschartres and I. Afterward, we wept for three days; but at that supreme moment when her heart had ceased to beat, and her breath no longer clouded the mirror, we felt nothing but the satisfaction of knowing that she had crossed the threshold of a better life without pain or anguish. I had feared the horrors of a death agony: Providence had spared her them.

Julie made her last toilette with the same care as in the best days. She put on her lace bonnet, her ribbons and rings. It is the custom with us to bury the dead with a crucifix and a prayer book. I brought those which I had preferred at the convent. Adorned for the tomb, she was still beautiful. No frown altered her pure and noble features; they expressed sublime tranquillity.

Christmas night, Deschartres came and called me. He was in a state of great exaltation, and he addressed me in a breathless voice: "How much courage do you have? Do you not think that we must render unto the dead a worship more tender than that of prayers and tears? Do you not believe that they watch us from above, and are touched by our fidelity and grief? If you do, come with me."

The night was clear and cold. The frost, which had formed a mask upon the snow, made walking so difficult that we slipped and fell several times on our way through the courtyard and into the cemetery.

"Easy now," said Deschartres, still exalted beneath a strange semblance of *sang-froid*. "You shall see the man who was your father." We drew near the ditch that had been dug to receive my grandmother. Within a little burial vault of rough stones was a coffin, which the new coffin was to join in several hours.

"I wanted to see it," said Deschartres, "and to supervise the workmen while they dug this ditch during the day. Look—your father's coffin is still intact; only the nails have fallen out. When I was here alone, I suddenly wanted to lift the lid, and I beheld the skeleton. The skull had come off of itself. I took it and kissed it. At once I felt an enormous relief, for I had never received his final embrace. Then I began to wonder if you had ever received it. Tomorrow this ditch will be filled, and doubtless it will not be dug again till it receives your own remains. So climb down; you must kiss the relic. You will remember this deed for your whole life. Someday the story of your father must be written, if only to cause your children, who will never know him, to love him. Climb down, give him whom you scarcely knew, and who loved you so greatly, a sign of your love and respect. Where he is now, I tell you, he will see you—and he will bless you!"

I was so moved and so uplifted that I found what my tutor was saying perfectly simple. I felt no repugnance at his idea, nothing in it seemed strange—indeed, I would have been remorseful and angry at him had he not acted upon this idea. We climbed down into the ditch, and I followed his example and religiously performed this act of devotion.

Thenceforth I remarked a complete change in Deschartres's beliefs. He had always been a materialist, and had not succeeded in hiding it from me, though he sought vague terms concerning the divinity and the immateriality of the soul. My grandmother was a deist, to use the expression of her day, and had forbidden him to make me over into an atheist. But he had had no end of troubles restraining himself, and had I once been prompted to deny the soul, he would unwillingly have confirmed my denial.

But now a sudden and extreme revolution came about in his character, and presently I heard him fervently uphold the authority of the Church. His conversion, like mine, had been a heartfelt impulse. Before the bones of a cherished being he had been unable to accept the horror of nothingness. My grandmother's death had revived the memory of my father's; he had found himself before this double grave, overcome by the two greatest sorrows of his life, and his fiery soul had protested, in spite of his cold reason, against the decree of eternal separation.

In the day that followed this strangely solemn night, we accompanied my grandmother's mortal remains to her son's side. All our friends came, and all the villagers attended. But the clamor; the grief-stricken faces; the beggers, who, eager to receive the customary distribution, pushed us almost into the ditch in their battle to be the first within arm's reach of the alms; the expressions of condolence; the genuine or affected airs of compassion; the noisy weeping; the banal exclamations of certain well-intentioned servitors—in sum, all those regrets which are for mere appearance' sake—pained me, and seemed irreligious. I was impatient to see them all gone.

As soon as the bustle had quietened in the house, and I was certain that I alone was up, I went down and shut myself in her room. It had not yet occurred to anyone to tidy it. The bed was unmade, and the first detail to catch my eye was the exact imprint of her body, which death had struck with a numb weight whose impress the mattress and the sheet still showed. I saw the negative of her whole shape, and as I kissed it, I thought I felt its lingering chill.

Half-empty vials stood by the bed. The incense which had been burned about the corpse filled the air. It was benjamin, which she had always preferred, and which had been brought back to her from India, in a coconut shell, by M. Dupleix. There was some left and I burned it. I arranged her vials in the order in which she had last asked for them, and I drew the curtain halfway, as she was wont to request. I lighted the night light, which still contained some oil; I stirred up the dwindling fire. Then I stretched out in the big armchair and pretended that she was still there and that I would hear her frail voice calling me once more as I dropped off into slumber.

I did not sleep, and yet I seemed to hear her breathe two or three times, I seemed to hear that sort of groan, a groan of wakening, that my ears knew so well. But nothing distinct materialized in my imagination, which was too eager to behold some sweet vision to arrive at the exaltation which could have produced it.

I had had in my childhood accesses of terror concerning specters, and had been visited at the convent with such apprehensions. When I had returned to Nohant all this had vanished so utterly that I regretted it, fearing, when I read the poets, that my imagination was dead. The religious and romantic act which Deschartres had made me perform the evening before was of a nature to call back the fears of childhood; but it did not: it had filled me with an absolute despair of being able to communicate directly with the beloved dead. Consequently I did not think that my grandmother could really appear to me, but I flattered hopes that my weary head might feel some tremor which would cause me to see her countenance once more, bathed in the light of eternal life.

But nothing came. Outside the north wind chirred. The foot warmer sang in the hearth, and so did the cricket, which my grand-mother had never allowed Deschartres to persecute, though it wakened her often. The grandfather clock struck the hours. The repeater watch fastened to the invalid's night table, which she had been wont to consult with her finger, was dumb. Presently I grew drowsy and fell into a sound sleep.

When after several hours I wakened, I had forgotten everything, and I raised myself on my elbows to see how well she was sleeping; whereupon it all returned to me, and I wept soothing tears upon the pillow which still bore the form of her head. Then I went out of the room, whereon the seals were affixed the following day; and I thought it was profaned by these formalities, with their crass motive.

My cousin René de Villeneuve, then my mother, with my uncle de Beaumont and my aunt Lucie Maréchal, arrived several days later. They came to be present at the reading of the testament and the removal of the seals. My new existence was to depend upon the content of this testament; I refer not to money—I didn't consider it, and besides, we knew of my grandmother's provisions in that regard—but to the issue of who was to replace her as my guardian.

It had been her greatest desire that I not be confided to my mother, and the way in which she had expressed this desire at the perfectly lucid period when she had drawn up her last will had profoundly shaken me. "Your mother," she had said, "is odder than you think. You really don't know her at all. She is so uncouth that she cares for her offspring after the fashion of a wild hen; she's devoted to her nestlings, but once they have fledged, and reason and instinctual tenderness are required, she flies to another tree and pecks them off. Three days with her and you'd be miserable. Her character, education, tastes, habits and thoughts will utterly shock you, when she is no longer curbed by my authority standing between the two of you. Don't expose yourself to such unhappiness; go live with your father's family; they want you for their ward when I am dead. Your mother will readily consent to this, as you may already suspect, and so may you retain with her a gentle, lasting bond that you will never have if you draw too close to her. I have it on good authority that I may entrust the remainder of your education, and the responsibility for setting you up in the world, to my cousin René de Villeneuve, whom I have named for your guardian; but I want your acquiescence in advance, for Madame de Villeneuve will most assuredly not take charge of a young person who follows her with reluctance."

In these moments of brief but lucent wisdom my grandmother assumed a complete ascendency over me. What gave weight to her words was my mother's curious and even wounding attitude, her unwillingness to support me in my spells of anguish, the scant mercies that my grandmother's illness excited in her, and the railing and sometimes threatening bitterness of her infrequent and singular letters. Undeserving of the dumb rage which seemed to be gathering within her, I was much distressed by it, and was forced to observe that she was either very unfair or, indeed, very odd. I knew that my sister Caroline was most unhappy with her; my mother had written: "Caroline is to be married. She is tired of living with me. I think, after all, that I'll be freer and happier when I live alone."

When, therefore, after several months, in the aftermath of my grandmother's death, my cousin René came to take me away, I was quite resolved to follow him. Yet my mother's arrival overwhelmed me. Her first embraces were so warm and true, and I was so happy to see my aunt Lucie again, with her Paris argot, her gaiety, vivacity, candor and motherly pamperings, that I flattered myself that I had recaptured my childhood dream of happiness in the bosom of my mother's family.

But scarcely a quarter of an hour had elapsed before my mother, much vexed by the fatigues of the trip, the presence of M. de Villeneuve, Deschartre's scowl, and especially her unhappy memories of Nohant, vented all the heaped-up bitterness of her soul upon my grandmother. Despite my aunt's efforts to calm her and to laugh off the effect of what she called "Sophie's exaggerations," she lost all self-command, and caused me to see that an abyss had imperceptibly grown between us, and that the poor dead woman's shade would long tenant it, and drive us to despair.

My mother's tirade against my grandmother dismayed me. I'd heard it before, but not always understood it. I had seen it only as the expression of a reprehensible rancor, a foible to bear with. But now the poor saintly woman was accused of having a depraved heart! Really my mother—I cannot conceal my feelings—really my mother could say the most appalling things in anger.

My firm resistance to this torrent of injustice only provoked her. I was, to be sure, much moved within, but seeing her so excited,

I thought I must contain myself, and show her, from the first storm, an unshakable will to respect the memory of my benefactress. As this revolt against her feelings was in itself an affront to her spite, I did not think I could imbue it with too much civility, apparent calm, or mastery of my secret indignation.

This effort of reason, this sacrifice of my inner anger to a feeling of duty, was the worst tactic I might have conceived with a nature like my mother's. It had been better to do as she did: to shout, storm, break something—in brief, to frighten her, and make her believe that I was as violent as she, and that she could not get the better of me.

"You don't know how to handle her," said my aunt when we were alone together. "You're too calm, too proud—precisely how not to behave with her! Listen, I know her! She's my elder sister, and she'd have made me perfectly wretched in my childhood if I'd done as you do; but whenever I saw that she was in her moods again, and itching for a row, I'd bait her until she exploded. The whole thing went faster. Then, when I saw that I'd really irked her, I got angry too, and all at once I would say to her: 'All right! Want to kiss and make up? Be quick about it, or I'll leave.' And she came around right away, and the fear of seeing me start up again would prevent her from starting up too often herself."

I could not avail myself of this counsel. I was not the sister, and consequently not the equal, of this ardent and unfortunate woman. I was her daughter. I could not put aside the sentiment and forms of respect. When she had come around of herself, I renewed my tenderness with all its testimonies; but it was impossible for me to force this affection by kissing lips still warm from abusing the one I venerated.

The reading of the testament stirred fresh storms. My mother, forewarned by someone who betrayed all my grandmother's secrets (I've never known who), had long known of the clause that separated me from her. She also knew of my adherence to this clause, whence her anticipatory ire.

She feigned to know nothing until the last moment, and we still flattered ourselves, my cousin and I, that the sort of aversion she had for me would make her eagerly accept this disposition; but she was fully armed for the reading. Doubtless she had been persuaded in advance to see the special clause as an injury that she must not accept. She declared in no uncertain terms that she would not let it get abroad that she was unworthy to keep her daughter; that she knew the clause was unlawful, since she was my natural and legitimate guardian; that she would go to the courts; and that neither entreaties nor threats could induce her to give up her right over me—which, in point of fact, was complete and absolute.

Who might have guessed, five years before, that this longed-for reunion was to cause me only woe and affliction? She reminded me of my old passion for her and bitterly upbraided me for having let my heart be corrupted by my grandmother and Deschartres. "Ah, my poor mother," I cried, "why did you not take me at my word in the old days? I would not have regretted a thing. I would have left everything for you. Why did you deceive me in my hopes, why did you forsake me so utterly? I admit I doubted your tenderness. Yet look at what you are doing: you are breaking, you are mortally wounding, the heart you would win over! You know full well that it took my grandmother five long years to make me forget one moment of her injustice to you; yet you shower me daily and hourly with your injustices to her!"

The persons who surrounded my mother behaved excellently toward me, but could not or did not know how to protect me. My aunt Lucie claimed that one should laugh off her sister's outbursts, and actually believed that I, her daughter, could do so. Pierret, who was usually fairer and more understanding than my mother, though sometimes just as susceptible and crotchety, mistook my sadness for coldness, and berated me for it with all his comical sound and fury, which succeeded only in amusing me. My dear Clotilde was powerless. My sister was cold and had responded to my welcoming effusions with a sort of distrust, as if she had expected some bad turn from me. Her husband was an excellent fellow, but he had no influence on the family. My great-uncle de Beaumont showed no tenderness whatever. He had always had a store of selfishness which refused to brook a sad and pale countenance at table without tormenting it, even to the point of ruthlessness. Also, he was aging fast, suffered from gout, and frequently stormed about in his rooms, heaping his cronies with abuse when they did not strain to divert him.

Yet my mother was not always tense and irritated. She had her good moments of candor and tenderness in which she accepted me once again. That was the worst. Had I been able to maintain a cold or indifferent front, I had perhaps achieved a stoic calm; but I could not. Did she shed a tear, did she show me one sign of anxiety or maternal care, then I began once again to love her and to hope. It was the way to despair: for on the morrow all was shattered and recalled into question.

She was deranged. She was going through a crisis which was exceptionally long and painful with her, though it never struck down her energy, her courage or her irritability. Her energetic frame could not cross the threshold of old age without a terrible struggle. Still pretty and quick to laugh, she as yet had no female jealousy of the youth and beauty of others. Hers was a chaste nature, whatever was thought and said of it, and her morals were irreproachable. She needed the violent emotions, and for all that her life may have been undone by them, they never surfeited the strange, and doubtless fatal, hatred that she cherished for the repose of the mind and body. She had always to renew her agitated atmosphere with new agitations: she would change lodgings; fall out with—or compose with—somebody or something; drive out to the country to spend a few hours and hasten home in no time, hating it; dine out, switching restaurants in middinner; and even alter her style of dressing utterly, from buckles to bandeaux, once a week.

She had little crazes which plainly bespoke this restlessness. She would buy a hat she thought charming; the same evening, it was hideous. She would remove first the bow, then the flowers, and finally the lace frills. She would rearrange it all with a good deal of skill and taste, and her hat would please her so all the day after. But the very next day that hat was hit by a whirlwind; and so it went, all the week long, until the unhappy hat, continuously transformed, became a cipher to her. Then she wore it with a deep contempt, and said she didn't give a button how she looked; until a new hat caught her eye and became her next craze.

Her hair was still black and very beautiful. She tired of being a brunette, and wore a blond wig which somehow failed to uglify her. She liked herself as a blonde for a while, then declared herself a "towhead" and settled on auburn. Then ash blond was the thing; next a warm black; and soon I saw that her hair changed color with every day in the week.

This infantile frivolity did not preclude drudgery and a painstaking application to household chores. She had her frissons also, and read M. d'Arlincourt with passion far into the night; which did not prevent her from being up again at six to worry her hat, to set off on her rounds or to take up her needle . . . laughing . . . despairing . . . boiling over.

When she was in good humor she was charming, and it was impossible not to be captivated by her gaiety, full of verve and picturesque flights of speech. Unfortunately this never lasted the day, and soon a thunderbolt hit you out of the blue.

And yet she loved me—or at least loved in me the memory of my father and my childhood; but also she hated in me the memory of my grandmother and Deschartres. She had brooded upon too many resentments, and devoured too many inward humiliations, not to require that her volcano expend itself in a long and terrible eruption. And so, accusing and condemning, she would enlist not only reality but figments too, and if she had indigestion she thought she had been poisoned, and verged on accusing me.

One night I thought that all the bitterness between us was to be forgotten, and that we would understand each other and love each other without suffering.

During the day she had been extremely violent, and, as usual, kind and reasonable when she had calmed down. She went to bed and asked me to stay by her side until she fell asleep, because she felt sad. I induced her, I don't know how, to open her heart to me, and there I read all the woe of her life and of her nature. She told me more than I wanted to know, but I must say that she did it with simplicity and a sort of singular grandeur. She flushed as she remembered old feelings . . . laughed . . . wept . . . accused . . . even argued . . . with much intelligence, sensibility and force. She wished to initiate me into the secret of all her misfortunes, and like one swept doomward by sorrow, sought in me the pretext for her sufferings, and from me the reinstatement of her soul.

At length, sitting down on her bed—and how beautiful she looked, with her red madras foulard drawn round her pale face, animated by those great black eyes!—she gathered up her plaint: "When all is said and done," she said, "I do not feel guilty of anything. I don't think I've ever wittingly done any wrong at all: I've only been pushed, pulled, often compelled to see and act. My only crime is to have loved. Ah, if I hadn't loved your father, I'd be rich, independent, carefree, and nobody would reproach me for anything! Before that day I hadn't a thought for anything. Pooh! I didn't even know what thinking was, I didn't know A from B. I was innocent as an unborn babe. I said my prayers mornings and evenings as they'd taught me to, and the good Lord never hinted that they didn't suit Him fine.

"But no sooner had I attached myself to your father, when woe and worry found me. People told me that I was unfit to love. Unfit to love! I didn't even know what they meant, and I paid them no mind. I felt my heart more loving than any of those dowagers', who loathed me, and whom I loathed back in full measure. I *was* loved. Your father used to say, 'Just shrug them off as I do.' I was happy, and I saw that he was too. How could I have persuaded myself that I was dishonoring him?

"Yet that is just what their every word insinuated when he was no longer alive to defend me. Then I had to start thinking, wondering, doubting myself, to feel humiliated and hate myself; or else hate them in their hypocrisy, and hate them with all my might.

"And then I who'd been so gay, so carefree, so frank, so sure of myself, became aware that I had enemies. I had never hated: now I began to hate everybody. I'd never given a thought to your society nobs with their moralizing, their fine manners, their pretensions. What I'd seen of them had always made me laugh, they were so funny. I saw they were wicked and false. Oh, let me tell you, if I've lived chastely since I was widowed, it's not been to please the nobs, who demand of others what they themselves can't live up to; it's because I couldn't do otherwise. I've loved only one man in my life, and after I lost him I didn't care for anyone or anything."

She burst into tears as she remembered my father. "Oh! How tender I would have been had we been able to grow old together! But God took him from me in my salad days. I do not curse Him; He is the Master; but I detest and curse the human race! . . ." And then she added, simply, as if weary of her effusion: "*Only think of it, only think.* . . . But luckily I don't think of it, not always."

It was the counterstatement to my grandmother's confession, which I had heard and accepted. Sorrow had set mother and wife in complete opposition: the one, unable to house her passion or find an object for it, had accepted the act of God, but felt her energy turn into hate for humanity; the other, with all her tenderness on her hands, had cried against God, but offered her fellow creatures treasures of charity.

I remained lost in the reflections excited by this double problem. Then my mother said abruptly:

"Well, I've told you too much, I can see it on your face, and now you condemn me and scorn me on good grounds! It's better that way. It's better that I just tear you out of my heart, and have no one to love after your father, not even you!"

I took her in my arms; she was taut, trembling.

"Scorn you?" I murmured. "How wrong you are! What I scorn is the world's scorn for you. Today I stand with you against the world, more even than I was at that time which you always say I forget. Then you had only my heart; today you have my reason and my conscience too. And *that* is the result of the 'fine education' you're so ready to rail at, *that* is the result of the religion and philosophy you so greatly detest. For me your past is sacred, not only because you are my mother, but also because I can reason, and I know that you are blameless."

"My God, what do I hear !" she cried, devouring my words. "Then what is it you condemn in me?"

"Your aversion for this world, your grudge against it, your grudge against the whole human race, on whom you seek vengeance for your sufferings. Once love made you happy and generous; now hate makes you unhappy and mean."

"It's true," she said, "it's only too true! But what can I do? One must love or hate. I cannot be indifferent and forgive out of laziness."

"Then forgive out of charity at least."

"Charity! Sure, charity for the wretched, the forgotten, the despised, because they are weak; charity for fallen girls who die in the mud because no one will love them; charity for those who suffer without reason—I'd give them the shirt off my back, and you know it well. But charity for *countesses?* Charity for Madame So-and-so, who's dishonored a husband as good as mine a hundred times? Charity for Monsieur So-and-so, who never found fault with your father's love till the day I insisted on becoming his wife? Oh, they are all scoundrels; they do such harm, they love to do harm, and all the while they go on about religion and virtue!"

"But look, don't you see that aside from divine law there is a law of fate which ordains the forgiveness of trespasses and the forgetfulness of personal sufferings, and that this law governs us, and punishes us when we have too greatly transgressed against it?"

"What's that? Speak plainly, girl."

"By closing our minds and hardening our hearts against wicked and blameworthy people, we get the habit of not recognizing perfectly innocent people, and heaping those who respect and cherish us with suspicion and rancor."

"Ha, you're trying to convince yourself!" she cried.

"Yes, I am; but I could be trying to convince my sister, or your sister, or Pierret. And anyway, don't you believe it yourself, don't you say it yourself when you're calmer?"

"It's true I provoke everyone when I set about it," she replied, "but I don't know how to do otherwise. The more I try, the more I fall into the same habit, and what I think is most unfair of me when I go to bed is what I think fairest when I wake up. My head works too hard; sometimes I feel it's exploding. I'm sound of mind when I don't reflect; but whether I start reflecting or not doesn't depend on me. The more I try to dodge thinking, the more I think. Forgetfulness must come of itself, through weariness. Is that what they teach in your books—how to think about nothing?"

The reader has seen, in this conversation, how impossible it was for me to bring reason to bear upon my mother's passionate instincts, for she took the rattle of her thoughts for reflection, and sought relief in a numb lassitude which robbed her of all sustained awareness of her own injustices. There was in her a store of admirable probity, but it was continually obscured by the fever of a deranged imagination which she was no longer young enough to fight, having lived, besides, in utter ignorance of the intellectual weapons she had needed.

Yet hers was a religious soul, and she loved God ardently, as a bulwark against her own and other injustice. She was blind to all clemency and evenhandedness but her own, and reckoning upon His unlimited compassion, gave no thought to rekindling and fanning in herself the spark of this perfection. Words availed nothing to convince her that there is some mutuality between our will and that of Him who bestows it. "God knows how weak we are," she would say, "since it pleased Him to create us so."

My sister's piety often nettled her. She loathed priests, and spoke to Caroline of "her" curates just as she did to me of "my" old countesses. Frequently she opened the Gospels to read a verse or two. This made her feel good or bad, in consonance with her mood. If calm, she softened at the thought of the Magdalene's tears and perfumes; if irritated, she scourged her neighbor as Jesus scourged the moneychangers in the Temple.

That night she blessed me as she fell asleep, thanked me for "the good I had done her," and declared that she would thenceforth be fair toward me always. "Don't worry any longer," she said. "You do not deserve all the grief I have caused you. You are fair, and your heart is in the right place. Love me; and know that at bottom I adore you."

This frame of heart lasted three days—long indeed for my poor mother. Spring had come, and my grandmother had always observed that at that season her character became even harsher, and at intervals verged on insanity. Now I saw that she had not been mistaken.

I believe that my mother sensed her derangement and wanted to be alone to hide it from me. She took me to Le Plessis, the country seat of M. and Mme. Duplessis, whom she had seen three days earlier at a dinner given by an old friend of my uncle de Beaumont, and left me the day after our arrival, saying, "You're pale: the country air will revive you. I'll fetch you next week."

She returned five months later.

Nine

I meet my future husband.—His prophecy.—Our friendship.—
My marriage.—Return to Nohant.—Seclusion at Nohant.—Birth
of my son.—Deschartres in Paris.—Deschartres's mysterious
death, perhaps a suicide.

DURING THIS PERIOD, M. and Mme. Duplessis came to spend several days in Paris, and though I was again living with my mother, they fetched me every morning to do the town, to dine "at the cabaret," as they put it, and to "mooch about" in the new quarters in the evenings. The "cabaret" was always the Café de Paris or the Frères Provençaux; the "mooching about" was simply the Opéra, the Théâtre de la Porte-Saint-Martin, or some mummers' show at the Cirque Olympique, which roused James Duplessis's war memories. My mother was invited to all these parties, but though she loved that sort of amusement, she usually let me go alone. It seemed she preferred to hand over all her maternal rights and duties to Mme. Duplessis.

One of these evenings, when we were taking ices at Tortoni's after the theater, Angèle Duplessis remarked to her husband, "Isn't that Casimir?" A slender, rather elegant young man, with a gay countenance and a military bearing, came up to shake hands with them and to reply to their questions concerning his father, a Colonel Dudevant, who, it appeared, enjoyed the warm regard of the family. He sat down next to Mme. Angèle and asked her in an undertone who I might be.

"Why, she is my daughter," loudly replied Angèle.

"In that case," he continued in the same undertone, "she is my wife. Remember, you promised me the hand of your eldest daughter. I was reckoning upon Wilfrid, but as this lass seems of more suitable age, I'll accept her instead, if you will give her to me."

Mme. Angèle burst out laughing, but the jest was prophecy.

Some days later Casimir Dudevant came out to Le Plessis and joined in romping childishly with me and the Duplessis children with a gaiety that boded well for his character. He did nothing to woo me, which would have troubled our informality, and indeed he did not even dream of it. A calm companionship grew between us, and he said to Mme. Angèle, who had long before taken to calling him her son-in-law, "Your daughter Aurore is a capital fellow"; and I replied, "Your son-in-law Casimir is a sweet-natured moppet."

I don't recall who loudly enlarged upon the jest; but old Stanislas, the Duplessis's paying guest, eager to descry some malice in it, called to me in the garden, where we were playing "prisoners' base": "Run, run after your 'husband'!" And Casimir, carried away by the game, shouted from where he stood: "Release my 'wife'!" By and by we were calling each other husband and wife with as little embarrassment or passion as young Norbert or Justine Duplessis might have displayed.

One day in the park Stanislas made some unkind remark to me on this subject, and I asked the old bear why he would put an ugly construction on the most trifling matters.

"Because you are a fool," he retorted, "to imagine you will ever wed that boy. He will get sixty or eighty thousand a year, and he will never have you for his wife."

"I give you my word of honor that I have not so much as dreamed of having him for my husband," I said. "And since a joke which would be in bad taste if all persons here were not as chaste as they are turns sour in your sour mind, I shall pray my 'father' and my 'mother' to put a speedy end to it."

James Duplessis, the first person I met as I went within, said in reply to my demand that old Stanislas was driveling.

"If you are going to heed all the sayings of that old Chinee," he said, "you'll not get a word out he can't find fault with. Forget what he said, and let's talk pounds and pence. It is true, Colonel Dudevant has a big fortune, and a big income too, half on his wife's side, half on his own; but on his side, much is personal and not land income; there are his state pensions as a retired officer, Officer of the Legion of Honor, Baron of the Empire, and so forth. In his own right he has only a rather fine estate in Gascony; and his son, who is not his wife's son but a natural child, is entitled to only half of this inheritance. Probably he will have it all, because his father loves him and has no other children; but his fortune will never exceed your own, and may well be smaller in the beginning. Thus there is nothing to bar your actually becoming man and wife, as we were saying in jest, and this match would be even more advantageous for him than for you. So no one can accuse you of 'running after' anybody. You may do as you please. Spurn the jest if it shocks you; ignore it if it is nothing to you."

"It is nothing to me," I replied, "and I'd only look foolish and lend it credit if I let it put me out."

And there the matter rested.

Casimir departed and returned. Upon his return he behaved more seriously with me, and asked me for my hand with great candor and clarity.

"I know it's unusual," he said, "but I want you to give me your own consent first with a free spirit. If you do not dislike me, yet have no ready answer, pay more attention to me, and tell me in a little while, when you have made up your mind, if you would give me leave to ask my father to make an overture to your mother."

This set me at ease. M. and Mme. Duplessis had spoken so highly of Casimir and his family that I had no reason not to accord him more serious attention. I found his speech and entire manner sincere. He never mentioned love, and confessed himself little inclined to sudden passion or enthusiasm, and in any case, ill fitted to express it seductively. He spoke of never-failing friendship, and compared the tranquil domestic happiness of our hosts to that which he would vow to procure me.

"To prove to you that I know my mind," he said, "I shall admit to you that I was struck at first sight by your kind and reasonable air. I thought you neither beautiful nor even pretty; I did not know who you were, I had never heard you mentioned; and yet when I said in jest to Madame Angèle that you would be my wife, I felt at once that if it should come to pass, I would be very happy. This vague idea returned to me each day, always with greater clarity, and when I joined in laughing and playing with you, it seemed to me that I had known you for ages, and that we two were old friends."

I believe that at that time of my life, as I was emerging from my long wavering between the convent and family life, any sudden declaration of love would have frightened me. I would not have understood it, it might even have seemed something silly or contrived. My heart had never taken one step beyond my ignorance; no tremor of my spirits was likely to trouble my views or allay my distrust of passion.

So I found Casimir's argument to my liking, and after consulting my hosts, I remained with him on that companionable footing which had become, in a way, our right. I had never been the object of those exclusive attentions, that voluntary and happy submission, which so surprises and touches a young girl's heart. Soon I could no longer refrain from regarding Casimir as the best and most trustworthy of friends.

With Mme. Angèle we arranged an interview between the Colonel and my mother, but formed no plans in advance, since the future would hang upon a whim of my mother, who might well bring all to naught. We knew that if she refused we would have to renounce such plans, and merely retain each other's esteem.

My mother came to Le Plessis and at once conceived a tender respect, as I did myself, for the handsome face, the silver hair, the kind and distinguished mien of the old Colonel. They chatted together and with our hosts. Afterward my mother said to me, "I gave my consent, but left a loophole. You see, I don't know what I think of the son. He is not good-looking. I'd have preferred a dashing son-in-law to give me his arm." Presently the Colonel gave me his own, and led me to a landscaped meadow behind the house, talking all the while of farming with James. He had trouble walking, having had violent attacks of gout. When he and James had left the other strollers, he spoke to me with great fondness, telling me that I pleased him very much, and that to have me for his daughter would make his happiness.

My mother remained several days, was pleasant and gay, provoked her future son-in-law by way of a test, found him a fine fellow, and upon her departure, gave us leave to stay together under the eye of Mme. Angèle. It had been agreed upon that we would not set a date for the wedding until Mme. Dudevant, who was spending a while with her family at Le Mans, should return to Paris. Until then, the parents would inform each other of the amount of the two fortunes, and the Colonel would decide the sum he would settle on his son while he lived.

At the end of a fortnight, my mother hit Le Plessis like a bomb. She had "discovered" that Casimir, in a riotous phase, had spent some time as a waiter in a café. I cannot conceive where she'd picked up this harebrained notion. I suspect she'd dreamed it the night before and on wakening had taken it for reality. Her allegation was greeted with peals of laughter, which enraged her. In vain did James endeavor to meet it seriously, to tell her that the Dudevants were scarcely ever out of his sight, and that Casimir had never fallen into any dissipation; in vain did Casimir himself protest that although there was no shame in being a café waiter, he, having passed directly from the military academy to the battlefield as a second lieutenant; having gone on the officers' reserve list to study the law in Paris, without delay; and having lived always with his father, from whom he received a handsome allowance, save when he accompanied him to Gascony, where he was treated as a son and heir, had never had—not for a week, not for a day—the "leisure" to wait tables; still she insisted, claimed she was being duped, and steering me outside, heaped abuse upon Mme. Angèle, her morals, the ill breeding of her family, and the "intrigues" of the Duplessises, who, she said, had made a business of marrying off adventurers to heiresses for a fat douceur, etc., etc.

She threw such a violent fit that I feared for her sanity and strove to coax her out of it by saying I would pack my bag and leave with her at once; that in Paris she might find all the information she wished; and that so long as she remained in doubt, we would not see Casimir. She calmed down at once. "Yes, yes!" she said. "Let's pack!" But scarcely had I begun to, when she said, "On second thought, I'm going alone. I don't like it here. You do, so stay. I will make inquiries, and let you know what I find out."

She departed that very evening, returned to make a few more

scenes of the same sort, and in general required precious little pray-
ing to leave me at Le Plessis until Mme. Dudevant arrived in Paris.
Then, seeing that my mother was about to conclude the marriage,
and was recalling me with an apparently serious intention, I went
to stay with her in a new apartment, rather small and ugly, which
she had rented in the Rue Saint-Lazare, behind the former location
of the Tivoli Gardens. From my dressing room windows I could
see this vast park, and during the day I could, for a slight entry
fee, stroll about there with my brother, who had just arrived and
taken up residence in an attic directly overhead.

Hippolyte had finished his term of service, and though about to
receive a commission, had not wanted to reenlist. He had grown
sick of the military profession he had once leaped at. He had reckoned upon a quicker promotion, and found the lot of a garrisoned
cavalryman, without hope of war and honor, mind-numbing and
without prospects. He could manage without hardship on his little
pension, and I invited him, unopposed by my mother, who liked
him very much, to live with me until he had decided upon a new
profession.

It was a good thing he stepped between my mother and me.
He was much better than I at jollying along her deranged character.
He laughed at her rages, flattered and bantered her, even scolded
her, for from him she would brook anything. His hussar's "cheek"
was not so easy to bruise as my girlish thin skin, and the insouciance
he displayed amid her tirades disarmed her so utterly that she forthwith gave them up. He composed my mind as best he could, and
told me I was foolish to take her moods so seriously, for he thought
them trifling matters compared to the brig and his regimental
"scraps."

Mme. Dudevant came to pay her official visit to my mother. She
was hardly her match in warmth or wit, but she had the manner
of a great lady, and looked like an angel of mercy. I fell headlong
for the sympathy that her martyred look, her frail voice and her
pretty face at once excited in all who met her, and excited in me
much longer than they deserved to. My mother was flattered by
her advances, which quickly found their mark: namely, her ruffled
pride. And so the alliance was resolved upon; recalled into question;
broken off altogether; and resolved upon once more, all to the tempo
of whims which lasted until autumn and which again made me

very sick and unhappy; for vainly had my brother convinced me that beneath it all my mother loved me and did not really mean a word of her own lavish abuse: I could not get used to those pendulating moods of wild gaiety and brooding anger, of expansive tenderness and apparent indifference or capricious dislike.

About Casimir she had nothing good to say whatsoever. She had taken a baffling dislike to him—his nose, she said, displeased her. She accepted his civilities, and amused herself with trying his patience, which was not great, and which yet held up, with Hippolyte's help and Pierret's intervention. But to me she condemned everything about him, and her accusations grew so outrageous that they only produced an indulgent smile in those whom she wished to embitter or to undeceive.

At last, after many humiliating parleys, she made up her mind. She would give my hand in exchange for a marriage settlement. M. Dudevant initially refused these terms on account of her mistrust of his son, which she expressed to him without mincing words. At my prompting, Casimir, too, vowed he would resist with all his might this conservative, property-minded measure, which almost always results in the sacrifice of moral freedom to the tyrannical immobility of real estate. I would not have sold the house and garden of Nohant for anything, but certainly a part of the land, in order to create for myself an income in proportion to the expenses entailed by the relatively large size of the domicile itself. I knew that my grandmother had always been discomfited by this disproportion; but my husband had to bow to the obstinacy of my mother, who was relishing her final act of authority.

We were married in September 1822, and after the wedding visits and cordialities, and an interval of several days spent with our friends the Duplessises, we left with my brother for Nohant, where Deschartres joyfully welcomed us.

I spent the winter of 1822–1823 at Nohant. I was rather ill, but lost in the sweet dreams and keen hopes of maternal love. The transformation which comes about during a woman's first pregnancy is usually total and sudden, and so it was for me. Mental needs, anxious thoughts, the eagerness to learn and observe—all these vanished before the sweet burden's first quiverings. During this period of waiting and hoping, Providence puts a woman's body and emotions before all else. And so I gave up sitting up nights, reading, pondering, gave up the intellectual life without need of any virtuous effort or regrets.

The winter was protracted and harsh. The ground, frozen hard, was long covered by high snowdrifts. My husband liked the country, though not as I did; mad for hunting, he left me for long hours, which I filled by making the layette. I'd never sewn before. Though my grandmother had told me that I ought to be able to do handi-work, she had never urged me to, and I had always assumed I was terribly clumsy. But when I had to clothe the little being whom I saw in all my dreams, I set about it with a sort of passion. Ursule would come by and show me how to whip or fell a seam. I was amazed when I saw how easy it was, but at the same time I under-stood that in sewing, as in all things, one must have the faculty of invention, and the mastery of the scissors stroke.

My husband got on well with Deschartres, whose lease at Nohant had nearly expired. I had warned him about Deschartres's arrogance and irascibility, and he had promised me to keep on his right side. He kept his word, but still it took him a while to assume authority in the management of the estate. Deschartres was now eager to attend to his own farm and no other. I obtained my husband's con-sent that he be allowed to live with us for the rest of his life, and I warmly urged him to concur. I couldn't imagine Deschartres sur-viving anywhere else—and there I was not wrong—but he declined my offer. "For twenty-five years I've been the absolute master of this estate," he said. "I've made all the decisions, with no check on my authority but that of two women, because your father never meddled in anything. As for your husband, he certainly doesn't bother me; he's never interfered with my stewardship. But now that it's drawing to a close, I'd surely annoy him, no matter how hard I tried not to, with my criticisms and objections. I'd be idle and bored, I'd be spiteful when my advice wasn't taken; and besides, I want to take command of my own destiny. You know I've always planned to make a fortune: well, I feel that the time is ripe." It was just as impossible to deflate my poor tutor's illusions as it was to buck his lust for domination. And so it was agreed upon that he would leave Nohant on Saint John's Day, that is, June 24, 1823, the last day of his lease.

We went to Paris ahead of him. After several days at Le Plessis with our friends, I rented a small suite in the Hôtel de Florence in the Rue Neuve des Mathurins, a town house owned by Gallyot, one of the Emperor's former chefs. This sterling gentleman had picked up a curious habit while supervising the Emperor's field kitchen: he never went to bed. As everybody knows, the Emperor's favorite snack was a golden roast chicken, and such a chicken was ready twenty-four hours in the day. A man's life had been devoted to the presence of a chicken upon the spit, and Gallyot, who was in charge of this man, had for ten years slept every night on a chair, fully dressed and ready to leap up. This hard regimen had not preserved him from obesity, yet he continued it for the rest of his life. Unable to lie down in a bed without gasping for breath, he claimed that he slept best with one eye open. It was in this Gallyot's town house, then, that I rented, in the rear of the garden, a little annex, where on June 30, 1823, my son Maurice made a lively appearance. It was the most beautiful moment of my life. After terrible labor pains and an hour of deep sleep, I awoke to find a little creature asleep on my pillow. I'd dreamed of him so much beforehand, and was still so weak, that I wasn't sure he was real. I was afraid that if I stirred, the vision might vanish, as it had so often vanished before.

I was kept in bed too long: they take more precautions with lying in at Paris than in the country. The second time I got up on the second day and was none the worse for it.

I nursed my son, as I later did his sister. My mother was his godmother and my father-in-law was his godfather.

Presently Deschartres arrived from Nohant, brimming with schemes to make his fortune. Stiff as a poker in his antique cornflower-blue suit with its gold buttons, he looked such a bumpkin that people stopped and stared in the streets. Unfazed, he walked on in state. He unswaddled Maurice and turned him round and round to make sure nothing needed reworking. He didn't pat him— I don't recall that Deschartres ever kissed or caressed anybody— but he held the sleeping baby on his lap awhile and considered him. Satisfied at last, he said, "It's time I lived for myself."

Colonel Dudevant was then in Paris with his wife, whom I did my best to love, though she was most unlovable. My father-in-law was a splendid fellow. We often ate at their house with Deschartres, whom the old colonel loved to tease. "You are a Jesuit!" he would say, and Deschartres would shout back, "Jacobin!" Neither epithet was very accurate.

Deschartres had found very pretty rooms for very little money at the Place Royale. He had bought furniture and even seemed to enjoy a measure of comfort. He told us about various little ventures of his, which, though they had failed of themselves, were sure to lead to a stunning coup. What was this coup? I wasn't sure: there was something about rapeseed oil and colza oil. Deschartres was tired of farming. He didn't want to sow and reap anymore; he wanted to buy and sell. He had fallen in with a crowd of "men with ideas"— people who, unfortunately, were just like him. He drew up plans, scribbled figures, and strange to say, lent ear and even money to strangers—he who had so little good will and was so impervious to others' advice! Often my father-in-law would say to him, "Monsieur Deschartres, you're a Johnadreams, and you're going to get yourself swindled." Deschartres just shrugged.

The Colonel indulged Maurice's every whim, but Mme. Dudevant couldn't bear tots, and as mine had had a few misadventures on the floor, she was so greatly repelled that she made me agree never to bring him along unless "precautions" had been taken. This proved hard: how to put an eighteen-month-old baby under oath?

In the spring of 1825 we returned to Nohant, and three months elapsed without my hearing from Deschartres. Surprised that my letters went unanswered, and unable to avail myself of my father-in-law's help—he had left Paris—I wrote the queries desk at the Place Royale.

Poor Deschartres was dead. All his slender fortune he had gambled and lost in unhappy enterprises. He had kept a total silence until his last hour. Nobody knew anything about him, nobody had seen him for months. He had bequeathed all his worldly goods to a laundress who had tended him devotedly. For the rest, not a word of reminiscence, complaint, appeal or farewell. Taking with him the secret of his disappointed ambition or betrayed trust, he had disappeared from the face of the earth, probably unperturbed, for in all that concerned himself alone, in bodily suffering as in financial setbacks, he was a true stoic.

His death affected me more than I cared to say. If at first I felt involuntary relief at being delivered from his tiresome dogmatism,

I also felt that with him I had lost the presence of a devoted heart and the society of a mind remarkable upon many accounts. My brother, who had hated him as a tyrant, was sorry he had died but did not regret him. My mother was unkind even to his shade, writing: "At last Deschartres is no more of this world!" Many did not let him off easy in their memory. The most allowed to so unsociable a being was that he had been a gentleman. Except for two or three peasants whose lives he had saved, and from whom he had refused payment, according to his custom, scarcely anybody mourned the Great Man, and I had to hide my tears to avoid being jeered at or wounding those he himself had too cruelly wounded. Yet he had carried off with him a large portion of my life: all my childhood memories, both pleasant and sad, and the whole stimulant, by turns vexing and beneficial, of my intellectual development. I felt that I was a bit more of an orphan than before. Poor Deschartres! He had thwarted both his nature and his destiny when he had ceased to live for others. He had thought of himself as an egoist, but he was wrong: he was incapable of living either by or for himself.

Though I could not obtain any account of his last moments, it occurred to me that he had taken his life. For several weeks he had been sick—sick at heart, most likely—but I could not believe that so robust a frame could be so quickly wasted merely by the approach of want. Besides, he must have received at least one letter from me inviting him to Nohant. Surely with his enterprising spirit, and his faith in the cornucopia of his genius, he would have recovered hope and self-confidence, had he but allowed himself time to reflect. It seemed more probable that he had given in to a moment of discouragement, and precipitated the catastrophe with some horse cure proper to dispel not only his illness and sorrow but his life as well. Yet he had lectured me so lengthily on the subject of suicide that I would scarcely have believed he could prove so fatally inconsistent, had I not recalled that my poor tutor was inconsistency personified. On another occasion he had said to me, "The day your father died, I loaded a chamber in my pistol." And once I had overheard him say, "If I ever thought I was incurably ill, I wouldn't burden anybody, but keep it to myself, and dose myself with opium to have done with it." It was his way to talk of death with the disdain of the ancients, and to commend those "sages" who had decamped from the world of appearances.

187

Ten

GUILLERY, my father-in-law's "chateau" in Gascony, was really only
a cottage. With its five big front windows, it looked rather like one
of those bungalows one sees in the outskirts of Paris. It was very
modestly furnished, like all the country houses of the South. Yet it
made a pleasant and quite comfortable home. At first the countryside
seemed wretched, but I soon got used to it. At the coming of winter,
which is the most agreeable season in that region of burning sands,
the pine woods and the forests of pine and cork oak assumed a
Druidical aspect under their lichens, while the earth, grown firm

188

and fragrant with the rains, was covered with a vernal vegetation which disappeared just at that time when spring comes to the North. The gorse bloomed; luxurious, violet-besprinkled mosses sprang up in the underbrush; the wolves howled; the hares bounded; Colette arrived from Nohant; and the horn sounded in the copses.

Here was a sort of hunting I could take to: no luxury, no liveried beaters, no scientific jargon, no red jackets, no sporting rivalries or pretensions; just hunting for hunting's sake. Friends and neighbors arrived the evening before, and the Colonel's people were dispatched to block as many burrows as possible; we set off at the crack of dawn, riding whatever sound-limbed horses were available and never blaming them for their falls, which were often unavoidable on paths where the loose sand quite concealed the tangled roots beneath.

We hunted by fair weather and foul. The wealthy peasants, who clearly were clever poachers as well, hurried along behind their little packs of dogs, which, despite their modest appearance, were obviously much more experienced than those of the hunters themselves. I'll never forget the punctilious Peyrounine arriving at the dawn rendezvous with his three "long-leashers," then taking the scent with a satisfied smile and a murmur: *"Aneim, ma Tan Belo!"* (*Aneim* is Gascon for *allons, courage.*)

We were many, but the woods were immense. I could follow a dog without getting lost merely by listening for Peyrounine's whistle. Now and again I would also hear his voice in the underbrush, exulting over the prowess of Tan Belo, his favorite bitch, and quietly airing his pride: "Ah, my beauty!"

My father-in-law was gay, irascible, tender, sensitive and fair-minded: I'd gladly have spent the rest of my life with this lovable old man, and I'm sure we'd never have quarreled. But I was doomed to lose all my natural protectors, and I was not to keep this one very long.

The Gascons are a first-rate lot, no more dishonest or boastful than any provincials—they're all a bit that way. They're witty, ignorant, very lazy, kind, generous, big-hearted and brave. At the period when I was in Gascony, the townsfolk were much more badly educated than those in my province, but their gaiety rang truer, and they were more responsive to friendship. Here, too, was a full contingent of village gossips, but they were much less malicious than ours, and indeed, if I remember rightly, they weren't very malicious at all.

The peasants, whom I couldn't really associate with, for it was only toward the end of my stay that I began to make out their dialect, seemed happier and more independent than ours. Those who lived around Guillery were quite well off, and none ever asked for help. On the contrary, they seemed to regard themselves as quite the equals of Mousu le Varon (Monsieur le Baron), and though extravagantly polite, had the air of extending him their protection, as if eager to reward a good neighbor. They showered him with presents, and he lived all the winter on the fowl and live game they brought him on New Year's Day. Indeed, New Year's Day saw an exchange of grub worthy of Pantagruel; Gascony must be the country of the goddess Manducée. The hams, stuffed hens, fatted geese, obese ducks, truffles, millet cakes and maize cakes rained down just as in that isle where Panurge had it so good; and the cottage of Guillery, seemingly so austere, boasted a kitchen to match the abbey of Thélème, whence no one, highborn or low, ever came out without a noticeable gain in weight.

This cuisine was not for me. The heavy sauces poisoned my maw, and often I didn't eat even though I'd just returned from the hunt. I usually felt sick, and grew thinner by the minute among countless cages wherein buntings and wood doves were busily feeding to death.

In the autumn of 1825 my husband and I made a side trip to Bordeaux. We went as far as Labrède, where the family of my friend Zoé had a country house. There I went through a period of terrible suffering from which this fine friend rescued me with her eloquence and courage. Her keen intelligence held sway over me for several years, and brought to my mind a balance that I'd sought vainly till then. I returned to Guillery exhausted but calm, having entertained, under Montesquieu's great oaks, cheerful thoughts quite unrelated to this philosopher. Yet I might have observed, by way of a pun, that the "spirit of the laws" had indeed entered into my new acceptance of my lot.

We had gone down the Gironde valley to Bordeaux, and to return as far as Nérac would take too much time, for being away from Maurice for as long as three days made me ill with anxiety. Therefore I returned to Bordeaux by land. Now, at this period the roads were few and ill-tended. We arrived at Casteljaloux at midnight, and alighting from the ramshackle stagecoach, I was delighted to see that my servant had come out to meet us with our horses. We had only four leagues left to make, but it was a stretch on a detestable road, upon a black night, and through an uninhabited forest of towering pines where prowled bands of Spaniards who might make most unpleasant company even in broad daylight. But the only living beings we saw were wolves. As the darkness forced us to ride at foot pace, these chaps came quietly along behind. It was my husband who observed, by the restiveness of his mount, that something was afoot. He told me to ride ahead and to give Colette a pat lest she take fright. Then, suddenly, two burning eyes appeared to my right and passed before me to my left.

"How many?" I whispered.

"Two, I think," came the answer, "but more may come. Just don't fall asleep; there's nothing else for it."

I was tired, so the warning was not superfluous. I kept on my guard, and we arrived at the house at four without mishap.

In those days such encounters were usual in the pine and cork-oak forests. Every day we heard the shepherds calling from copse to copse to warn of the enemy's approach. These shepherds were picturesque fellows with their belted, open-sided tunics, and the rifles they now bore instead of the traditional crook.

For a while Guillery was well defended. There was a mongrel called Pigon who was positively heroic when it came to wolves. At night he went out alone to draw them in the woods, and in the morning would return with tufts of fur and shreds of flesh hanging from his iron-spiked collar. But one evening, alas, someone forgot to put on his armor, and the intrepid dog never returned.

The winter was a bit harsher than is common in that country. The Garonne overflowed, and consequently its tributaries did too. We were cut off for several days, and the famished wolves grew very bold, eating all our young dogs. The house was in the middle of the country, without courtyard or enclosure of any sort, so these animals could come right under our windows and howl. There was one who amused himself one night by gnawing at the door to our rooms, which was at ground level. I was reading in one room while my husband slept in another. I opened the inner door to call Pigon, thinking he had returned and wanted to come in. I was about to open the outer door when my husband wakened and shouted, "What the deuce are you doing? It's a wolf!" Such is the calm induced by habit that my husband turned over and fell back asleep and I took up my book, while the wolf continued to gnaw at our door. He couldn't get very far—it was pretty solid—but he did leave the marks of his attempt. I doubt he had any wicked designs; he was probably just teething.

One day when my father-in-law the Colonel was midway on the road toward one of his friends, who lived a half league off, he encountered one, two, three, then suddenly no less than fourteen wolves! He paid them little heed: wolves don't really attack; they just follow along and wait until the horse grows restive and throws his rider or stumbles and falls. Then you have to rise quickly; otherwise they go for the jugular. Well, the Colonel, whose horse was used to such encounters, went calmly forward; but as he stopped at his friend's house to ring, one of his fourteen escorts leaped at his horse's flank and snapped at the hem of his coat. He had no weapon but a riding whip, which he cracked at the enemy without effect, so he got the idea of dismounting and shaking his coat at his assailants. They scampered off at once; yet it seemed to him hours before that door opened, and when it did he fetched a deep sigh of relief!

This adventure had occurred long before; at the time of which I write he was so gouty that two men were required to lift him onto his horse and get him off it. Yet once up on his little mirror-bright bay mare with her blond mane, despite his great surcoat, his long olive-drab gaiters, and his white hair streaming on the breeze, he had a truly martial bearing, and rode with more skill and gentleness than anyone else.

I've mentioned the bands of Spaniards who roamed the countryside. They were Catalans chiefly, nomads from the far foothills of the Pyrenees. Some came to get day labor, and were fairly reliable despite their ferocious appearance; others arrived with herds of goats, which they put to pasture in the vast moors round about, often venturing as far as the skirts of the copses, where their livestock did a great deal of damage. To parley with them was most unpleasant. They would retire in silence, and deftly advise you with catapults and throwing sticks to leave them alone. They were much feared. I can't say if they still make the moors their common, but I do know that this abuse went on for several years more, and that some

landowners were wounded, and a few even killed, in these skir-
mishes.

Guillery, then, was a place of wolves and brigands, yet we were
happy there. Visits were exchanged. The landowners had absolutely
nothing to do; indeed, they cultivated a taste for doing nothing,
and spent their time making excursions, hunting, and regaling one
another.

I experienced much in the next few years at Nohant. It seemed
to me that I lived a century under the empire of the same thought,
so weary was I of a gaiety without heart, of a home without intimacy,
of an encroaching loneliness which din and drunkenness rendered
only more absolute. Yet there was no real misconduct to complain
of, and even had there been, I would not have allowed myself to
see it. The dissipation of my brother and of those swept away by
him had not yet reached the point where I no longer felt myself
inspire in them a sort of fear which was not condescension but
instinctive respect. For my part, I was as tolerant as I could be.
As long as they were merely tiresome, jabbering, loud, even sick
and altogether disgusting, I tried to laugh, and even grew used to
putting up with a jesting tone which actually revolted me. But when
nerves came into play, when lewdness and grossness appeared, when
even my poor brother, long submissive and repentant before my
remonstrations, became brutal and wicked, I turned a deaf ear, and
not bothering to hide my feelings, marched up to my little room
as soon as I could.

There I could easily busy myself and divert my mind from the
din without, which often lasted until six or seven in the morning.
I had grown used to working at night beside my sick grandmother;
now I had other invalids, not to tend, but to hear in their ravings.

Yet my moral solitude was profound, absolute, and would have
been fatal to a tender soul still in the flower of youth, had it not
been filled with a dream become a passion, not in my life, since I
had sacrificed my life to duty, but in my thoughts. An absent being,
with whom I held unceasing converse, and to whom I offered all
my thoughts, musings, humble virtues and platonic enthusiasm; an
excellent being whom I adorned with every perfection that human
nature does not comprise; a man, then, who appeared to me several
days, several hours sometimes, in a year, and who, as romantic when

by my side as I was myself, had left my piety undismayed and my conscience untroubled, was all the support and solace of my exile in the world of reality.

This absent—not to say invisible—being, whom I had made the third term of my existence *(God, he, and I),* grew weary of this superhuman aspiration toward sublime love. He was generous and tender enough not to say it, but his letters became rarer, his words more urgent, or colder, according to the sense I wished to find in them. His passions needed nourishment other than enthusiastic friendship and the epistolary life. He had made a vow which he had kept religiously, and without which I would have broken with him; but he had made no vow restricting the joys or pleasures he might find elsewhere. I sensed that I burdened him terribly, or else that I was no longer anything but a mental amusement. I inclined too modestly toward the latter opinion; later I learned I had been wrong. But I only congratulated myself the more on having broken the bond about his heart and about the furtherance of his destiny. I loved him a long while more, in silence and abashment. Then I thought of him calmly, gratefully, and I never think of him now but with friendship and love.

When this calm but irreversible rupture was accomplished, I tried to return to my life, which no exterior thing had disturbed or modified; but I could not. My little room would have me no longer.

I was then living in what had been my grandmother's boudoir, because it had only one door and could not be used as a thoroughfare under any pretext. This boudoir was so small that with my books, herbals, butterflies and pebbles (I was amusing myself with natural history, though without learning a thing), there was no room for a bed. A hammock answered to the purpose. For a desk I used a chiffonier, which I long shared with a cricket who had grown tame from watching me. He lived on my sealing wafers, which I made certain were always of the whitest, fearing lest he be poisoned. He would come and eat on my paper while I was writing, and then go sing in a favorite drawer. Sometimes he walked upon my writing, and I would shoo him off before he was tempted to taste fresh ink. One evening I did not see him or hear his flutter, and sought him everywhere. I found nothing of my friend but his two rear legs sticking out from between the sash and the window frame.

He had never told me he went out, and the housemaid had crushed him when she closed the window.

The cricket's song symbolically foreshadowed the end of my stay at Nohant. That autumn I was inspired by new ideas; changed my way of living; went forth; and rode often. I roughed out a sort of novel which never saw the light of day; then, rereading it, became convinced that it was worthless, but that I could do others much less poor; and in sum, that it was no poorer than plenty of novels which kept their authors alive. I realized that I wrote them fast, easily, lengthily, without fatigue; that my thoughts, though benumbed in my brain, wakened in the course of writing, and hung together; that in my life of meditation, I'd largely observed, and understood rather well, the natures I'd encountered, and that I knew human nature well enough to depict it; and lastly, that of all the trades that I might master, literature offered me the greatest chance of success, as a métier, and, to speak plainly, as a livelihood.

Since well before my marriage, I had felt that my situation, my small fortune, my freedom to do nothing, my supposed right to command a certain number of human beings—peasants and servants—in sum, my role as heiress and lady of the manor, despite its negligible consequence, went against my tastes, my logic, my talents. Let the reader recall how my mother's poverty, which had separated her from me, had affected my brain and my heart, and how, in my innermost soul, I had rejected the notion of inherited wealth, and long reckoned upon fleeing comfort for the world of work.

To these romantic ideas had succeeded, in the early days of marriage, the will to oblige my husband, and to be the housekeeper that he wished me to be. Household cares have never bored me, and I am not one of those sublime spirits who cannot come off their clouds. Granted, I saw a good deal in clouds; but that is one more reason for me to feel my feet on the ground. Often indeed, worn out and agitated, I would have agreed with what Panurge said upon the raging sea: "Happy is he who plants cabbages! He has one foot on dry land, and the other is no farther away than the length of a shovel blade!"

But that shovel blade, that something between the land and my second foot, was just what I needed and could not find. I needed some motive, some aim as simple yet logical as "planting cabbages," to know what I lived for. In taking pains to economize on everything, as I had been advised, I came to realize that it is impossible to be thrifty without sometimes being selfish; the closer I came to the soil, and grubbed at the problem of how to make it pay, the more clearly I saw that it pays scarcely anything, and that tenant farmers who have little or no soil to till cannot survive on the strength of their arms alone. Nohant's yield was too slight, the day laborers too unreliable, exhaustion and illness too inevitable. My husband was not inhuman, and did not call me to account for small expenses; but when at the month's end he saw my books, he lost his head and made me lose mine too; my income, he said, was too small by half for my largesse, and there was no chance we might stay on at Nohant if Nohant did not pay. It was the truth; but I could not take it upon myself to reduce my tenants to subsistence and to refuse even that to my hirelings. I did not resist his demands or his counsel, but I was at my wits' end. I was impatient, but compliant. He knew it, and took advantage of it.

My stewardship lasted but one year. My budget was ten thousand francs; I spent fourteen, and went about as shamefaced as a child caught in the pantry. I offered to quit; he accepted. I gave up control of my holdings, and even renounced a trust of fifteen thousand francs which had been allotted to me for my wardrobe under the marriage settlement. It was more than I needed, and I preferred to leave it to my guardian's discretion than to come begging. From this period until 1831 I hadn't a penny to my name, and never took one from our common purse without first asking my husband's permission; and when, after nine years of marriage, I asked him to acquit my personal debts, they came to no more than five hundred francs.

I do not report these trifles that I may complain of having been made to submit to some constraint or to have suffered from some meanness. My husband was not mean; he refused me nothing. I had no needs, I desired nothing outside the household budget he had drawn up, and content to forgo all responsibility, I left him unlimited authority. Thus he had got the habit of regarding me as his ward, and had no reason to be vexed at so tranquil a child.

Amid the nunnish life that I led at Nohant—which wanted neither cell, nor vow of obedience, nor of silence, nor of poverty—a need to live on my own grew at last within me. I suffered from being useless. Unable to help the poor of our district in any other way, I had set up for a sort of country doctor, and my patients, who did not pay, had swelled to such numbers as to crush me with fatigue. To save money I had become something of an apothecary too, and wore myself out in the preparation of salves and syrups. I did not tire of this trade—I was dreaming, and cared not where I dreamed—but I told myself that if I had some money of my own, my patients would be better cared for and my practice might avail itself of some real knowledge.

Furthermore, slavery is something antihuman which one accepts only on the condition that one may dream of freedom. I was not my husband's slave, he gladly left me to my readings and my juleps; but I was enslaved in a preordained social condition, and it was not he who could emancipate me. If I'd asked him for the moon, he'd have laughed and replied, "Produce its price, and I'm your man"; and if I'd allowed myself to say that I wanted to see China, he'd have answered, "Get the money, get Nohant to bring it in, and go to China."

Thus I'd mulled over the problem of having my own means, however slender, that I might spend, without outside control or twinges of conscience, on an artistic pleasure, on alms to a deserving person, on a good book, on a trip, on a gift to some impecunious friend—on all those trifles one cannot do without, yet without which one is not man or woman, but very angel or beast. In our wholly factitious society, to have no cash at all means frightful want or absolute powerlessness. To be without responsibilities is its own sort of serfdom—something approaching the shame of a suspension of civil rights.

I'd also told myself that the day would come when I could no longer stay at Nohant—this on account of what still seemed passing woes, yet which, at times, I saw aggravated alarmingly. I'd have had to turn out my brother, who, straitened by the poor management of his own estate, had come to live with us to save money, as well as another friend of the family, for whom I felt, despite his bacchic frenzies, a very real regard. He was a man who like my brother had heart and wit to spare one day in three, or four, or five—however the wind blew, as they put it. Now, as it happened, there were "hocused breezes," which occasioned plenty of foolery, "hocused faces," which they could not encounter without craving a nip, and when they had taken a nip, it turned out, oddly enough, that the

wine was "most hocused" of all.* Really there is nothing worse than
these kindly, witty drunkards—you can't get angry with them. My
brother became literally crying drunk, and I was forced to shut
myself up in my cell to keep him from crying on my shoulder all
the night long—at those times, that is, when he had not taken that
dosage which made him want to strangle his best friends. Poor Hippolyte! How charming he was in his good days, how unbearable
in his bad hours! Well, the way he was carrying on, and despite
certain indirect consequences of his behavior, which were more
serious than his jabberings, weeping fits and rages, I preferred exile
to turning him out. Besides, his wife lived with us too—his poor,
excellent wife, who had but one joy in life, that of being in such
frail health that she spent more time abed than afoot, and slept a
sleep so leaden that she hardly saw what was going on.

With an aim to emancipate myself, and to remove my children
from what might prove a baneful influence, and certain that I'd
be allowed to go away on condition I did not request a share, even
a very unequal one, of my income, I'd tried to put myself to some
little trade. I'd tried translations: they were too time-consuming,
and caused me too much trouble and too many pangs of conscience;
quick portrait sketches in chalk or watercolors: I caught the likeness
cleverly, and passably drew my little heads, but they were unorigi-
nal; dressmaking: I was fast, but did not see nicely enough, and
learned that what I made could bring in less than a franc a day;
and—with my mother in mind—millinery: but she had not been
able to set up again, lacking a small capital. For four years I groped
about and toiled and moiled over nothing worth a straw, to discover
in myself a talent for . . . anything. For a moment I thought I'd
found it. I'd painted ornamental flowers and birds, in microscopic
compositions, on those lacquered wooden cigar cases that they man-
ufacture in Spa. Among them were some very pretty ones, which
I showed to the varnisher on one of my trips to Paris. Admiring
them, he asked if that was my trade; and I said yes, to see where
it would lead. He told me he would place these objects in his window
and see what price they might fetch. In a few days he informed
me that he had turned down an offer of eighty francs for a cigar

---

* An untranslatable pun on *salé*. I have assumed, without hard evidence, that
the primary meaning in this context refers to the "hocusing" of strong drink with
some sort of opiate, presumably tincture of laudanum. —Translator.

case; I'd pulled the floor price of a hundred francs out of the air, thinking it would never fetch a hundred sous!

My situation was simple: since I brought to my literary projects neither well-trained talent, nor specialized study, nor memories of a life of surface agitation, nor a knowledge of the world, I had no ambition. Ambition must repose upon self-confidence, and I was not so silly as to reckon upon my slight genius. I felt I was rich in a very limited fund: that of the analysis of feeling, the portrayal of a certain number of characters, the love of nature, the familiar presentation, as it were, of the scenes and customs of country life: but that sufficed for a start. "As I go on," I thought, "I will see more people and things, I will extend my social circle, I will multiply the locations of the scenes, and besides, if need be I can always fall back on 'the historical novel' and study the details of history, and I will use my mind to divine the thoughts of men who are no longer."

When my resolution to go seek my fortune—that is, the income of three thousand francs I'd always dreamed of—was ripe, to declare it and act upon it was the matter of three days. My husband was required by the marriage settlement to pay me an allowance of fifteen hundred francs. I asked for my daughter, and permission to spend three months in Paris twice a year, with two hundred and fifty francs extra for every month I was away. The affair was concluded with dispatch. He thought it was a whim I'd soon tire of.

My brother agreed. "You think you're going to live in Paris with a child on an average of two hundred and fifty francs a month—you who don't know the price of a chicken? It's too absurd! You'll be back empty-handed before the fortnight's out, and Casimir's firmly resolved to turn a deaf ear to any requests for a bigger allowance."

"That may be," I said, "but I'm having a go. Lend me your apartment in your town house for ten days, and look after Solange* till I've found rooms. I'll be back soon enough, as you say."

My brother was the only one who tried to combat my resolution. He felt a bit ashamed of the disgust that the household had aroused in me. He did not want to confess it to himself, but he had just

* Her daughter, born in 1828. —Translator.

199

unwittingly confessed it to me. His wife was more understanding: she had confidence in my courage and my destiny. She felt that I was availing myself of the only means to dodge, or to forestall, an even more painful decision.

My daughter still understood nothing; and Maurice would have understood nothing, had not my brother taken care to tell him that I was going off for a long while, and might never come back. He said this in hopes that my poor child's grief would hold me back. Maurice's tears broke my heart, but I contrived to calm him and to make him trust my word.

I arrived in Paris shortly after the row in the Palais du Luxembourg and the trial of the cabinet ministers.

Eleven

*The garret on the Quai Saint-Michel and the eccentric life that
I led for several months before settling in there.—A disguise,
and its extraordinary success.—The Baroness Dudevant forbids
me to compromise her name in the arts.—My pen name.—"Jules
Sand" and "George Sand."—The cholera.—The Cloître de Saint-
Merry.—I change garrets.—Four Berrichons in the literary
world.—M. Delatouche.—Le Figaro.—A walk in the Latin Quarter.—Balzac.—Balzac redecorates.—Balzac's several sides.—Delatouche conceives a dislike for him.—Dinner, and a phantasma-
goric evening at Balzac's.—Delatouche encourages and paralyzes
me.—Indiana.—They are mistaken who say that it represents me
and my story.—Theory of the beautiful.—Theory of the true.—
What Balzac thought of them.*

I LOOKED for lodgings, and soon settled in above the Quai Saint-
Michel, in a garret apartment in the large corner house at the entrance to the bridge, opposite the morgue. I had three quite decent
little rooms which opened onto a balcony overlooking a long stretch
of the Seine and from which I could gaze on the monumental buildings directly opposite: Notre-Dame, Saint-Jacques-la-Boucherie,
Sainte-Chapelle, etc. I had a piece of sky, a view of water, air, swallows and what greenery grew upon the rooftops; I did not feel too
much in the Paris of civilization, which would have suited neither

my tastes nor my means, but rather in the picturesque and poetic Paris of Victor Hugo—the Paris of the past.

I think my rent was three hundred francs a year. The five flights of stairs were terrible, but I had no choice, even with my plump baby girl under my arm. I had no maid; my concierge, who was very loyal and tidy and kindhearted, helped me with the housework for fifteen francs a month. I had my dinner brought up from an eating house—the shopkeeper, too, was clean and honest—at two francs a day. I washed and ironed all the fancy linen myself. And so I managed to live within my allowance.

The hardest thing was to buy furniture. Elegance was out of the question, of course. I obtained credit, and managed to pay; but this settling in, modest though it was, took a while to organize, and I spent several months at Paris and Nohant before I could transplant Solange from her "palace" to this new state of poverty without her being upset by or even noticing it. Little by little everything was put in place, and once I had her with me, with meals and service arranged for, I was able to lead a sedentary life, going out only to take her walking in the Luxembourg Gardens, and sitting with her every evening while I wrote. Then Providence smiled on me. While tending a pot of mignonette on my balcony, I met my neighbor, who, more elegant than I, was growing an orange tree on hers. Her name was Mme. Badoureau, and she lived with her husband, a schoolmaster, and a charming daughter of fifteen, a sweet blond girl who shyly averted her eyes and who was soon very taken with Solange. This excellent family suggested that Solange come to play with the children who called on them for private lessons; for she easily tired of our tiny garret, where she had nothing to do. This made the child's life no longer merely bearable but positively pleasant. These good people lavished every favor and tenderness upon her without allowing me to pay them, though such a consideration would have been well earned, and quite in keeping with their profession.

Until then—that is, until my daughter came to Paris—I lived less easily and actually quite oddly, but in a way which led directly to my goal.

I refused to go over my budget, or to borrow. (A debt of five hundred francs—the only debt of my life—had worried me awfully! What if M. Dudevant should refuse to pay it! In fact, he paid it gladly; but I dared mention it to him only when I was very ill and feared "to die insolvent.") So I looked about for some sort of paid handiwork, but found nothing. (I'll say in a moment where my literary luck stood.) I had a little portrait in the window of the café on the Quai Saint-Michel, in the very house where I lived; but custom never came. I had botched my concierge's likeness, and so courted the ill will of the whole neighborhood!

I wanted to read, but had no books. Anyway, it was winter, I was counting my fire logs, it was spendthrift to stay at home. I tried the Bibliothèque Mazarin, but it was so cold there I'd have been better off on the towers of Notre-Dame. The place had its old "navvies," bookworms who settled in at a table, snug, motionless, mummified, unaware that their blue noses were crystallizing. I envied their petrifaction; I watched them sit down or stand up, as if worked by springs, to see if they were not of wood.

Then, too, I was eager to cast off my provinciality and to be acquainted with all the ideas and forms of my time. I felt that they were necessary, and I was curious about them; but except for the most striking achievements, I knew nothing about the arts in their modern shape. Above all, I hungered for the theater.

I had no illusions that a poor woman could indulge such longings. Balzac used to say, "You can't be a woman in Paris on under twenty-five thousand." And this paradox, that a woman was not really a woman unless she was smartly dressed, became a reality for the woman who would be an artist.

Yet I saw that my young male friends from Berry—my childhood companions—were living in Paris on as little as I, and knew about everything that could possibly interest young people. The literary and political events, the excitements of the theaters and picture salons, of the clubs and of the streets—they saw it all, they were there. I had legs as strong as theirs, and good feet which had learned to walk sturdily in their great clogs upon the rutted roads of Berry. Yet on the Paris pavement I was like a boat on ice. My delicate shoes cracked open in two days, my pattens sent me spilling, and I always forgot to lift my dress. I was muddy, tired and runny-nosed, and I watched my shoes and my clothes—not to forget my little velvet hats, which the drainpipes watered—go to rack and ruin with alarming rapidity.

I had experienced such things before I had ever dreamed of moving to Paris, and had once asked my mother, who lived there in elegance and ease on thirty-five hundred francs, how one might dress in the most modest style in that dreadful climate without keeping to one's room six days a week. "It's easy at my age, and with my habits," she replied, "but when I was young and your father was hard up, he hit on the idea of dressing me as a boy. My sister did the same, and we went everywhere with our husbands: to the theater—oh, anywhere we wanted. And it halved our bills."

At first I found this idea merely amusing. Then I saw it was the answer. Having been dressed as a boy in my childhood, and having hunted in knee breeches and shirt with Deschartres, such dress was hardly new to me, and I was not shocked to put it on again. At that time, the fashion was perfect for such a disguise: men wore long squarish coats called Petersham greatcoats, which went all the way down to their heels and revealed so little of their figures that my brother had once laughingly said to me, as he was putting on his coat at Nohant, "Handsome, eh? It's the fashion, and it doesn't pinch. The tailor measures the sentry box, and the whole regiment is fitted splendidly!"

So I had a "sentry-box coat" cut for me out of a heavy drab stuff, with matching trousers and waistcoat. With a gray hat and wide woolen tie, I was a perfect little first-year student. I can't convey how much my boots delighted me: I'd have gladly slept in them, as my brother did when he was a lad and had just got his first pair. With those steel-tipped heels I was solid on the sidewalk at last. I dashed back and forth across Paris and felt I was going around the world. My clothes were weatherproof too. I was out and about in all weather, came home at all hours, was in the pits of all the theaters. Nobody heeded me, or suspected my disguise. I wore it well, and its lack of coquetry, and concealment of my figure, warded off suspicion. I was too ill-dressed, and too simple-looking (I'm usually that way, on a cloud, or ready to gape at anything), to draw or hold anyone's attention. Women are not good at disguising themselves, even on stage. They will not sacrifice their wasp waists, their dainty feet, their pretty swaying, their lustrous eyes; yet only by giving up these qualities, especially the lustrous eyes, may they evade detection. There is a way of slipping hither and thither without one head turning your way, and of speaking in low, dull tones which do not shrill like a flute upon such ears as may overhear you. Besides, if you do not want to be noticed *as a man,* you must first get the habit of not being noticed *as a woman.*

I never sat alone in the pit, not because people were any ruder there than elsewhere, but because in those days the clappers, both paid and unpaid, used to provoke each other. There was much shoving on opening night, and I had not strength enough to fight the crowd. I always kept within the phalanx of my Berrichon friends, who did their best to protect me. One evening, however, when we were near a chandelier, it happened that I yawned openly— an innocent, sincere yawn!—and the "Romans," or paid clappers, were ready to do me in. "Street Arab!" they shouted. I realized then how angry and hotheaded I could grow when picked on, and if my friends had not been numerous enough to stare down the claque, I'm sure I'd have got myself thrashed.

Then the Baroness Dudevant came inquiring why I was so long in Paris without my husband. But the affair was smartly disposed of. I told her my husband had no objection.

"But is it true you intend to print books?"

"Yes, Madame."

"Té!" she cried (a Gascon expletive she used habitually, which meant "You don't say!"). "How very droll!"

"Yes, Madame."

"Well and good; but I hope you'll not put the name I bear upon printed covers."

"Oh, never, Madame! No danger of that."

There were no further exchanges. She departed for the South, and I have not seen her since.

The name I was to put upon "printed covers" had scarce concerned me. In any case, I had resolved to remain anonymous. I wrote a draft of a first book, which Jules Sandeau, whom the publisher Delatouche had dubbed Jules Sand, entirely rewrote. This book attracted another publisher, who asked for another novel under the same pen name. I had already written *Indiana* at Nohant, and wanted to offer it under the required pseudonym, but Jules Sandeau modestly refused to acknowledge the paternity of a book with which he'd had nothing to do. This did not suit the publisher at all. An author's name is a strong selling point, and as the pen name was now selling briskly, it must needs be kept. Delatouche was consulted, and he instantly found a solution: Sand would stay, but I would take another surname for myself alone. I picked George without further ado; Greek for "farmer," it seemed synonymous with Berrichon. Jules and George, both personally unknown to the public, would pass as brothers or cousins.

When Solange and I had moved in over the Quai Saint-Michel, I hoped to return to my sedentary habits, but life outside soon grew so tragic that it colored my own existence. The neighborhoods about us were among the first to be seized by the cholera. It stole rapidly toward us and mounted our house floor by floor. It carried off six people, stopping at the door of our garret as if disdaining so meager a prey.

Nobody among the little group of my countrymen that had formed about me yielded to the dreadful panic of those days, which actually seemed to summon the plague, and usually did bring it on. We were all worried for each other, but never for ourselves. Thus, to avoid unnecessary anxiety, we agreed to meet every day, if only for a moment, in the Luxembourg Gardens; when one of us failed to appear, the others ran to his rooms. Not one of us ever had a trace of a symptom. Yet none of us had altered his diet, or taken any special precautions against the epidemic.

But oh, what a horrid sight was that endless convoy passing beneath my window and crossing the Pont Saint-Michel! On some days the great movers' conveyances, now become the hearses of the poor, followed each other without letup; and what frightened me most was not the corpses, piled like sacks pell-mell within, but the absence of any kin behind these tumbrels; it was the drivers whipping up the horses, and quickening the pace with a curse; it was the passers-by, rushing frightened from the hideous cortege; it was the rage of the workingmen, who were convinced that measures had been taken on high to poison them, and who shook their fists at the sky; and when these menacing bands of men had passed, it was the despondent or apathetic expressions that stupefied all faces.

I had considered fleeing for my daughter's sake; but everybody said that travel was more dangerous than salutary, and I, too, told myself that if the breath of the plague should find us before we departed, we might unknowingly carry it to Nohant, which it had not yet reached (and never did).

And besides, amid common dangers for which there is no help, one quickly bears up. My friends and I decided that since the cholera carried off the poor sooner than the rich, we were among the easiest prey, and, consequently, should accept this fact without being overcome by a disaster which surrounded not only us, but also those enraged and despairing working folk, who believed they were the object of some special curse.

Right in the midst of this horrible episode came the saddening incident of the Cloître de Saint-Merry. I was in the Luxembourg Gardens with Solange late in the afternoon. She was playing in the sand while I watched her, my back against the broad base of a statue. I was well aware that some sort of tempest was brewing in Paris, but had hardly thought it would reach my neighborhood so quickly. Sitting there engrossed, I failed to see that all the strollers had hurried out of the park. Then I heard a charge being sounded, and snatching up my daughter, saw that we were alone of our sex in that huge garden, and that a cordon of troops was sweeping across it, from grating to grating. I hurried back toward my garret through the confused crowds, threading the alleys so as not to be knocked down by the streams of curious onlookers, who would gather tightly at some spot, then suddenly panic and rush elsewhere, trampling one another. At every step I met frightened people, crying, "Go back! The troops are firing on the crowd!" But the biggest danger was actually that the shops were being shuttered fast enough to crack the skulls of the passers-by. Solange lost heart and began to wail. By the time we reached the quai, people were fleeing every which way. I went on, certain that the worst thing was to stay in the streets, and ran into our house without stopping to discover what was happening. I was not even scared, for I had not yet seen street warfare, and had never dreamed of what I was about to witness: the madness which seizes the shocked and frightened soldier, and turns him into the most dangerous enemy that innocent onlookers can meet during a riot.

At first I thought only of calming my poor child, who by now was sick with fear. I decided to tell her that what was happening on the quai was a bat hunt—she had seen her father and her uncle Hippolyte so engaged on the terrace at Nohant—and I succeeded in lulling her to sleep to the sound of rifle fire. I propped a mattress from my bed in the window of her room to catch any stray bullets, and spent much of the night on the balcony trying to grasp what was happening in the darkness below.

What happened there is known to all. Seventeen insurgents had seized the guard post by the little bridge of the Hôtel-Dieu. A column of the National Guard surprised them during the night. "Fifteen of these luckless men," writes Louis Blanc in his *Histoire de dix ans*, "were cut to pieces and thrown into the Seine; the other two were trapped in the nearby streets, and their throats slit."

I did not see this horrible scene, shrouded as it was in nocturnal shadows, but I heard the furious clamor and the terrifying death rattles; then a deathly silence descended upon the city, which had fallen asleep from the sheer exhaustion of so much fear.

More remote and indistinct sounds signaled continued resistance at some unknown spot. In the morning it was safe to go out and buy food for the day, though it seemed likely that the events would keep all citizens indoors. To judge by the forces the government had marshaled, they were determined to crush a handful of insurgents who would fight to the death. The latter hoped their desperate heroism might spark a new revolution: perhaps a republic for the people, a monarchy for the Duke of Bordeaux, or an empire for the Duke of Reichstadt. As usual, each faction had plotted the uprising, and each coveted the prize; but when it was clear that that prize was death on the barricades, the factions lay low, while the heroes were martyred in full view of the people of Paris, who were horror-struck by their "victory."

The view from my perch on the morning of June 6 filled me with dread. The populace was forbidden to go out, and troops guarded all the bridges and all the ways into the adjacent streets. From ten in the morning until the "execution" was over, the long prospect of the deserted quais in the bright sunlight resembled a dead city, as if the cholera had indeed carried off the last inhabitant. The sentries guarding the ways out of the area seemed stupefied, phantasmal. Motionless as stone along the parapets, they gave no word or gesture to dispel the bleak semblance of desolation. The only sign of life was the swallows, who skimmed over the water in uneasy haste, as if the unwanted calm frightened them. Hours of cruel silence passed, troubled only by the sharp cries of the swifts about the roofs of Notre-Dame. Then, all at once, the startled birds flew back into the ancient towers; the soldiers shouldered their glinting rifles along the bridges; orders were given in hushed tones. The ranks opened to let in bands of cavalry who met and passed, the returning troops weary and blood-spattered, the fresh ones white with rage. The captive citizenry reappeared at the windows and the rooftops, eager to lose themselves in the scenes of horror about to take place on the far side of the Île de la Cité. The dreadful din had begun. At increasingly regular intervals, the infantry opened a deadly fusillade. Sitting in the doorway to the balcony, and keeping Solange busy in her room so that she could not look out, I counted each assault and the cries that answered it. Then a cannon thundered. I saw the bridge congested with tumbrels returning across the Île de la Cité and leaving a trail of blood, and I assumed that so murderous an insurrection must have many adherents; but these were its dying blows, and I could almost count the victims of each assault. Then silence again; people came down from the rooftops into the streets; the concierges, their faces perfect caricatures of Property in Panic, called to one another triumphantly, "It's done with!"; and the victors, who had done nothing but look on, reappeared in an uproar. The king took a stroll upon the quais. The bourgeoisie fraternized with the hoi polloi at every street corner. The troops were dignified and solemn, having thought for an instant that it was the July Revolution all over again.

For several days, the ways into the Place and the Quai Saint-Michel showed large bloodstains, and the corpses in the morgue, stacked with their heads at the windows like a solid wall of gruesome masonry, oozed a red stream which meandered out under the arches and down nearly to the river. The odor was so fetid, and I was so sickened—as much, I confess, by the poor weary soldiers as by their defiant prisoners—that I could not touch food for a fortnight. Much later I still could not look at meat; it seemed to have that hot, acrid stench of butchery that had greeted me, amid the first tardy gusts of spring, when I awoke on the seventh and the eighth of June.

The next winter was so cold in my garret that I soon realized I could not afford the necessary firewood. Delatouche had left his flat, which was also by the Seine, but only four flights up, with a southern exposure which gave upon some gardens. It was more spacious, was comfortably furnished and contained just what I'd long yearned for—a closed "Prussian" stove of enameled iron. He gave me his lease, and I moved in over the Quai Malaquais. Maurice, whose father had put him in a school in Paris, soon came to greet me there.

But here I am, already at the time of my entry into the literary world! In haste to depict the external circumstances of my life, I've said nothing at all about my first modest efforts in this direction. It's time I spoke of my new acquaintances, and of the hopes that nourished me.

There were three of us Berrichons in Paris—Félix Pyat, Jules Sandeau and myself—all apprentices at letters under the direction of a fourth Berrichon, M. Delatouche. This master should have been—and doubtless wanted to be—the link among us all, and we expected to become one family under Apollo, and he the paterfamilias. But his embittered, sensitive and unhappy character betrayed both these desires and the needs of his heart, which was kind, generous and tender. After setting us one against the other somewhat, he set upon us one after the other.

I have told, in a rather detailed obituary on M. Delatouche, all the good and the bad that was in him. I told the bad without defaulting in my debt of gratitude, or in the warm feelings which I returned him in the years before his death. To show how the bad—that is, his anxiety, unhealthy sensitivity and misanthropy—was both fatal and unwitting, I quoted passages from his letters, where in strong and graceful words he portrayed himself in all his greatness, and in his suffering. I had already written about him during his life with the same respect and affection. I never had cause to reproach him, and would never have known in what I had displeased him, had I not observed, during his final and rapid decline, that he was a hopeless hypochondriac.

Delatouche had just bought *Le Figaro*,* and he wrote each issue virtually by himself beside the fire, chatting the while with his editors and many callers. These callers—some charming, some ludicrous—were the unsuspecting butt of us dependable "devils." Entrenched in the alcoves of his apartment, we never missed a word, and did not hesitate to sally forth.

I had a little table and a little rug by the fireplace, but I was

---

* *Le Figaro* was still a skimpy newspaper with very few subscribers.

none too steady at my work, about which I really knew nothing. Delatouche had more or less to collar me and dump me into my chair; he would toss me a subject and give me a slip of paper on which I was to get it down. I would scribble ten pages—not one word to the point—and throw them on the fire. The others had wit, verve, facility; they talked and laughed; Delatouche sparkled with sarcasm. I listened very amused, but wrote nothing good; and at the month's end got twelve and a half francs, fifteen at the most, for my part in the collaboration; and even that was too much!

With us Delatouche became young again, even playing baby tricks. I remember a dinner we gave him at Pinson's, and a fantastical moonlit walk through the Latin Quarter. We were trailed by a cab he had hailed and which he kept till midnight, unable to get rid of our joyous, foolish company. He climbed into the cab twenty times, and each time we coaxed him out. We were going nowhere, just to show him it was the most wonderful way to walk. And he enjoyed it too, for he gave in with little resistance each time. The cabman, victim of our teasing, sat like Patience on a monument. I remember that when we arrived, who knows how or why, at Mount Sainte-Geneviève, we began to file in and out of the cab—it was going very slowly in the empty street, doors open, folding steps down—singing something impish in a mournful tone: I don't remember why it seemed so funny, or why Delatouche was laughing so merrily, but I think it was with the sheer joy of being silly for once in his life. Pyat insisted that he, Pyat, had a goal, which was to serenade all the greengrocers in the neighborhood; and he went from shop to shop singing at the top of his voice, "A greengrocer is a rose."

It was the only time I ever saw Delatouche in high spirits, for his wit was so splenetic that even in playful moods he often seemed mortally sad. "How happy they are!" he said, slipping his arm about me as the others romped ahead. "They've put a little wine in their water, and they're drunk. But what heady wine is youth! And how wonderfully one laughs when one doesn't need anything to laugh *at!* Oh, if only one could enjoy oneself so two days running! But as soon as one knows what or whom one is laughing at, one doesn't laugh anymore—no, one wants to cry."

Delatouche's great sorrow was to grow old. There was no help for it; he used to repeat, "One is never fifty, only twice twenty-five." Despite this mental revolt, he seemed even older than he was. Already ill, and aggravating his illness by the impatience with which he bore it, he was often touchy in the morning, and I quietly made myself scarce. Then he would call me over or come and humor me, never apologizing, but atoning for having hurt me with a thousand gracious favors and paternal pats.

Later, when I tried to find out why he suddenly soured on me, I was told that he had been in love with me, and secretly jealous, and wounded by my not guessing his secret. Not so. At first I was wary of him; M. Duris-Dufresne, airing his own prejudices, had put me on guard against him. I was told that I should have seen through him (not a coquette, I've often failed to discern men's secrets in time). But I was certainly able to tell whether he accepted my trust without ulterior motives, and I soon observed that "the governor's" jealousy (we called him "the governor") was wholly intellectual, and aimed at anyone, of whatever age or sex, who came his way.

He was a friend, but more a teacher, and a temperamentally jealous one at that, like old Porpora, whom I depicted in one of my novels. When he had nurtured someone's mind or developed his talent, he refused to allow anyone else to inspire, help or even dare approach his protégé.

One of my friends who knew Balzac somewhat had introduced me to him, not as some back-country muse, but as a fine fellow from the provinces who marveled at his own talent. This was the truth. Although Balzac had not yet produced his masterpieces, I was keenly struck by his new and original manner, and I already considered him a master worth studying. Balzac had not charmed me as Delatouche had, but he seemed just as witty, and his character more forthright and balanced. Everyone knows how he brimmed over with self-satisfaction, a satisfaction so well founded that one gladly forgave him for it; and how he liked to talk about his books, to tell them in advance, to invent them while chatting, and to read them in drafts and galleys. Simple and good-natured as a child, he asked advice of children and ignored the answer, or took it up only to combat it with stubborn superiority. He never taught; he talked of himself, himself alone. Only once did he forget about himself, to speak to us of Rabelais, whom I had not yet read. He was so marvelous, so breath-taking, so lucid, that we agreed, on leaving

212

him, that he would have just the future he dreamed of; he knew too well what was *not* himself not to make of himself a great individual.

He was then living in the Rue de Cassini, in a cheerful little mezzanine apartment beside the Observatoire. One fine morning, having sold his *Peau de chagrin* at a good price, he despised his lodgings and wanted to leave them; but on second thought he was content to change his poet's rooms into a suite of boudoirs fit for a marquise. One day he invited us to take some ices within these walls, now hung with silk and fringed with lace. I laughed and laughed; it did not occur to me that he took his need for ostentation seriously, or that it was more than a passing fancy. I was wrong; such whims became the tyrants of his life, and for them he often sacrificed the most basic comforts. Thenceforth he lived like that, lacking everything in the midst of his extravagance, and forgoing soup and coffee rather than silver and china.

Soon reduced to the most incredible shifts and devices that he might not part with the trinkets that delighted his eye, this fantasist lived by his wits in the palace of faerie; a stubborn man, he would put up with anything in order that his life might keep something of his dream.

Childish, powerful, always craving some gewgaw, never jealous of another's glory, sincere even to modesty, boastful even to braggadocio, confident in himself and confiding in others, effusive, kindhearted and quite mad—though with an inner sanctuary of reason wherein he retired to reign over his work—cynical in chastity, drunk on water, intemperate of work and sober in all other passions, romantic and positivistic to equal excess, credulous and doubting, full of contrasts and mysteries—such was the young Balzac, already a puzzle to those who tired of his too constant study of himself, which did not seem as interesting to all as, in reality, it was.

Indeed, in those days many otherwise competent judges of literature denied Balzac's genius, or at least did not believe that his career would unfold with the power that it did. Delatouche was one of the most backward of these judges. He spoke of Balzac in tones of frightening hostility. Balzac had been his disciple, and their recent breakup, whose cause was to remain a mystery to Balzac, had left an open sore in Delatouche. Delatouche could not provide one solid reason for his resentment, and often Balzac said to me, "Watch out! You'll see—one fine morning, without suspecting anything, without knowing why, you'll discover he's your mortal enemy."

I thought Delatouche was wrong to denigrate Balzac, who spoke of him gently, and with regret; but Balzac, too, was wrong to believe they had become irreconcilable enemies. He could have won Delatouche back, with time.

But not just then. I kept trying to tell Delatouche how to bring about their reconciliation. The first time he flew out of his skin. "Then you've seen him!" he cried. "You still see him! That's the last straw!" I was afraid he'd throw me out the window. He calmed down, went off in a sulk, came back, and finally granted that I could "have my Balzac" since my friendship for Balzac clearly did not diminish the sympathy he craved for himself. But each time I initiated or accepted a literary attachment, Delatouche threw a tantrum. Anyone he had not introduced to me he took for an enemy, even if that person was indifferent to me.

I rarely mentioned my literary projects to Balzac. He scarcely acknowledged them, and did not dream of seeing for himself if I had talent. I did not ask his advice; he would have candidly told me—as much out of modesty as out of egoism—that he kept it for himself. For he had a way of being modest beneath a shell of presumption—I observed this later, with pleasant surprise—and as for his egoism, he could also be devoted and generous.

His society was very agreeable, though fatiguing for me, who did not know how to answer cleverly enough to vary the subject; but his soul was serene, and I never saw him sulk. With his fat belly, he would climb to the top of the house on the Quai Saint-Michel and arrive panting, laughing, and bursting with tales before he could catch his breath. He would take up the scribblings on my table to see what they were; but then, still absorbed in the book he was writing, he would begin to recount it, and I found these narrations more instructive than all the objections which Delatouche, that heartbreaking niggler, offered against my inventions.

One evening when we had dined at Balzac's after a strange fashion—I think it was on boiled beef, a melon and iced champagne—he put on a brand-new dressing gown and showed it off to us with a little girl's joy. He wanted to go out so costumed, a candlestick in hand, to guide us as far as the grating around the Palais du Luxembourg. It was late, the spot was deserted, and I observed to him that he would get himself murdered going home. "Humbug," he replied. "If I meet with thieves, they'll take me for a madman, and they will fear me; or for a prince, and they will respect me." And so he accompanied us, carrying his lighted candle in a pretty candelabrum of chased silver gilt, and talking of the four Arabian horses that he did not own, would soon own, never did own and, for a while, firmly believed himself to own. He'd have taken us to the far corner of Paris if we'd let him.

I've said that Delatouche drove one to despair. But he was also *in* despair, for himself, and he worked so hard on everything he undertook that he became disgusted with it. Sometimes he would allow himself to tell the plots of his novels in advance, more discreetly and to fewer people than Balzac, but with even greater glibness if he saw that they were listening. It was unwise to shift a chair, to stir the fire or to sneeze at such moments; he would break off at once and inquire, with almond-oil politeness, if you had a cold, or pins and needles in your leg; then, feigning to have forgotten the plot of his novel, he would want ever so much begging before pretending to remember it. Balzac had a thousand times his talent for writing, but not the thousandth part of his gift of gab. The stories that Delatouche told so marvelously seemed truly marvelous, whereas what Balzac told, in his often impossible way, usually represented merely impossible projects. But when Delatouche's work was published, one searched in vain for the charm of what one had heard, and one had just the opposite surprise in reading Balzac. Balzac knew that he set forth his ideas poorly— not without fire or wit, but without order or clarity. So he preferred to read, with manuscript in hand; whereas Delatouche, who did a hundred novels without ever writing them, almost never had anything to read—at best a few pages which did not realize his project and which visibly pained him. He had no facility; consequently he had a horror of it, and showered the most buffoonish abuse and the most poisonous comparisons upon the prolific Balzac (not to mention Sir Walter Scott, whom he secretly adored).

I always thought that Delatouche threw away too much real talent in talk. Balzac threw away only his silliness. Talk was his escape valve; he kept his deep wisdom for his work. Delatouche exhausted his fund in excellent performances; for though he, too, was rich in wisdom, he could ill spare such generosity.

And then, his health had fatally paralyzed his wings just as he was spreading them. He wrote some lines of good poetry, fluent yet solid, but mingled with others which were strained and pretty empty; some very remarkable and original novels, but also weak and slipshod ones; and some ingenious and trenchant articles, and others so personal that they were incomprehensible and so without interest for the public. That his elite intelligence could fly both so high and so low must be explained by the cruel ebb and flow of his illness.

Delatouche also had the misfortune to be too interested in what other people were doing. At that time he read everything. As a publisher he received whatever came out, but pretended not to look at the new books and merely passed them to whoever of his editors was at hand. "Here's some medicine for you," he'd say. "You're young, it won't kill you. Say what you want about it; I've no interest in it myself." But when the review was handed in, he would criticize the critique with such precision that we knew he had downed the medicine before anyone, and had even savored its tempting, acrid taste.

I'd have been a fool not to listen to whatever Delatouche told me. But his perpetual analysis of everything, his dissection of others and himself, and all his telling criticism—which resulted only in self-negation and the negation of others—singularly saddened my soul. The baby harness was beginning to pinch. I was learning all about what I shouldn't do, but nothing about what I should do, and I was losing my self-confidence.

I was and am grateful that Delatouche made me put off certain projects; it was a great favor, for in those days writers wrote the oddest things. The eccentricities of the young Victor Hugo had excited the younger generation, who were bored with the threadbare ideas of the Restoration. Chateaubriand was no longer sufficiently romantic, and even the new master, Hugo, was barely romantic enough for the fierce appetites he had whetted. The brats of his own school (whom he would never have accepted as disciples, and they knew it well) wanted to "sink" him by outdoing him. They racked their brains for absurd titles and disgusting subjects, and soon this hunt for the most preposterous sign of individuality swept up even the talented, who, attired in outlandish finery, rushed into the fray.

Since the teachers themselves had set such a bad example, I was sorely tempted to do as the other pupils were doing, and I searched for far-fetched subjects which I never could have rendered. Among the critics of the day who resisted this upheaval, Delatouche showed discernment and taste in defending what was genuinely good and beautiful both in his and in his adversaries' school. With his jests and warnings he kept me on the straight and narrow path. But at the same time he threw me into fresh quandaries. "Avoid imitation like the plague," he would say. "Use your own stores: read in your life, in your heart, and tell your impressions." Once he said out of the blue: "Your feelings are too absolute, your personality too isolated; you don't know society and you don't know people. You haven't lived and thought like everyone else. Your head is empty." I thought he was right, and I went back to Nohant resolved to make tea boxes and lacquered snuffboxes.

At last I began *Indiana,* without a plan, without a hope, without any preliminary sketch. I barred all precepts and examples from my mind, and gave up rummaging in other people's literary manners for a theme, and in my own story for a protagonist. Of course, some readers insist that Indiana was I, and her story my own, but that is simply not so. I have presented many types of women, but I have never appeared upon my own stage in feminine garb. I am too romantic to have discerned a novel's heroine in my looking glass. I never thought I was lovely, lovable or logical enough in my character, taken as a whole, or in my actions, to be poetical or interesting. Oh, I could have powdered my nose, and dramatized my life, but to no avail, I'm sure: I'd never have brought it off. My self, met face to face, would always have chilled me.

Far be it from me to say that an artist has not the right to portray himself or to tell his life story. Let him crown himself before the multitudes with the blooms of the Muse—if only he be clever enough not to be readily recognized beneath these adornments, or beautiful enough not to look silly. But as for me, I was of too motley stuff to suit any such idealization. Had I wished to show my serious side, I'd have written about one who till then had resembled the monk Alexis (in my not very entertaining *Spiridion)* more than Indiana, the passionate Creole. And if I'd wanted to show my other side, my need for gaiety, foolery, clowning, I'd have invented a type so inauthentic that I could never have found words for her, nor any sensible behavior.

I hadn't a shred of a theory when I started to write, and I don't think I've ever had one when inspiration made me take up my pen. For all that, my instincts have led me to the theory I'm about to set forth, and which I've generally followed unconsciously. Even as I write, this theory is still being discussed.

According to it, the novel is a work of poetry as much as analysis. Authentic, even real, characters and situations are required, ranged about a figure who must exemplify the chief feeling or idea of the book. This figure usually represents passionate love, for almost all novels are love stories. This love must be idealized, and the author should not fear to give it all the energies to which he himself aspires, and all the pain he has witnessed or felt. But this love must never be debased by fortuitous events; it must triumph or die, and the author should not fear to give it exceptional importance, unusual power, and charms or sufferings beyond the common run of human things, and even beyond the bounds of probability.

In sum, the idealization of feeling is the true subject. The storyteller's art consists in setting this subject against a background of reality so vivid that it takes on the color of truth.

Is this theory valid? I think so; but it is not and should not be taken as the only one. Balzac, in time, caused me to understand, by the truth and force of his ideas, that one can sacrifice idealization of subject to truth of scene—to the criticism of society and even of mankind.

Balzac summed this up when he said to me:

"You seek man as he should be; I take him as he is. Believe me, we are both right. Our paths meet in the end. I love exceptional people too; I *am* one. Besides, I need them—to set off my vulgar people—and I never sacrifice them needlessly. But these vulgar people interest me more than they do you. I magnify and idealize them in reverse, in their ugliness or folly. I give their deformities frightening or grotesque proportions. That you could never do, and you do well not to gaze too closely on the beings who give you nightmares. Idealize only toward the lovely and the beautiful: that is woman's work."

Twelve

I WANTED to see Italy, which like all artists I thirsted for, and which quenched my thirst, but not as I'd expected. I soon tired of pictures and monuments. The cold gave me a fever, then the heat prostrated me, and the beautiful sky ended by boring me. But I found a mellow solitude in a corner of Venice, and it would have kept me there for a long time if I'd had my children with me. Let no one worry, I shall not reproduce any descriptions from *Lettres d'un voyageur* or from the novels I've set in Venice. I mean merely to offer a few details from my own life.

On the steamboat from Lyons to Avignon I met one of our most remarkable writers, Beyle, whose penname was Stendhal. He was French consul at Civitavecchia and was returning to his post after a short stay in Paris. His mind shone, and his conversation was not unlike that of Delatouche, with less delicacy and grace but more depth. At first glance he seemed the same man, fat, but fine-boned under a mask of suet. But Delatouche was sometimes rendered beautiful by a sudden melancholy, whereas Beyle wore a satirical, scoffing expression no matter when you looked at him. I chatted with him part of the way, and found him most amiable. He mocked my illusions about Italy, assuring me that I'd soon have enough of it, and that artists "in search of the sublime" in that land were just idle tourists. I was not convinced, for I saw that he had tired of his exile and was returning to Italy without enthusiasm. He made great fun of the typical Italian, whom he found unbearable, and toward whom he was most unfair. He predicted that I'd suffer in a way I never did—that I'd be deprived of pleasant conversation, and of what, as he thought, composed the intellectual life: books, newspapers, whatever is the talk of the town. I saw at once how much Italy must have lacked for a mind so original, charming and affected, and so far from friends who could appreciate or excite it. He was particularly affected in his sham disdain for vanity, and sought to find in everybody some pretension on which to train his galling wit. But I don't think he was nasty: he was trying too hard to seem so.

All that he predicted would prove boring and intellectually empty in Italy nourished me instead of frightening me; for I was going there, as on all my trips, to flee the close inquiring wit he thought I hungered for.

We dined with some other choice travelers in a bad village inn, the steamboat pilot not wanting to go under the Saint-Esprit bridge before daylight. There Stendhal became madly gay, drank somewhat, and dancing around the table in his big fur-trimmed boots, became somewhat grotesque and not a bit pretty.

At Avignon he took us to see the cathedral in its fine site. There, in a corner, an old Christ in painted wood, life-size and truly hideous, furnished him the matter of the most incredible ranting. He had a horror of those repellent images whose barbaric ugliness and shameless nudity were cherished, as he claimed, by the people of the South. He would readily have thrashed this statue.

Frankly, I didn't mind when Beyle took the Genoa road. He feared the sea, and my aim was to go quickly to Rome. So we separated after several days of playful acquaintanceship; but as the depths of his mind betrayed what he really fancied, which was lewdness or the dream of it, I confess that I'd had enough of him, and that if he had gone by water, I might have gone by mountain. For the rest, he was a superior man, more shrewd and ingenious than just in his judgments; of original talent, writing poorly but telling his tales so as to create an impression and excite his readers.

Venice was indeed the city of my dreams, and all that I had already visioned of her still colored her image in my eyes, both mornings and evenings, upon balmy days and in her darkly mirrored storms. I loved this city for itself, and it is the only one in the world that I can so love, for town life has always produced upon me the effect of a prison which I suffer only on my fellow prisoners' account. But in Venice one could live for a long time; and I understand why, in her hour of splendor and liberty, her children almost personified her in their love, and cherished her not as a thing but as a living being.

Presently I took a fever and then a bad illness with dreadful headaches which I had not previously known, and which have since lodged in my brain in the form of frequent and often unbearable migraines. I expected to remain only a few days in that city, but unexpected events detained me there.

Alfred de Musset was much more gravely affected than I by the air of Venice, which strikes down many foreigners, a fact of which too few are aware.* He became seriously ill; a typhoid fever put him within an inch of his life. It was not only the respect due to a noble genius which inspired me with a great solicitude and which gave me—and I so sick myself—unexpected energy; it was also his

* Géraldy, the singer, was in Venice at the same period, and took, at the same time as Alfred de Musset, a contagion no less serious. As for Léopold Robert, who had settled there and who blew out his brains shortly after my departure, I doubt not that the air of Venice, too exciting for certain constitutions, greatly contributed to the tragic spleen that seized him. For some time I lived opposite the house he occupied, and saw him row by in a boat every day. In a blouse of black velvet and hat of the same, he reminded me of some Renaissance painter. His face was pale and sad, his voice harsh and shrill. I wanted very much to see his picture of the *Fishers of Chioggia*, which was talked about as if it were a mysterious wonder, for he had hidden it away with a sort of strange, angry jealousy. I could have taken advantage of his boat rowings, whose hours I had come to know, and stolen into his studio; but I was told that if he were to learn of the disloyalty of his hostess it would drive him mad. I was wary of doing anything to put him out of temper; and thus inquiring of certain persons who saw him at all hours, I learned that he was already considered a lunatic of the saddest sort.

charm and the moral sufferings continually inflicted upon his poet's constitution. I spent seventeen days at his bedside without taking more than one hour of rest out of twenty-four. His convalescence lasted about as many days, and I recall that directly after his departure my fatigue produced a singular effect upon me. I had accompanied him late in the morning as far as Mestre in a gondola, and I came home through the little canals in the heart of the city. These narrow canals, which serve as streets, are crossed by little one-arch footbridges. I was so blear-eyed after nights of vigil that I saw everything upside down, particularly this arcade of bridges, which rose up before me like a series of inverted arches.

But spring came, the northern Italian spring, which is perhaps the loveliest in the world. Long wanderings in the Tyrolian Alps, and later in the Venetian archipelago with its sprinkling of charming islets, restored me and enabled me to write. And indeed I had to; I'd gone through my slender means, and had not the price of a ticket to Paris. I took small, more than modest rooms in the center of town. And there, alone in the afternoons, going out only in the evenings to take the air, and working at night to the song of the tame nightingales that people all the balconies of Venice, I wrote *André, Jacques, Matéa,* and the first *Lettres d'un voyageur.*

Since my marriage I'd had no immediate subjects of discord with my mother, but her agitated character had caused me constant suffering. She came to Nohant and there indulged in unwitting unfairness and unwarranted sharpness with the most innocent persons. Yet when I called her to account for this, I gained a certain sway over her. Besides, I still loved her with a passion which all my complaints could never destroy. My renown had produced in her the strangest pendulation between joy and rage. She began by reading malicious reviews with their false hints about my morals. Convinced that I deserved them all, she showered me with reproaches, and sent or brought me scrapbooks of abusive articles which otherwise would never have reached my door. I would ask her if she'd read the book in question but she'd never read what she damned. Protesting that she'd never open it, she'd begin to read it, fall blindly in love with it as only a mother can, and declare the thing sublime and the reviews infamous; and so it went with each new book.

And so it went with everything. Whatever trip or visit I made, whomever she met at my house, whatever hat or shoes I was wearing, occasioned a harassment which would have degenerated into a serious quarrel had I not promised that I would change my plans, acquaintances and clothes to suit her. I had nothing to lose since she forgot everything the next day. But I needed endless patience to brave at each interview an unpredictable gust. Patience I had; but I was mortally saddened never to meet with her charming wit and tender impulses except among perpetual storms.

She lived for several years in a house, 6 Boulevard Poissonière, which has been torn down and replaced by the railwayman's house for the bridge. She almost always lived alone, unable to keep a servant longer than a week. She tidied her little apartment herself, cleaned it with painstaking care, and filled it with flowers. It faced due south, bright with skylight or sunlight, and she kept her windows open to the summer heat, the dust, the din of the boulevard, and could not get enough of Paris into her room. "I'm Parisian to the marrow," she would say. "Everything in Paris which depresses others, I thrive on. I'm never too hot or cold here. I prefer the dusty trees in the boulevard, and the black gutters that water them, to all your frightening forests and your rivers, where I'd likely drown. I don't care for gardens anymore; they remind me of cemeteries. The silence of the country scares and bores me. Paris always feels like a celebration, and this bustle which I find so cheering draws me out of myself. No one knows better than you that the day I start thinking, I'll die." Poor mother, she was to spend her last days deep in thought!

Though several of my friends, witnesses to her rages or unkindnesses toward me, reproached me for being too soft-hearted toward her, I could not overcome a keen excitement every time I visited her. Sometimes, finding myself by chance under her window, I'd discover I was dying to see her; I'd stop, afraid of the tirade which perhaps awaited me; but almost always I gave in. Whenever I'd held out and not seen her for a week, I'd rush to her full of secret impatience. I realized the power of this instinct in the distress I felt each time I arrived before the door to her house. It was a little iron door with a grating which opened upon a descending stair. At the bottom lived a merchant of plumbing fixtures, who fulfilled, I believe, the duties of a concierge, for a voice always cried to me out of the shop, "Not in!" or "In, go on up!" I would go through a little courtyard, climb a flight of stairs, go down a passage, and climb three flights more. It gave me time to think, and always in the dark passage I would ask myself: "Well, what look awaits me up there today? Good, bad? Smiling, stricken? What excuse will she find to rail at me?"

But then I'd recall the warm welcomes she gave me when she was in a good mood. What cries of joy, what shining looks, what motherly kisses! Those cries, those looks, those kisses, were surely worth the risk of two hours of bitterness. Then I burned to see her, the stairs became unbearable, I raced up; I arrived more excited than breathless, and my heart almost burst as I rang. I listened through the door and already knew my fate, for when she was in good humor she recognized my ring and I heard her exclaim as she pulled the latch, "Ah, it's my Aurore!" But when she was in her black moods she did not recognize my noise, or pretended not to, and called, "Who is it?"

That "Who is it?" fell like a stone upon my breast, and often a while elapsed before she voiced her complaint or calmed down. When I'd drawn a smile from her at last, or when Pierret arrived and took my side, her reproaches turned to gaiety, and I took her out to a restaurant and to the theater. Such an evening she called a "pleasure party," and she enjoyed herself as she had in her youth. And she was so charming then that all the rest was forgotten.

But on certain days we could not see eye to eye. This always happened just when her welcome had been warmest, when my ring had elicited her tenderest tones. Then she would be seized with a need to keep me there and torment me, and seeing the storm gather, I would slip away, flustered or drained, and hurry down the stairs as impatiently as I had climbed them.

To give some idea of her strange accusations, it will be enough for me to relate a characteristic one, which proves how little her heart was engaged in the vagaries of her imagination.

I was wearing a bracelet of Maurice's hair—blond, silky, with delicate highlights, and of a hue and fineness that only a little child's can have. Alibaud had just been executed, and my mother had heard that he'd had long hair. I've never seen Alibaud; I've heard he was swarthy; but wouldn't you know that my mother, in a tizzy over this drama, fancied that the bracelet was woven of his hair! "And what clinches it," she said, "is that your chum Charles Ledru was that murderer's defense counsel." In those days I wouldn't have recognized Charles Ledru had I passed him in the street; but there was no way to dissuade her. She demanded that I throw the dear bracelet on the fire; it was all the golden fleece of Maurice's babyhood, and she'd seen it on my arm ten times without thinking anything of it. I had to run out to escape her clutching at my wrist. Often I ran out laughing; but while I was laughing, I felt great tears roll down my cheeks. I could never get used to seeing her angry and unhappy just when I was about to pour out my heart to her—a heart often aching with some secret bitterness, which she probably would not have understood, but which one hour of her love would have driven away.

The first letter I wrote upon resolving to oppose my husband in court was to her. The affection she returned me was spontaneous, total, unwavering. Whenever I came to Paris during this contest she was all I might have hoped for. Thus almost two years went by during which my mother once again became for me what she'd been in my childhood. Instead she began to plague Maurice, whom she wanted to govern in her own way, and who resisted her rather more than I'd have wished. But she adored him all the same, and I allowed her to indulge in this mischief just to be sure she wasn't ill. Sometimes I'd say to Pierret: "My mother's adorable now, but she seems less lively, less gay. Are you sure she's not ailing?"

"Ailing? Not 'er, she's ridin' 'igh. She's finally got through the age when they feel the great crisis, and now she's like she was when she was young—just as lovable, and almost as lovely."

And it was true. When she had preened a bit, and she dressed bewitchingly, heads still turned in the boulevards, uncertain of her age and struck by her perfect features.

When I came up to Paris in late July 1837, brought by the terrible tiding of her approaching end, the latest bulletins had yet given me great hope. I dashed to her house and leaped down the little stair off the boulevard; but here I collided with the merchant of plumbing fixtures.

"Not in," he said. "Don't you know, Madame Dupin's never in anymore." I thought it was his way of announcing her death, and her open window, which I had taken as a good omen, returned to my mind as the emblem of an eternal departure. "No, it's not that," he said. "She's no worse than she was. She only wanted attendance in a nursing home, away from the noise, and with a garden. I thought Monsieur Pierret had written you."

Pierret's letter hadn't reached me. I ran to the nursing home, expecting to find my mother convalescing, since she'd apparently been keen to enjoy a garden.

I found her in a horrid, stuffy cubicle, lying on a mean little bed and so changed that I hardly recognized her. She was a hundred years old. She threw her arms about my neck, and said, "Ah, I am saved! You have brought me life!" My sister, who was at her bedside, explained to me in a low voice that the choice of this dreadful domicile was the invalid's whim and not a necessity. Our poor mother, imagining in her feverish hours that she was surrounded by thieves, had hid a bag of money under her pillow, and refused to take a better room for fear of revealing her means to these imaginary bandits.

I had to play along with her fantasy for a while; but gradually I wore it away. The nursing home was pleasant and spacious. I rented the best suite on the garden side, and she consented to be moved thither the next day. I called in old Dr. Gaubert, whose gentle and understanding face pleased her, and who persuaded her to follow his instructions. But afterward he led me out into the garden and said, "Don't fool yourself, she cannot recover. The liver is dreadfully swollen. But the worst is over, and she will die painlessly. All you can do is to retard the fatal moment by caring for her soul. As for bodily care, do whatever she asks. She hasn't the strength to request anything that could really harm her. My part is to prescribe insignificant remedies, and to look as if they'll work. She's impressionable as a baby. Keep her mind on the hope of a rapid recovery. Let her go gently, without knowing that she is." And he added with his characteristic serenity (for he was fast sinking himself, and knew it well, though he religiously hid it from his friends): "To die is not so terrible a thing."

I passed the word to my sister, and thereafter we had but one thought: to distract our invalid and to allay her suspicions. She wanted to get up and go out. "That is dangerous," said Gaubert. "She may die in your arms; but to keep her body in a state of dullness that her mind cannot accept is worse still. Go ahead. Do what she asks."

We dressed our mother and bore her into a hackney coach. She wanted to go to the Champs Élysées. There for an instant she was revivified by the stream of life about her. "How beautiful it all is," she said, "these noisy carriages, these dashing horses, these elegant women, this sun, this golden dust! One cannot die here. No! In Paris one does not die!" Her eyes sparkled and her voice rang. But as we drew near the Arc de Triomphe she went pale as death and said, "I can't make it. I've had enough." We were horrified; she seemed about to breathe her last. I signaled for the carriage to stop, and the invalid revived. "Let's go back," she said. "Someday soon we'll come out here again. Oh, we'll drive all the way to the Bois!"

She went out a few more times. She was growing visibly weaker, but the fear of death vanished. The nights were bad, troubled by fever and delirium, but in the daytime she seemed reborn. She became ravenous; my sister was troubled by her odd requests for food and scolded me for bringing her whatever she asked for, but I scolded my sister back for crossing her so much, and indeed, she fetched a sigh of relief when she saw our mother, now surrounded by fruits and tidbits, brighten at the sight of them, and touch them, and say, "I'll eat something in a moment." She never did. She had tasted them with her eyes.

We brought her down into the garden, and there, in an easychair in the sunshine, she fell into reverie, and then into deep meditation. She waited till she and I were alone to tell me what she was thinking. "Your sister is religious," she said, "but I have lost all religion since I realized I was about to die. I can't bear to see a priest's face, do you hear? If I must go, I want smiles about me. After all, why should I be afraid to stand before my Maker? I've always loved Him." And she added with simple vehemence, "He can blame me for whatever He wants, but I defy Him to say I haven't loved Him!"

The destiny which pursued me did not allow me to console my dying mother without struggles and distractions. My brother, who was acting in the strangest and most contradictory fashion, wrote me a note: "I am advising you, without your husband's knowledge, that he is about to leave for Nohant to carry off Maurice. Don't let on; it would put me in his bad books. But I think it's my duty to warn you of his scheme. You must decide if your son is not too weak with rheumatic fever to go back to school."

Indeed, Maurice was in no condition to return to school, and I feared the effect upon his jittery nerves of a painful surprise and a sharp quarrel with his father. But I could not leave my mother. One of my friends went with the post chaise to Ars, and took Maurice to Fontainebleau, whither I went, under a false name, and procured him accommodations at an inn. The friend was kind enough to stay with him while I returned to my sick mother.

I arrived at the nursing home at seven in the morning. I had traveled by night to save time. I saw that her window was open, and recalling the window on the boulevard, I sensed that all was over. Two days earlier, while I was embracing her my mother had said, "I feel very well now, and I have the pleasantest thoughts I've ever had. I've started to like the country, though I never could bear it before. The feeling just came over me while I was coloring a chromo. It was a pretty Swiss view, with trees and mountains, cottages, cows and waterfalls. That picture keeps coming back to me, and I see it prettier than it was, prettier than nature itself. When I close my eyes, I see landscapes you couldn't imagine, that even you couldn't describe . . . too lovely, too grand! And it gets better every minute. I must go back to Nohant and visit the caves and waterfalls in the little wood. You have won Nohant back now; I'd be happy there. You're leaving in a fortnight, aren't you? Good, you'll take me with you."

It was fiercely hot that day. Dr. Gaubert had told my sister and me to dissuade her from going out driving unless it rained. So when the heat only redoubled its fury, I pretended to go hail a hansom and returned saying it was impossible to find an empty one.

"Oh, I don't care," she said. "I feel so well I've no desire to stir. Run off to Maurice, dear. When you return I'm sure you'll find me cured."

The next day she was perfectly calm. At five in the afternoon she said to my sister, "Dress my hair. I want my hair done nicely." When it was done she looked in the mirror and smiled. Her hand dropped the mirror, and her soul flew out of her. Gaubert wrote me at once, but I suppose I crossed the post wagon on the road. I arrived to find her "cured" indeed: cured of the cruel task and the awful weariness of living in this world.

Pierret did not weep. Like Deschartres at my grandmother's deathbed, he seemed not to understand that he was to be parted forever from the object of his love. He followed her bier to the cemetery the next day and returned laughing heartily about something or other.

Poor Pierret! He never got over her death. He went back to the White Horse, to his pipe and beer. He was as gay, as gruff, as scatterbrained and noisy as ever. The next year he visited me at Nohant. On the surface he was still the same Pierret, but all at once he said, "Come, let's talk about your mother! Do you remember . . . ?" And he began to reminisce about her ways, her foibles, and all the outbursts of which he had been the willing victim; and he recalled her sayings, he recalled the inflections of her voice, and he laughed with all his heart; and then upon a joke he took up his hat and went out. I followed after him, for I saw that he was trembling; and I found him sobbing in a corner of the garden.

There is another soul, no less pure in its essence, no less troubled when in this world, whom I meet with equal calm in my conversations with the dead, and in my anticipation of that better world wherein we shall surely know one another in the rays of a diviner light.

I speak of Frederic Chopin, guest of the last eight years of my seclusion at Nohant under the Monarchy.

In 1838, as soon as I had won custody of Maurice, I decided to find him a winter milder than our own, that I might preserve him from a return of the rheumatic pains of the previous year. I wished at the same time to find a tranquil spot where I could make him study somewhat, and his sister with him, and where I myself could do a bit of work.

As I was preparing for my departure, Chopin, whom I saw every day, and whose genius and character I dearly loved, said several times that if he were going instead of Maurice, he would soon be cured himself. I believed him, and I was wrong. I did not take him in Maurice's stead, but at Maurice's side. His friends had long been urging him to spend some time in the south of Europe; they thought him consumptive. Gaubert examined him and assured me he was not. "But you will save him," he said, "if you give him fresh air, daily walks and plenty of rest." The others, well aware that Chopin would never leave the social life of Paris unless someone whom he loved and who was devoted to him dragged him away, warmly urged me not to refuse his unhoped-for wish.

Events were to prove that I was wrong to yield to their hopes and to my own solicitude. It was hard enough for me to go abroad with two children, the one already ill, the other bursting with health and wild spirits, without fretting my heart and playing doctor to a third.

But Chopin was enjoying a moment of good health which set everyone at ease. Except for Grzymala, who was doubtful, we all had high hopes. Still I prayed Chopin to ponder his moral strength, since for several years he had never thought without dread of leaving Paris, his doctor, his relations, his apartment, his piano. He was a creature of habit, and the slightest change was a terrible thing in his life.

I left with my children, telling him that I would go to Perpignan, and that if he did not arrive there within a few days, I would cross into Spain. I had chosen Majorca on the word of people who thought they knew the island's climate and comforts, but who knew nothing of them at all.

Our friend Mendizabal, a man as noble as he is renowned, was bound for Madrid, and offered to accompany Chopin as far as the frontier, should he decide to realize his dream of traveling.

I have little to say about Majorca, having written a long volume about this journey. I have related my anguish for the sick man whom I was escorting. As soon as winter arrived—and it announced itself suddenly with torrential rains—Chopin showed, with equal suddenness, all the symptoms of a pulmonary congestion. I wonder what would have become of me had the rheumatic pains seized Maurice; there was no doctor we trusted, and the simplest physic was unobtainable. Even the sugar was bad and often made one sick.

Maurice, thank heaven, braving wind and rain from dawn to dusk, recovered fully. Neither Solange nor I feared the showers and the flooded roads. We had found decent and very picturesque lodgings in an abandoned and partially ruined charterhouse. I gave the children their lessons in the mornings; they played for the rest of the day while I worked; in the evenings we would run together through the moonlit cloisters, or read to one another in one of the cells. Our life of romantic solitude would have been most agreeable, despite the wildness of the countryside and the meanness of the natives, had not the sight of our companion's suffering, and certain days when we feared for his life, robbed me of all the pleasure and good of the trip.

The artist was a detestable invalid. Just what I had feared most—though not, unhappily, enough—came to pass: he lost heart. Though he bore pain with passable courage, he could not overcome his anxiety-ridden fancies. For him the cloister was full of terrors and phantoms even when he was well. He did not talk of his anxieties, but I divined them. Returning with my children from our nocturnal explorations in the ruins, I would find him, at ten in the evening, sitting pale at the keyboard, his eyes struck with dread and his hair standing on end. It would take him a few seconds to recognize us.

Then he would try to laugh, and play us the sublime things he had just composed—or, to put it more truly, the terrible and heart-rending obsessions which, as if unknown to him, had stolen over him in that hour of loneliness, sorrow and fright.

It was there he composed the loveliest of those few pages which he modestly called Preludes. They are masterworks. Several of them offer to our thoughts visions of long-departed monks, and the sound of those snatches of funereal plainsong that so oppressed him; some are melancholic and mild; they came to him at hours of sun and health, with the children's laughter floating over the window sill, with the distant thrum of guitars, with the pale roses abloom in the snow.

Others are sad and mournful, and while beguiling your ear they rend your heart. There is one which came to him of a dreary evening of rain, which plunges the soul into despondency. That day Maurice and I had left him in good health, to go to Palma to buy some necessities for our encampment; we had made three leagues in six hours, only to return in the midst of a flood, and we arrived in the dark, shoeless, forsaken by our coachman, through undreamed-of dangers. Mindful of our invalid's anxieties, we made haste. Those anxieties had been fearful indeed, but they had subsided into a sort of calm despair: he was playing a wonderful prelude, and he was weeping. Seeing us come in, he stood up with a loud cry, then said in a strange and distant voice: "Ah, I knew it! I knew you were dead!"

When he regained his spirits and saw the state we were in, he grew ill in retrospect of the dangers we'd been through; but he confessed to me afterward that while awaiting us he had seen it all in a dream, and that at length, unable to tell this dream from reality, he calmed down and half slumbered while playing the piano, convinced that he was dead. He saw himself, floating on a lake; heavy drops of cold water were dripping on his chest; and when I made him listen to the sound of these drops, which were actually falling all the while on the roof, he denied having heard them. He was even angry when I described this phenomenon with the words "mimetic harmony." He protested vehemently—and quite rightly too—against the childishness of such imitations for the ear. His genius was indeed full of the mysterious harmonies in nature, but they were rendered by the sublime equivalents of his musical thought, and not by servile mimicry of the sounds about him. His composition of that evening certainly echoed the drops of water which were drumming on the resonant tiles of the charterhouse; but they had been rendered in his imagination, and in his song, by tears falling from heaven on his heart.

At times, in his youth, he had had cheerful and balanced ideas. He had done some Polish songs and unpublished romances which were charming, vital, companionable and of an adorable gentleness. Some of his last compositions were once again like crystal springs reflecting a bright sun. But how rare, how short, were the tranquil ecstasies of his contemplation! For him, the song of the lark in the sky, and the downy floating of the swan upon still waters, were no more than lightning flashes of serene beauty. He was saddened more keenly by the cry of the ravening, plaintive eagle on the rocks of Majorca, the bitter shrilling of the north wind, and the disconsolate, snow-covered yews, than he was gladdened by the fragrant orange trees, the gracile vine shoots and the Moorish cantilena of the field hands.

Such was his character in all things. Alive for an instant to sweet affection and the smiles of destiny, he was afflicted for days, for weeks, by the crassness of an indifferent listener or the vexations of daily life. And strange to say, a great cause for sorrow did not grieve him so much as a little one. It seemed he had not the strength first to grasp it and then to feel it. The heave of emotion was out of scale with its spring. As for his deplorable health, he heroically accepted its real dangers, but ate his heart out over its slightest fluctuations. Such is the destiny of all beings whose nervous system is developed to excess.

With his extreme awareness of detail, his horror of poverty, and his need of refined comforts, he natually came to abhor Majorca after a few days of illness. But there was nothing for it; he was too weak to travel. When he was better, contrary winds blew against the coast, and for three days the steamboat was unable to leave Majorca's one port, if port it could be called.

Our stay in the charterhouse of Valldemosa was a torture for him and a torment for me. Charming, gay and sweet in society, Chopin, when sick, was cause for despair. No soul was more brilliant, delicate or unselfish, no friendship more faithful and loyal, no wit more brilliant in its moments of gaiety, no intelligence more serious and complete in its domain; but alas! no humor was more changeable, no imagination darker or more delirious, no feelings more susceptible, no heart more insatiable. Yet none of it was his fault; it was the fault of his illness. He was all raw nerves; the fold of a rose petal, the shadow of a fly, frayed them the more. He found everything under the Spanish sky, except for me and my children, unpleasing and repellent. He was dying not so much of the discomforts of our sojourn as of his own impatience to be gone.

At last we managed to get ourselves to Barcelona, and thence, by sea again, to Marseilles, at the end of winter.

Chopin always wanted Nohant and could not bear Nohant. He was the social man par excellence: not the man of crowded and formal gatherings, but of intimate ones, of salons of twenty people, of the hour when the crush is over and the habitués press about the artist and draw out of him with fond entreaties what is purest in his inspiration. It was then that he gave all his genius and talent. It was then, having plunged his audience into deep meditation or painful sorrow—for often his music depressed your spirits terribly, especially when he was improvising—it was then, all at once, as if to remove the thought and impress of his suffering from the others and himself, that he would turn toward the mirror when he thought no one was looking, muss his hair and loosen his cravat, and suddenly reappear as a phlegmatic Englishman, an impertinent old man, a silly, gushy Englishwoman, a sordid Jew. They were always sad types, however comical, but perfectly understood, and so delicately portrayed that one never tired of admiring them.

To tear Chopin away from so much indulgence, to attach him to a simple, studious routine—he who had been reared in the laps of princesses—was to deprive him of the stuff of life; of a made-up life, it is true, for like a rouged and powdered lady, he put away, once home, his sparkle and bite, to yield the night to sleeplessness and fever; but also of a life that would have been livelier, though shorter, than one spent in the seclusion of a closed family circle. In Paris he went through several such circles a day, or at the least, selected each night a fresh one for a backdrop. And so he had a circuit of twenty or thirty salons to intoxicate and bewitch with his presence.

Chopin was not born to love one woman, and his love was doled out in proportion to that which he himself demanded; but he wore his heart on his sleeve. True, he regained his balance quite easily: a wrong word, an ambivalent smile, could disenchant him utterly. He would fall passionately in love with three women during the same soiree, yet depart by himself, forgetting all three and leaving each with the impression that she alone had charmed him.

As a friend he was the same way, aglow at first meeting, then cool, then warm again, living in a continual infatuation, bewitching to whoever was its current object, but also in secret rancors which poisoned his dearest affections.

A story that he told me will show how carelessly his heart measured its own offerings against those it demanded of others.

He had fallen headlong for the granddaughter of a celebrated musician, and was considering asking for her hand. At the same time he was toying with the notion of marrying, also for love, a woman in Poland. Uncommitted, he wavered between these two passions. The young Parisienne favored his suit, and he was getting on splendidly with her when one day he called on her with another pianist more renowned than himself, and she was fool enough to offer the other a chair first. He never called on her again, and forgot her at once.

It has been claimed that I portrayed his character with great analytical accuracy in one of my novels. This is an error. Certain readers merely believed they recognized some of his traits; and Liszt, proceeding along the same lines, which are rather too conven-ient to be reliable, in his *Life of Chopin* (which, though somewhat rank in style, is yet full of good things and good pages), went far astray with the best will in the world.

I have described, in my *Prince Karol,* the character of a man determined in his nature and exclusive in his feelings and demands. Such a man Chopin never was. Nature does not delineate as art does, however realistic that art may be. She has her whims and inconsistencies, which, though perhaps merely apparent, are yet most mysterious. Art may correct such inconsistencies, but only because it is too limited to render them.

Chopin was a summation of those magnificent inconsistencies which God alone can permit Himself to create, and which have their peculiar logic. He was modest by principle and gentle by habit, but he was also haughty by instinct, and full of a legitimate and unconscious pride. Hence his sufferings, which his reason never mastered, and which never fixed upon any specific object.

And besides, Prince Karol was no artist. He was a dreamer, nothing more; devoid of genius, he had not the rights of genius. He was thus a character more real than likable, and so little the portrait of a great artist that Chopin, reading the fresh pages of my manuscript each day upon my writing cabinet, never considered if Prince Karol might be himself—he who was so suspicious!

Yet later, by reaction, he fancied—so I'm told—that he was. Certain enemies (for there were enemies of mine about him who claimed they were his friends—as if it was not murder to embitter that sick heart!) caused him to think that the novel was a revelation of the sort of man he was. Doubtless at that time he recalled the book only vaguely—he had forgotten it—but he was poring over it in no time.

But oh, that story is so little our own! Indeed, ours was just the opposite. We had neither the same surroundings nor the same sufferings. Our story, our own true story, had not the makings of a novel; its essence was too simple and too serious ever to offer occasion for a quarrel between us and about us. I accepted whatever Chopin thought and did outside my own life. Sharing neither his tastes, nor his ideas (but for those about art), nor his political principles, nor his appreciation of the world as it is, I never attempted to remake any part of him. I respected his individuality as I respected that of Delacroix and of my other friends who trod a different path than my own.

On the other hand, Chopin accorded me and, if I may say so, honored me with a kind of friendship that was exceptional in his life. He was always the same man for me. Doubtless he had few illusions about me, since I never fell in his esteem. That is what made our harmony last so long.

And so there was never a mutual reproach save, alas, one—and that was the first and the last. Such a lofty affection had to destroy itself, rather than exhaust itself in unworthy disputes.

But if toward me Chopin was devoted, gracious, attentive and deferring, he had not forsworn his harshness toward those who surrounded me. With them his changeable soul, by turns generous and mean, swung to and fro unchecked between infatuation and hatred. Nothing of his tormented inner life, of which his artistic masterpieces were the vague mysterious expression, was ever betrayed by his lips. Such was his reserve for seven years that only I could divine that torment, soothe it and retard its gathering storm. Oh, why did external circumstances not part us before the eighth year!

My attachment was able to work the miracle of making him somewhat calm and happy only because God had blessed it by preserving his health for a while. Yet he was visibly falling into a decline, and I no longer knew what remedies might assuage his nervous susceptibility. The death of his friend Dr. Matuszynski and then that of his own father were two terrible blows. Catholic dogma makes death seem terrifying and dreadful, and Chopin, instead of dreaming of a better world for these pure souls, had frightening visions, and I was obliged to spend many nights in a room adjoining his own, ever ready to forsake my work to chase the specters from his sleep and sleeplessness. For he imagined his own death accompanied by every superstitious fancy of Slavic poetry. Pole that he was, he lived in the nightmare world of legend. The phantoms called to him, entwined themselves about him, and far from seeing his father and his friend smile upon him in the light of faith, he waved their emaciated faces from his own, and flailed in their icy arms' embrace.

Nohant had become unpleasing to him. His return in the spring was to give him a few moments of bliss. But once he set to work, all grew dark about him. His creation was spontaneous, miraculous. He found without search or foresight. It came out of the keyboard, sudden, complete, sublime, or it sang in his head as he sauntered, and he hastened back to cast it on the instrument and hear it aloud. But then began the most crushing labor I have ever witnessed. It was a train of efforts, waverings, frustrated stabs at recapturing certain details of the theme that he had heard; what he had conceived as a unity he now overanalyzed in his desire to get it down, and his chagrin at not being able to rediscover it whole and clear plunged him into a sort of despair. He withdrew into his room for days, weeping, pacing up and down, breaking his pens, playing a measure a hundred times over, changing it each time, then writing it out and erasing it as many times, and beginning all over again on the morrow with painstaking and desperate perseverance. He would spend six weeks on a page, only to hark back to what he had first roughed out.

For a long time I had enough influence with him to make him consent to trust this first rush of inspiration. But when he no longer inclined to believe me, he gently reproached me with having spoiled him and with not being severe enough with him. I tried to distract him, to take him walking. Sometimes, with my brood waiting outside in a country gig, I would rend him against his will from this agony; I would drive him down to the banks of the Creuse, and after two or three days lost in the sunshine and the rain upon those dreadful roads, we would arrive, laughing and famished, at some magnificent spot, where he would seem reborn. The first days he would be exhausted; but at least he slept! The last day, returning to Nohant, he would be alive and young again, and would find the way out of his quandary without much effort; but it was not always possible to convince him to leave that piano, which more often made his torment than his joy, and little by little he began to show ill humor when I disturbed him. I dared not insist. Chopin in a rage was fearsome, and since with me he always restrained himself, he seemed likely to burst and die.

My life, always active and cheerful on the surface, had become more painful than ever underneath. I despaired to give others the happiness I had renounced for myself; for I had more than one cause for deep sorrow which I strove to overcome. Chopin's friendship was never a refuge for me in sadness. He had plenty of ills of his own to bear. Mine would have broken his back, and therefore he knew little about them, and understood less. Besides, he would have seen all from a different vantage than my own. My real strength came from my son, now of an age to share with me the most serious interests of life, and who bore me up with his even temper, his precocious power of reason and his unfailing gaiety. He and I do not see alike in all matters, but we have kindred constitutions, many of the same tastes and needs, and what is more, so fast a natural bond that no dispute between us can last out the day, nor resist a moment's talking heart to heart. If we dwell in different gardens of thought and feeling, there is at least a large and ever open door in the wall between: the door of immense affection and absolute trust.

After his latest relapses the sick man's mind clouded over, and Maurice, who had loved him tenderly until then, was suddenly wounded by him in an unforeseen way and over a trifle. They made up; but the dike was breached, and the flood was not long in coming. Now Chopin was often irritated without cause, and sometimes he was unfairly vexed by other people's good intentions. All this was allowed; but at last Maurice, weary of pinpricks, spoke of throwing up his cards. This could not and did not happen. But Chopin would not admit my legitimate and necessary intervention. He dropped his head and said I no longer loved him.

What blasphemy after eight years of maternal devotion! But his offended heart was unaware of its own ravings. I thought that a few calm words exchanged at a distance would heal his wound, restore our friendship and set his memory right. But then came the February Revolution, and Paris grew temporarily odious to this mind so incapable of bending to any sort of social transformation. Free for ten years to return to Poland, or at least certain that he would be tolerated there, he had preferred to languish far from his adored family and bear the sorrow of seeing his country altered and denatured. He had fled tyranny; now he was fleeing liberty!

I saw him briefly again in March 1848. I shook his trembling, icy hand. I wanted to talk; he escaped. I suppose it was my turn to say he no longer loved me, but I spared him this suffering, and left all in the hands of Providence. I was never to see him again.

As a ministrant to the sick—for such was my mission during a substantial portion of my life—I have had to accept without too much astonishment, and most of all, without too much resentment, the transports and torpors of a soul at grips with fever. I have learned at the bedside to detect where lies the empire of a healthy and free will, and to forgive what are only the agitations and ravings of one who is foredoomed.

I was repaid for my years of vigil, anguish and self-forgetfulness with years of tenderness, trust and gratitude, which one hour of unfairness and abandon have nowise canceled in God's eyes. God has not punished; God has seen more than that one bad hour whose suffering I do not wish to recall. I bore it, not with cold stoicism, but with tears of suffering and ardor in my secret prayers. And it is because I have said to the departed, "Go, and be blessed!" that I hope to find, in the hearts of those who will close my eyes, the same blessing in my final hour.

About the same time that I lost Chopin I lost my brother, in an even sadder way: his reason had been spent already for some while; alcohol had ravaged and destroyed that fine nature and made it hover between idiocy and madness. He had passed his last years quarreling with and being reconciled with my children, his family and all his friends. As long as he came to see me, I prolonged his life by secretly watering his wine—his palate was so coarsened that he failed to notice—and if he made up for quality with quantity, at least his drunkenness was less oppressive, less intense. But I only retarded the fatal moment when, nature having lost its resilience, he could no longer recover his lucidity even when sober. He spent his last months sulking at me and writing me unimaginable letters. The February Revolution, which he was no longer able to understand, brought down his tottering faculties. At first an impassioned republican, he behaved like so many others, who had not, like him, the access of madness as an excuse—that is, he grew frightened of it; and he began to fancy that the People wanted him dead! The People—from whom he was descended on his mother's side, like me, and with whom he lived in the public house a good deal more than any mere fraternization required—became his bugbear, and he wrote me that he "had it on the best authority that certain political friends of mine wanted to murder him." Poor brother! And when this hallucination passed, others followed without letup, until even his deranged imagination was extinguished, and was replaced by the unconscious stupor of his death throes.

It is altogether natural for one who has lived a half century to see herself deprived of many of those with whom she has lived in her heart; but we are traversing an age when violent commotions have shaken us all, and left every family bereaved. Especially in the past few years, revolutions, bringing dreadful days of civil war in their wake, assaulting vested interests, rousing violent passions, and seeming fatally to call down great epidemics after crises of rage and sorrow, after the proscription of some, and the tears or terrors of others—revolutions, which summon great wars, and which, as they succeed one another, destroy the souls of some while harvesting the lives of others—have put one half of France in mourning for the other.

For my part, I no longer count upon my fingers the bitter losses I have lately sustained, for they are upward of five score. My heart is a cemetery, and if the dead do not unsteady me, and rend me away into the tomb which has swallowed up the half of my life, it is because that other life is peopled for me by so many beloved souls that at times I fall under the illusion that it is my present one. This illusion is not without a certain austere charm, and in my thoughts I meet as often with the dead as with the living.

During the years whose principal agitations I have just sketched, I locked within my breast other, more poignant sorrows, whose revelation would serve no purpose in such a book as this. These sorrows were foreign, so to speak, to my life: no force of mine could have deflected them, and they entered my destiny unattracted by any magnetism of my own. In some respects we make our own life; in others, we submit to the life that others make for us. I have told or given some inkling of everything that has come into my life of my own will, everything drawn thereto by my own instincts. I have told how I have borne whatever was inherent in my own nature. I have said all that I wanted to say or should have said. As for those mortal sorrows which other natures caused to weigh upon me, they are the story of the secret martyrdom to which we all submit, either in public or in private, and which we must suffer in silence.

Index